Moses of South Carolina

★ ★ ★

MOSES

of South Carolina

A Jewish Scalawag
during Radical Reconstruction

Benjamin Ginsberg

The Johns Hopkins University Press

Baltimore

The Johns Hopkins University Press
2715 North Charles Street
Baltimore, Maryland 21218-4363
www.press.jhu.edu

Library of Congress Cataloging-in-Publication Data

Ginsberg, Benjamin.
  Moses of South Carolina : a Jewish scalawag during radical reconstruction /
Benjamin Ginsberg.
      p.   cm.
  Includes bibliographical references and index.
  ISBN-13: 978-0-8018-9464-0 (hardcover : alk. paper)
  ISBN-10: 0-8018-9464-6 (hardcover : alk. paper)
  1. Moses, Franklin Israel, 1838–1906. 2. Governors—South Carolina—
Biography. 3. Legislators—South Carolina—Biography. 4. South Carolina—
Politics and government—1865–1950. 5. Reconstruction (U.S. history,
1865–1877)—South Carolina. 6. Republican Party (S.C.)—History—19th century.
I. Title.
  F274.M67G56 2010
  975.7'041092—dc22   2009030638
  [B]

A catalog record for this book is available from the British Library.

Special discounts are available for bulk purchases of this book.
For more information, please contact Special Sales at 410-516-6936
or specialsales@press.jhu.edu.

For Sandy

CONTENTS

PREFACE

A graduate student once called my attention to a "white national-ist" Web site where he had found—along with articles denying the Holocaust, astounding new proof of the international Jewish con-spiracy, and the like—a piece praising a portion of *The Fatal Em-brace: Jews and the State,* my 1993 book on anti-Semitism. In par-ticular, the article found much merit in my brief discussion of the life of Franklin J. Moses, the so-called Robber Governor, a half-Jewish fellow who served as South Carolina's chief executive from 1872 to 1874. My white nationalist fan explained that most books and articles about Jews, especially those written by other Jews, tended to ignore Jewish criminality and cupidity. My discussion of Franklin Moses, according to this writer, was a rare exception, dealing forth-rightly with the schemes and crimes of a shady Jew.

I was somewhat taken aback. Every author, of course, likes ap-plause, but this was coming from a rather unsavory quarter. Besides, I had always been rather fond of Frank Moses. Perhaps he was my Rahel Varnhagen. Since I first became aware of Moses, I have often wondered if history had treated him fairly. Much of the story of Reconstruction, as Eric Foner has noted, was written by its enemies, who had political reasons for distorting the historical record.*

Those wracking their brains but unable to recall the name Frank Moses should not be concerned. Moses, a well-known figure in his own time, was the subject of many tongue-wagging articles and

*Eric Foner, "South Carolina's Black Elected Officials during Reconstruc-tion," in *At Freedom's Door: African American Founding Fathers and Law-yers in Reconstruction South Carolina,* ed. James L. Underwood and W. Lewis Burke (Columbia: University of South Carolina Press, 2000), 166–75.

numerous editorial cartoons in the nation's press, prompted by his then-astonishing propensity to socialize freely with blacks and to treat them as his equals. Today, however, outside his home state, Moses has been forgotten. He left few papers. The surviving Moses materials in the South Carolina state archives are mainly requests for pardons and state appointments addressed to the governor. As far as I can determine, Moses has been the subject of only three studies—a 1933 article in the *North Carolina Historical Review* by the well-known southern historian R. H. Woody; a Princeton undergraduate thesis written in 1950 by Julian Thomas Buxton, who was from Moses's hometown of Sumter, South Carolina; and a brief 1981 conference paper. Perhaps the best primary material on Moses consists of the weekly editorials and news articles he wrote while serving as editor of the *Sumter News* in 1866 and 1867. Moses's editorials trace the shifts in his political views and his eventual turn to Radicalism in 1867.

In South Carolina itself, where Civil War and Reconstruction history is still vividly, if not always accurately, recalled, Moses the scalawag robber governor is remembered as an odious figure who led the state to financial and moral ruin. Indeed, in South Carolina the name Franklin Moses can still draw heated reactions, as I discovered one afternoon when speaking on the topic to a Johns Hopkins alumni group in Charleston. One elderly and somewhat inebriated gentleman actually began to shout at me for defending the despicable Robber Governor.

At any rate, I resolved to learn more about Frank Moses and this book is the result. My white nationalist friends can relax. Frank Moses was not an honest man. Moses, however, was not simply a dishonest man. Had Moses's friends, rather than his enemies, controlled the press and the post-Reconstruction historical record, Moses might have been remembered fondly as the "racial and social equality governor" or the "land redistribution governor," rather than the Robber Governor.

Frank Moses died a lonely exile from his state and, eventually, from the historical record. Moses was not a saint, but he deserves better treatment than he has gotten. I hope this book will bring Moses a measure of posthumous rehabilitation—usually the only form of rehabilitation available to those who wind up on the losing side of history.

In the course of writing this book I benefited from conversations with several of my Johns Hopkins University colleagues, in particular Matthew A. Crenson and Robert Kargon, and from the advice of the anonymous reader selected by the Johns Hopkins University Press. I also thank Suvi M. Irvine, who was a wonderful research assistant, and Robert J. Brugger, who has been a fabulous editor. My thanks also to Arthur and Joan Sarnoff who gave me an opportunity several years ago to present my preliminary thoughts on this project to a gathering at their home on Sullivan's Island, South Carolina—an appropriate setting to begin the story of Frank Moses.

CHAPTER ONE

A Southern Moses

IN THE 1870s, during the heyday of Radical Reconstruction, Franklin Moses Jr., a member of an old South Carolina Jewish family, was a major figure in state politics. Moses, a scalawag (a native white who supported the northern occupation) and Radical Republican, was an influential participant in the South Carolina Constitutional Convention of 1868. He subsequently served as Speaker of the South Carolina House of Representatives and in 1872 was elected governor of the state. Moses was only half-Jewish and an apostate to boot. But if he sometimes forgot his Jewishness, his friends and neighbors were happy to remind him. The press, not fooled by Moses's claim that he was an Episcopalian, sometimes referred to him as an "Israelite" and occasionally as "Franklin Moses, Jewnier." Not wishing to have a Jew, even an Episcopalian Jew in her parlor, Moses's Protestant mother-in-law never allowed him into her home.[1]

Though largely forgotten outside his home state, Moses undertook much of importance in his own time. Before the war, Moses had been a "fire-eater," as outspoken proponents of secession were called. As the confidential secretary to South Carolina's governor, Moses may well have written the order to state militia forces to open fire on the *Star of the West*, the U.S. naval vessel attempting to bring supplies to the besieged federal garrison at Fort Sumter. Moses later claimed, with some foundation, to have been the person who actually hoisted South Carolina's Palmetto flag over Fort Sumter when the garrison surrendered in 1861.[2] After the war, though, Moses was among the most arrant of the South's Republican radicals. One historian called him the "most perfect scalawag" in all the South.[3]

His efforts on behalf of South Carolina's blacks made Moses a pariah among white Carolinians. As they fought tooth and nail against Republican rule, Moses's enemies hoped to discredit him by dubbing him the Robber Governor. The label stuck. South Carolina's history texts continue to this day to censure Frank Moses for his alleged cupidity. In a 1998 survey undertaken by a South Carolina newspaper, the Robber Governor was named the worst chief executive in the state's history.[4]

We like to think that those who do good *are* good. Certainly, the sanitized versions of history taught to schoolchildren present the important figures of American history as saints in their personal lives. This is one reason Americans are continually disappointed when it is revealed that today's heroes all have feet of clay. But the relationship between public accomplishments and private (or even public) morality is usually complicated. Often, great deeds are achieved by individuals of dubious moral character while their more ethical fellows achieve nothing or even do harm.

Without question, Frank Moses was corrupt. He accepted bribes, skimmed money from South Carolina bond sales, and accepted kickbacks from firms that did business with the state. But so what? Moses also launched social programs, integrated state institutions, and built a black militia that, for a time, protected freedmen's political rights against the efforts of white paramilitary forces such as the Ku Klux Klan to extrude blacks from the political arena. Moses supported the then-novel idea of publicly funded old age pensions.[5] In the face of vehement white opposition, Moses helped make it possible for blacks to attend the state university. Even some of the activities that Moses's enemies labeled corrupt were designed more to build a party machine in a decidedly hostile environment than to line Moses's own pockets. At the end of his life, Moses said he thought he had done more good than evil, and it would be difficult to contradict him.

In truth, Moses did not even deserve to be called the Robber Governor for his financial crimes. If he was a thief, he was a small-timer compared to the great political crooks of his, and perhaps our own, time. Moses was assigned his sobriquet by political enemies more for his social sins than his financial improprieties. White southerners of his day hated Moses because he flagrantly violated southern racial taboos. Many Republican politicians of the period talked the talk of racial justice but did not especially like black people or have much to do with them. Moses walked the walk. He invited black men and women into his home and interacted with black people on a basis of total equality. If Moses was a robber, what he stole was not so much white South Carolinians' money as their sense of racial exclusivity.

And to declare Frank Moses South Carolina's worst governor is inappropriate. In a state whose post–Civil War executives included "Pitchfork" Ben Tillman, an uncouth and vicious thug, and Wade Hampton, the leader of a bloody insurgency against lawful authority, Moses hardly seems to merit a prominent place in the gubernatorial rogue's gallery.[6] Writing in 1874, George W. Curtis of *Harper's Weekly* characterized South Carolina politics as a clash between "the party of the thieves [the Republicans] and the party of the murderers [the Democrats]."[7] Given this choice we might, like Curtis, prefer Moses and his petty thieves to Hampton and his murderers.

For those unfamiliar with the events discussed in this book, a bit of history may be in order. South Carolina is a small state, but its fractious citizens have played a large role in America's history. The nullification crisis, fomented by the Palmetto state's politicians, threatened to provoke a civil war during the Jacksonian era. Two decades later, when a war between the states actually erupted, the first shots were fired by South Carolina's militiamen. And in the decade following the war, circumstances in South Carolina had an enormous impact on the national government's effort to "reconstruct" the defeated South.

After the Confederacy's surrender, the federal government, under the auspices of the Republican party's radical wing, developed a plan of Reconstruction designed to disempower the prewar southern political class while building Republican regimes throughout the region. These regimes were to be led by a coalition of southern whites who supported Reconstruction—reviled throughout the South as scalawags—and white emigrants from the North—the so-called carpetbaggers. This leadership cadre would, in turn, be supported by the votes of newly enfranchised former slaves and protected by federal army garrisons, at least until the new governments were sufficiently stable to stand on their own.[8]

Most southern whites were implacably opposed to Radical Reconstruction. They were determined to recapture control of their affairs and to return blacks to a subordinate position in southern society. Ultimately, southern whites achieved both goals. By 1877 Reconstruction governments had been overthrown throughout the South and the cornerstones of the southern apartheid system were being put into place. The collapse of Reconstruction had profound consequences for America's future development, paving the way for the emergence of the solidly white and politically conservative South that served as a barrier to political and social reform in the United States for much of the twentieth century. For blacks, the consequences were devastating. Within a few years after the end of Reconstruction, most southern blacks had been stripped of their newly won civil and political rights. Nearly another century would pass before these rights would be restored.

The failure of Radical Reconstruction certainly cannot be traced solely to events in South Carolina. Many of the forces that undermined Republican policy had their origins far outside the Palmetto state's borders. But South Carolina was Reconstruction's last stand. The collapse of Republicanism in South Carolina meant the full restoration of white Democratic rule to the South.

South Carolina in the 1870s was a case where events "on the ground" overtook and overturned the grand visions of policy makers in Washington. The course of Reconstruction was determined in isolated camp sites and church yards where freedmen learned about politics, and dusty hamlets like Edgefield, South Carolina, where black and white militia men fought pitched battles. State politicians like Frank Moses were buffeted by shifts in federal policy in far-off Washington, while facing the daily reality of gun battles in the Edge-fields of the state. It is at this political level, midway between grand vision and dusty reality, that politicians struggle to shape events only to find their efforts undermined from above or thwarted from below.

Jews and Blacks: Allies at the Margins

At first blush, it may seem peculiar to encounter a Jew, even a half-Jewish apostate, at the center of events in South Carolina more than a century ago. At the time of the Civil War fewer than fifty thousand Jews lived in the entire South, and only a few hundred Jewish families could be found in South Carolina. But lack of numbers has never prevented Jews from playing an important role in political life. Indeed, Jews have both built governments and led revolutions in societies where they were small and shunned minorities. Jews have talent and ambition and a centuries-long tradition of education, and they tend to prosper if allowed even the slightest opportunity.

One secret of Jewish success is social marginality. The Jews are, to a greater or lesser extent, "outside society," as Hannah Arendt put it.[9] Marginality can expose Jews to suspicion, hostility, and discrimination. At the same time, though, talented marginals may see politics and society with clearer eyes and from a better vantage point than those who are fully immersed in their own culture. The marginal may envision possibilities others do not and be willing to undertake a course of action others will not. Benjamin Disraeli, Arendt's exemplar of the brilliant Jewish marginal, or "exception Jew" as she called him, famously rejected the accepted wisdom of his political party and his social class to assert that, if enfranchised, British industrial workers would become champions of the established order. Disraeli proved to be correct. "In the inarticulate mass of the English populace, he discerned the Conservative workingman as the sculptor perceives the angel prisoned in a block of marble," observed the *London Times* after Disraeli's death.[10]

Even in America, the most inclusive of nations, Jews are social marginals, uncertain about their precise place in the social order. On the one hand, most Jews seek acceptance and inclusion in the American mainstream. They want to be considered 100 percent American, to be "just like everyone else." The problem is that many of these same Jews also want to retain communal institutions, religious practices, and ethnic ties that will always make them a bit different from everyone else—perhaps only 98 percent American. And even those who do believe that they are 100 percent American are never completely confident that their gentile neighbors agree. Note the howls of protest and indignation from the American Jewish community in response to the publication of a book by two obscure professors asserting that the pro-Israel lobby, backed mainly by American Jews, worked to subordinate America's foreign policy interests to those of Israel.[11] One suspects that an exposé of the activities of the Irish lobby would have been greeted with yawns by Americans of Irish descent. The Irish today are 100 percent American and feel no need to prove it.

The Jews are less certain of their status and still uneasy after nearly four centuries on American soil. Even as they do their Christmas shopping, the Jews have a lingering sense that they are on the outside looking in. And short of surrendering their institutions, practices, and communal ties to join the deracinated multitude—something that most Jews will not do—America's Jews are condemned to remain marginals, not quite 100 percent American. This marginality makes the Jews nervous, an anxiety perhaps reflected in the prominence of Jews among political journalists, social scientists, and historians. Jews seem to feel a strong compulsion to study America under a microscope rather than to take its beneficence at face value. Their marginality also gives the Jews an unusually critical perspective. It is no accident that in America, as elsewhere, Jews are found in great numbers among social critics, investigative journalists, political activists, radical intellectuals, and the like. The Jews imagine alternative possibilities and, perhaps, better futures.

Franklin Moses was a man at the margins of society. He stood at the fringe of the southern aristocracy but was never invited to join. Moses was always on the outside looking in. And like Disraeli and other Jewish marginals, Moses came to envision a society different from the one in which he had been raised. The freedmen were Franklin Moses's angels in marble. Where his fellow southerners saw ignorant savages, Moses saw citizens. Where his fellow Republicans saw children in need of tutelage, Moses saw political allies. From the margins of southern society, Franklin Moses built America's first black-Jewish alliance, a prototype for the alliances that were to help reshape American politics in the decades to come.

Over the past century, despite the existence of more than a little black anti-Semitism and a measure of Jewish racism, blacks and Jews have frequently been politically linked in the United States. For example, a majority of the whites in President Barack Obama's inner circle are Jews as were virtually all of Dr. Martin Luther King's most important white advisers. Their own marginality has given American Jews reason to ally themselves with blacks. To begin with, Jews often perceive a stake in championing the cause of blacks. When mobilized, black resentment and restiveness can become a powerful force for social change. And to some extent, though not always, the changes sought by blacks have been congenial to the interests of Jews.[12] During the 1960s, for example, Jewish organizations recognized that the civil rights movement's goal of outlawing discrimination based on race would serve the desire of Jews for fuller inclusion in American society. By supporting African Americans in the battle for civil rights, Jews were fighting to demolish the barriers that stood in their own way as well.

But Jews do not view blacks merely instrumentally. As victims of oppression and even slavery, themselves, Jews cannot help but have a certain sympathy for blacks and, though this is rarely spoken, also a somewhat embarrassed sense of gratitude. In America, blacks have borne the brunt of the racial hatred that, elsewhere, was reserved mainly for Jewish people. In America, one might say, the presence of blacks made the Jews whiter.[13] Because of this underlying sympathy, even when Jewish support for blacks was initially motivated by self-interest, Jews have been easily caught up in the battle and often allowed their sympathies to outweigh their interests. The current generation of African Americans may not remember that during the civil rights struggle the majority of the whites who risked their lives as freedom riders were Jews, as were nearly two-thirds of the whites who went into the South during the violent Freedom Summer of 1964. These supporters included Michael Schwermer and Andrew Goodman who, along with their black friend James Chaney, were murdered by racist thugs in Mississippi.[14]

Frank Moses initially aligned himself with blacks because he believed that such a relationship would serve his political interests. Before the Civil War, Moses tried unsuccessfully to be part of the southern social and political elite. He lived at the aristocratic fringe. The war changed everything. The war reduced Moses's chances for admission to the top tier of southern politics and society. At the same time, though, that society was being shaken to its foundations. The bottom rail, as Moses's contemporaries would have put it, was threatening to rise to the top. Viewing southern society from the margins, perhaps Moses saw an opportunity to build a new order, with himself at the top. This course of action would be fraught with risk. It would require him to seek and win black support and to alienate himself from white society. After much hesitation, Moses decided to make himself a leader among the former slaves and, with their backing, to remake South Carolina. His ambitions thwarted in the old white South, Moses aspired to construct a new black South Carolina in which he would be a leader.

While Moses first saw his relationship with blacks in purely tactical terms, in due course, his sympathies for the freedmen grew. More than one white Republican gave lip service to the idea of equal political rights for blacks because black votes were needed to maintain Republican power. But Moses was among the few who also advocated social equality. He sought to open public institutions to blacks and was one of the very few white politicians in the South—or North—who personally socialized with blacks. And it was his blatant disdain for the southern apartheid system, not his small-time thievery, that caused Moses to be shunned and hated by South Carolina's whites.[15]

For a time, what might be called an alliance of the oppressed and the marginal played a powerful role in South Carolina politics, as it did in the nation as a whole a century later. Indeed the alliance between blacks and Jews in mid-nineteenth century South Carolina was, in some instances, exceptionally close. Two of Moses's principal associates, South Carolina secretary of state Francis Cardozo and state land commissioner and U.S. representative Robert DeLarge, were the sons of black mothers and Jewish fathers. Cardozo, in fact, was a member of the same distinguished southern family that later produced U.S. Supreme Court Justice Benjamin Cardozo.

Like Disraeli, some ambitious marginals are able to achieve enormous success. The ability to see what others do not can be advantageous. Marginality, though, can also be a precarious position. Seeing the world differently from others, being out of step, is often dangerous. Even the biblical Moses fled Egypt when he discovered that an Egyptian prince with the sensibilities of a Jew had little chance of surviving in the land of the pharaohs.

Frank Moses had a vision of the world that differed from that of his neighbors, but he lacked the ability to bring about its realization. Perhaps, following the example of his biblical namesake, he should have fled the South. In retrospect, to have had any chance of success given the implacable hostility of the white South and the eventual indifference of the North, radical Republicans needed to be, well, more radical. Southern Republicans needed to create powerful black military forces capable of defeating the Ku Kluxers, "rifle clubs," "red shirts," and other paramilitary formations fielded by their white antagonists. Southern Republicans needed to expropriate the plantations upon which their rivals' economic power was based and divide the land among the freedmen to bolster their fortunes. Southern Republicans needed to adopt confiscatory tax systems to pay for social policies. They needed to be ruthless and unrelenting in their efforts to stamp out the factionalism in their own ranks that sapped Republican strength.

Moses took many steps in the right direction, but he could not do enough. Concerned with their own electoral prospects, the northern Republicans whose support was essential to their fellow partisans in the South would not tolerate a program of land confiscation and had little sympathy for the creation of black armies. Moses could not possibly have succeeded. Considering the task at hand, even the biblical Moses might have faltered. If God had been serious about suppressing southern white resistance and preventing the freedmen from being returned to bondage, perhaps he should have sent Lenin rather than Moses.

In the end, Frank Moses failed. He was exiled from South Carolina and reviled for his apostasy. His relatives changed their surname to avoid the taint of an association with the Robber Governor. For Frank Moses, as for so many Jewish marginals, having a different—even if better—view of the world was a curse rather than a blessing.

Jews in the South

The southern society into which Franklin Moses Jr. was born was reasonably hospitable to Jews, allowing a small number to approach, if not reach its topmost rungs. In the antebellum South, most Jews were small peddlers, tailors, or shopkeepers—proprietors of what was regionally known as the "Jew store."[16] Often, an entire extended family might live in a few small rooms above the shop. In other instances, a group of unmarried Jewish men would share rooms above a shop or in a boarding house to save money. A relatively small group of Jewish families of Sephardic (Spanish and Portuguese) origin, however, had settled in the South in the late seventeenth and early eighteenth centuries. By the nineteenth century, members of these families had become intellectuals, professionals, and important merchants. Though the total number of Jews in the antebellum South was small, so was the South's merchant and professional class. Hence, Jews figured prominently within this stratum and achieved a measure of acceptance within southern society.

As is typical of highly stratified, landlord-peasant societies, the eighteenth-century Ukraine is an example, the antebellum South was a region in which technical, commercial, and intellectual skills were in relatively short supply. Popular education had been almost completely neglected in the region, so that outside the planter class and the small business and professional stratum that served it, illiteracy was the norm. The sons of members of the planter class were usually educated by private tutors, academies, and colleges. But most members of this class regarded education more as a form of preparation for membership in polite society than as a source of training. As a result, secondary education in the South was extremely weak, and with the exception of the University of Virginia, colleges had nowhere near the quality of their northern counterparts.

Given the lack of intellectual resources and training in the surrounding gentile society, the tiny Jewish community, which, as usual, insisted on educating its children, comprised a significant and visible fraction of the doctors, traders (including slave traders like the Davis family of Richmond that was singled out for censure by Harriet Beecher Stowe in *Uncle Tom's Cabin*), newspaper editors, shopkeepers, business people, lawyers, and so forth. To a substantial extent, the South's professional stratum served the moneyed and propertied classes in this highly stratified society. Like other business and professional people, Jews depended on the patronage and favor of the southern landowners who dominated government, politics, and the southern economy. The landowners controlled access to politics, were the source of most legal business, and were the chief market for services and goods, including slaves, in the South.

In the 1990s some radical blacks charged that Jews controlled the slave trade in the antebellum South.[17] This charge is without much foundation. Like other small businessmen of the period, Jewish merchants did deal in slaves. Because they had little capital to invest, Jewish merchants often established themselves as auctioneers, commodities brokers, and consignment sellers—fields in which little start-up capital was required. Unfortunately, slaves were such an important part of the routine commerce of the South during this period that such merchants routinely bought and sold human beings. In cities throughout the South, Jewish auctioneers and brokers were visible participants in this aspect of the slave trade. However, the bulk of the slave trade, including most of the interstate traffic in slaves, was not controlled by small commodities brokers, who dealt in slaves as well as other goods. These brokers accounted for only a tiny fraction of the traffic in human beings. The great bulk of the slave trade was organized and controlled by a small number of large firms that specialized in this form of commerce. A small number of Jewish firms, to be sure, were involved in this business. The Davis family of Richmond, as well as the Cohens of Atlanta, the Goldsmiths of Mobile, the Mordecais of Charleston, and the Moses family of Lumpkin, Georgia, were successful slave traders. But the majority of the large slave trading companies were non-Jewish. Such firms as Franklin and Armfield, the largest slave trading enterprise in the entire South—a firm that sold more slaves than all the Jewish firms combined—did not employ Jews. Like other southerners, some Jews did own slaves. According to some scholars, though, the number was small. Free blacks owned more slaves than did Jews in the Old South.[18]

Though they were not prominent in the slave trade, Jews did serve the slaveholders. In the antebellum period, a number of Jews became important political and intellectual spokesmen for the planter stratum. Because education and intellectual skills were relatively more scarce among native-stock southern whites than among their northern counterparts, Jews often had more opportunity for advancement in the South than in the North. As was true in other times and places, members of the southern elite often found Jews to be the most reliable agents and spokesmen precisely because Jewish subordinates were more dependent on their patrons. Jewish politicians, editors, and lawyers usually had no independent base of support and were no threat to their patrons' interests.

This helps explain why America's first two Jewish senators were southerners, rather than northerners. Judah Benjamin of Louisiana and David Yulee of Florida were important spokesmen for planter interests in the U.S. Senate in the 1850s. (Yulee, whose name had been Levy, had converted to Christianity.) Similarly, David Kaufman of Texas and Philip Phillips of Alabama spoke for the interests of southern planters in the U.S. House of Representatives, defending states' rights and the expansion of slavery into the territories. Phillips actually crafted Stephen A. Douglas's Kansas-Nebraska Act of 1854, which created the new territories of Kansas and Nebraska. The act effectively repealed the Missouri Compromise of 1820, which had prohibited slavery in the western territories latitude 36°30' north. The Kansas-Nebraska Act provided for "popular sovereignty" when it came to slavery in the territories, allowing each new territory's settlers to decide for themselves whether their territory should be slave or free. The Kansas-Nebraska Act was hailed in the South but led to protracted guerilla warfare between pro- and antislavery forces in what came to be known as Bleeding Kansas.

Jacob Cardozo, a nationally prominent South Carolina editor and political economist, published scholarly defenses of slavery.[19] He asserted that the institution was to be praised on both economic and ethical grounds. Economically, wrote Cardozo, slavery brought wealth to the region and, on aggregate, left slaves better off than people only the lower rungs of northern wage earners.[20] Ethically, said Cardozo, the case was clear-cut. Slavery was not only sanctioned, but actually instituted by God. "The reason," he wrote, "the Almighty made the colored black is to prove their inferiority." (History does not record what Cardozo's nephews, the sons of his brother and a free black woman, thought of their uncle's ideas about race.) After the war, Cardozo continued to support the cause of the planters. In his 1866 volume *Reminiscences of Charleston*, Cardozo expressed his sympathy for the losses suffered by the South's former ruling class: "The owner of two hundred to five hundred slaves with a princely income, has not only to submit to the most degraded employments, but he frequently cannot obtain them. In some instances, he has to drive a cart, or attend a retail grocery, while he may have to obey the orders of an ignorant and course menial. There is something unnatural in this reverse of position—something revolting to my sense of propriety in this social degradation."

In a similar vein, the antebellum playwright and journalist Isaac Harby, editor of the *Southern Patriot,* penned biting attacks on the abolitionists. Thomas Cooper DeLeon wrote novels that presented slavery in a positive light. DeLeon's best-known work was *Belles, Beaux, and Brains of the 60s.* In that work he sought to refute charges that slavery was cruel. These charges, he maintained, were nothing but mythology and abolitionist propaganda. One bit of evidence for the lack of substance to these accusations of southern cruelty, DeLeon pointed out, was that in creating the fictional character of Simon Legree for her novel *Uncle Tom's Cabin,* even so fervent an opponent of southern slavery as Harriet Beecher Stowe was compelled to describe the cruel overseer as a northerner. And Samuel Mordecai, a Richmond journalist, was one of the most important writers for the *Farmer's Register,* a publication devoted to the needs and interests of slave owners.

In the business world, Jews played an important role in areas involving technical expertise or technological innovation. In prewar South Carolina, for example, Jewish businessmen were at the forefront of efforts to modernize and industrialize the state's agrarian economy. Moses Mordecai, a pioneer in the commercial use of the steamship, won the government contract for the transport of mail between New York and Charleston. Solomon Solomons, an engineer, directed the construction of the North Eastern Railroad. Michael Lazarus was another pioneer in the development of commercial steam transport and opened steamboat navigation on the Savannah River. Joshua Lazarus founded the Gas Light company in Charleston and illuminated the city's streets.

Before the war, Jews' talents had made them important political and intellectual spokesmen for the southern cause. Though the Jewish community was small, its intellectual skills were important in a region where such skills were in short supply. For similar reasons, during the Civil War itself a significant number of Jews served in prominent positions in the Confederate government and as high-ranking officers in the Confederate army.[21] Jews were especially important in those capacities requiring substantial technical or intellectual competence. Edwin DeLeon was a Confederate propagandist and diplomat in Europe, serving as special envoy to the court of Napoleon III. David DeLeon served as Confederate surgeon general. Isaac Baruch was assistant surgeon general. Lionel Levy was Confederate judge advocate. Abraham C. Myers was Confederate quartermaster general. L. C. Harby of South Carolina served as a commodore in the Confederate navy, commanding a fleet of river gunboats. J. Randolph Mordecai served as assistant adjutant general. Raphael Moses was the chief commissary officer for General Longstreet's corps. All told, twenty-four Jews served as senior officers in the Confederate army, while only sixteen served in comparable positions in the much larger Union army—this at a time when the Jewish population of the North was nearly three times as large as that of the South. The highest-ranking Jewish Confederate was, of course, Judah Benjamin, who served successively as Confederate attorney general, secretary of war, and secretary of state.

The Jews of South Carolina

The first Jews seem to have arrived in South Carolina in the 1690s.[22] Religious tolerance was a fundamental tenet of South Carolina's constitution, which had been written by John Locke. As a result, the colony was a magnet for religious dissenters like the French Huguenots and Palatine Germans. A small number of Sephardic Jews also reached the colony, where they set up shop as merchants and tradesmen, mainly in Charleston. In 1750 Charleston's Jews built a synagogue and organized a Hebrew Benevolent Society. The congregation's first rabbi was Moses Cohen. His great-grandson

Abraham C. Myers, a West Point graduate, fought in the Seminole and the Mexican Wars before joining the Confederate Army. Fort Myers, Florida, was named for him.

During the Revolutionary War the Jewish community, like its gentile counterpart, was divided, but many supported the colonial cause. A number of Jews fought in South Carolina's militia companies. One company from Charleston contained so many Jews that it was dubbed the Jew Company.[23] Perhaps the best-known Revolutionary-era Jew in South Carolina was Francis Salvador. A Sephardic Jew who had emigrated from England, Salvador was a member of the 1775 Provincial Congress of the self-proclaimed independent state of South Carolina. Salvador is thought to have been the first Jew elected to public office in North America.[24] Salvador was killed in a battle with loyalist forces and their Native American allies early in 1776, quite probably becoming the first Jewish military casualty of the Revolutionary war. Jews had not been warmly received by all Charlestonians. In 1778 the *Charleston Gazette* published an anonymous complaint that too many Jews were migrating to the city. "The tribe of Israel," said the writer, was "fleeing [from Georgia, then under attack] for an asylum with their ill-got wealth—dastardly turning their backs upon the country when in danger, which gave them bread and protection."[25] Charleston's Jews replied indignantly that they were second to none in their willingness to fight for their country. After the Revolution, Charleston's Jews lived well, despite an occasional indication that some of their neighbors harbored anti-Semitic prejudices.[26]

By the early nineteenth century, several hundred Jews lived in South Carolina. Some had become moderately wealthy and had encouraged their sons to enter the learned professions, in particular the law. In the years preceding the Civil War, the Jewish community prospered. Jews were among the state's leading merchants, teachers, bankers, physicians, journalists, and lawyers, and several had become active in state and local politics. Among South Carolina's notable Jewish politicians were Chapman Levy, who served in the state legislature from 1829 to 1833 and from 1836 to 1838; Myer

Jacobs, who served in the legislature from 1833 to 1839; M. C. Mordecai, a state legislator from 1835 to 1846 and a state senator from 1855 to 1858; and, of course, Franklin I. Moses, a state senator for twenty years.

At the beginning of the Civil War, the Jews of South Carolina were, if anything, more zealous than their coreligionists in seeking to serve the South. Many of South Carolina's Jews had opposed secession. When their state went to war, however, nearly all Jewish men of military age donned Confederate uniforms.[27] Several distinguished themselves in battle. For example, E. W. Moise of Charleston, a distant cousin of the Moses clan, commanded the 7th Cavalry regiment in the Army of Northern Virginia. Moise, a Douglas Democrat, had been an outspoken opponent of secession. Once the war began, however, he organized and, at his own expense, outfitted a cavalry company—named the Moise Rangers—that subsequently became Company A of the 7th Cavalry. Moise saw action in numerous engagements, including Gettysburg where he was wounded, and earned many commendations and promotions. Brevetted to the rank of colonel, Moise ultimately became one of the state's Civil War heroes and a friend and confidante of Gen. Wade Hampton, future governor and South Carolina's highest ranking military officer.[28] Moise was known throughout the Confederate cavalry for having commandeered a Yankee gunboat, an unusual feat for a horse soldier. In February 1864 the gunboat *Smith Briggs*, part of a federal flotilla on Chuckatuck Creek near Smithfield, Virginia, was retrieving a group of Union soldiers from a raiding mission. Moise and his cavalry troopers charged down a hill, boarded the boat, and turned its cannon on the other federal ships, driving them off.[29]

Many of South Carolina's Jews were not as fortunate as Moise. The roster of South Carolina's Jewish soldiers killed in the war is a long one. Simply reading a portion of the list in sterile alphabetical order begins to tell the story. Baum, Marcus, killed at the battle of the Wilderness; Blankenshee, H., killed at First Manassas; Blamkenstine, Jacob, Chancellorsville; Brown, Mendel, Atlanta; Cohen, Henry, Savage Station; Cohen, Isaac, Fort Fisher; Cohen, Jacob,

Fort Fisher; Cohen, Marx, Bentonville; Cohen, Robert, Secession-ville; Hoffman, Michael, Black River. The list goes on.[30] Within the Moses family itself, fifteen men went to war. Of these, four were killed and five others wounded.[31]

The Moses Family

Long before the Civil War, the Moses family was among the most prominent Jewish clans in South Carolina. Franklin Moses's great-grandfather, a Charleston merchant by the name of Meyer Moses, served in the state militia and acquitted himself well when the town was besieged by British forces during the Revolutionary War. Moses gained the notice of Gen. Thomas Sumter, commander of South Carolina's militia forces. At the time of Moses's death in 1787, Sumter wrote to the family attesting to Moses's service to the revo-lutionary cause. "After the fall of Charleston, his treatment of the wounded and prisoners was extremely friendly and humane . . . [in] that on these occasions he expended a considerable sum relieving them."[32] Frank Moses's paternal grandfather, Maj. Myer Moses, was also well regarded by his fellow Carolinians. That Moses served as a militia officer in the War of 1812 and later was active in Charles-ton politics and civic affairs. The extended Moses family included many prominent attorneys, merchants, civic leaders, and military officers.

Frank Moses's father, Franklin Israel Moses, was one of South Carolina's leading politicians and jurists. The elder Franklin was born in Charleston in 1804; he graduated from South Carolina Col-lege in 1821. As was common during that era, after graduation, Moses studied law in the office of an experienced attorney, in this case, James Petigru. He was admitted to the bar in 1825.[33] Soon thereafter he opened a practice in Sumter District, in the hamlet of what was then known as Sumterville, an area later incorporated as the City of Sumter. Moses proved to be an able lawyer and his prac-tice prospered.[34] He soon became a member in good standing of the district's small business and professional community and, despite some familial opposition on both sides, married Jane McLelland, the daughter of a well-to-do, local gentile family. Making use of his business and social connections, Moses went into politics. In 1842 he was elected to the South Carolina Senate from Claremont, which was then a part of Sumter District. He served in the state senate until 1862, chairing the senate judiciary committee for most of those years. He was also a professor of law and a trustee of South Carolina College and was chosen captain of the Claremont Cavalry, a largely ceremonial militia troop that paraded through town in flashy uniforms on patriotic occasions.[35]

During the course of his political career, Moses generally articulated the views of the state's wealthy and powerful planters upon whose favor both his legal and political careers depended. In 1832, for example, he was a secretary of the Union Convention, which met in Charleston to oppose the Nullifiers who were ready to dissolve the Union over the tariff issue. Moses's political patrons, men of substance and property, opposed the tariff but were certainly not ready to destroy the Union. The state's elite, moreover, saw the proponents of nullification, the Nullies, as radicals intent on upending the state's power structure.[36] Similarly, in 1852, when the issue of slavery in the territories split the state between the Secessionists and Unionists, Moses articulated the antisecession views of most members of the planter class. By 1859, though, as the sentiments of this class began to shift, Moses became a leader of the secessionist cause in the state senate. "The time has come," Moses declared in a December 1859 speech to the senate, "and this remark comes from me with a very good grace, for I had not believed [that] I would see the day when I would ask to be delivered from this Union; but it has come, and we must meet it as becomes the Senate of South Carolina."[37]

Moses's law practice made him a wealthy man. He was able to purchase property and list himself as a planter and attorney in the district's records. At the same time, his political acumen made Moses an influential figure in Sumter District and in the state as a whole. He was often characterized and sometimes denounced by contemporaries as the leading political force in Sumter. In due course, Moses persuaded other members of his family to move to the district, and for many years, Moses and his brother Montgomery practiced law together. The historian Barnett Elzas declares that "as a public man Senator Moses was remarkable for his carefulness, watchfulness, thorough preparation and attention, and for his fidelity to the interests of his constituents.[38] The South Carolina legal historian U. R. Brooks writes, "His square dealings and industry[,] always exercised for the benefit of his clients, made him a very popular man."[39] Moses was also something of a scholar, writing a number of philosophical treatises and a volume on South Carolina election law.[40] Despite his accomplishments, Moses was not universally admired. Some charged that the Moses brothers would often represent opposite sides in a case, thus ensuring the firm's success in court.[41] A critic of Moses's son described the younger Moses as "a liar [and] a sneak" who lacked "moral sense," and said that he was "a true son of old Franklin Moses."[42]

The future governor was born March 17, 1838. His mother was a devout Methodist and his father was apparently willing to leave religious matters to his wife. Accordingly, Franklin was raised in the Methodist church. The elder Moses made an effort to downplay his own Jewishness, which was a bit of a hindrance in South Carolina society. He changed his middle name, Israel, to the initial J, and gave that same middle initial to his son. Hence, young Franklin was sometimes referred to as Franklin J. Moses Jr., though that appellation was not actually correct.

Young Moses, as he was more typically called, seems to have led an uneventful and privileged life at the edges of the planter aristocracy. His education began with a private tutor and continued in a private school in Columbia. He then attended South Carolina College for two years where he participated in the Euphradian Debating Society, a group that prided itself on producing many of South Carolina's most important political figures.[43] After two years, Moses left college to begin studying law in his father's office.

Moses was apparently an excellent horseman and was an avid

participant in the colorful equestrian tournaments and "jousts" that were an important form of entertainment for the wealthier residents of country towns like Sumter. He joined his father's Claremont cavalry troop and cut a dashing figure during parades. In this period, upper-class southerners were avid readers of Walter Scott's *Ivanhoe* and other historical romances with medieval settings.[44] They fancied themselves noble lords and ladies undertaking brave deeds and defending their castles from attack. For equestrian tournaments, young men dressed in what they imagined to be knightly attire, sometimes modeled after some heroic historical or literary figure. Amusingly, given his future identification with efforts to secure justice for black Carolinians, young Moses often chose to dress as Othello, Shakespeare's tragic Moor of Venice.[45] This choice, however, did not prevent his election as an officer of the Claremont Cavalry.

Equestrian tournaments were often followed by gala balls in which the ersatz lords and ladies had an opportunity to dance, mingle, and flirt. Apparently young Moses excelled in these pursuits as well. He was romantically linked to several women before marrying Emma Buford Richardson in 1859. The wedding took place at the Church of the Holy Comforter, an Episcopal church where Sumter's elite worshiped. Franklin had no difficulty shedding his Methodist ties and becoming an Episcopalian. Religion, as one historian put it, was one of Moses's "lesser worries."[46] Miss Richardson was the daughter of J. S. G. Richardson, an attorney and court reporter with an excellent, statewide reputation and impeccable social credentials. Moses's father was very pleased with the match, which he viewed as enhancing the family's political and social standing. Moses's new mother-in-law, however, was not at all happy. She refused to recognize her daughter's marriage to a Jewish parvenu and never allowed her son-in-law into her home.

The issues surrounding young Franklin's marriage help to illuminate the position of the Moses family in South Carolina society. The Moses family was wealthy and respectable but the elder Moses was a Jew and was not a member of the state's ruling planter gentry. Moses might take care of the planters' legal affairs and speak for their interests in the state legislature. He might even purchase a plantation. He did not, however, belong to the planters' social circle. He was, in effect, a court Jew, privileged and well regarded but not a member of aristocratic society. Young Moses grew up on what one historian called the "aristocratic fringe."[47] This is a position that typically breeds resentment, ambition, or both. One thinks, for example, of the young George Washington who aspired, without much success, to be accepted into the elite social circles inhabited by his half brother, Lawrence. The envy and resentment Washington felt at the time seem to have been the origins of the relentless drive to achieve rank and fame for which he was subsequently noted.[48] In a similar vein, Frank Moses averred years later that most of his actions in life had been driven by "pride—a personal and family pride."[49]

Secession

During the crises of the 1830s and early 1850s, the propertied interests that dominated South Carolina politics had urged moderation in the South's response to northern criticism and to efforts to limit the expansion of slavery. But by the late 1850s, the views of South Carolina's planters had shifted dramatically. The new Republican party, a political entity that made opposition to slavery a major plank in its political platform, won the 1858 national congressional elections. In 1859 news of John Brown's raid at Harper's Ferry, Virginia, threw the entire South into an uproar. And in early 1860 the Republicans nominated as their presidential candidate Abraham Lincoln, who was seen throughout the South, albeit incorrectly, as a mortal foe of slavery. These developments led even the most moderate among South Carolina's planters to believe that secession from the Union might become necessary. In 1859 planters supported the gubernatorial candidacy of F. W. Pickens, who had been a Nullie in 1852 and been dismissed as a hothead by men of property and substance. Before the war, South Carolina's governors were chosen by the state legislature. When Pickens became governor, a general agreement emerged among the planters that if Lincoln was elected, the state would secede and would defend itself if attacked.

The elder Moses, who had strongly supported Pickens's election, used his influence to persuade the governor to appoint young Frank as one of his personal secretaries and aides-de-camp. Since Pickens's handwriting was virtually illegible, Moses wrote many of Pickens's letters, papers, and orders, which gave the young assistant constant access to the governor. His position also conferred upon Moses the honorary rank of lieutenant colonel in the South Carolina militia and made him a visible figure in the state capital where he was known as an ardent secessionist. At the age of twenty-two Frank Moses's career in South Carolina politics seemed well launched. He was in the right place, expressed the right ideas, and had the right patrons. His future seemed assured.

In November 1860 Lincoln won the presidency. The next month, in a statewide convention, South Carolina voted to secede from the Union. The elder Franklin Moses, reflecting the new consensus among his planter patrons, had offered the state senate resolution calling for a convention and was a major figure at the convention itself. South Carolina now considered itself an independent nation and was prepared to go to war to maintain its independence. Before Lincoln was inaugurated, six other states—Texas, Louisiana, Mississippi, Florida, Alabama, and Georgia—followed South Carolina out of the Union and banded together as the Confederate States of America. This new Confederacy chose Jefferson Davis, a U.S. senator from Mississippi, as its president. Despite these developments, many politicians in both the North and South continued to hope that some compromise might be reached and the crisis defused. Several of the southern states, including Virginia, the South's most important state, had not yet seceded, and unionist politicians continued, in the spring of 1861, to search for some formula to avert the breakup of the United States. Perhaps such a formula might have been found, but events in Charleston's harbor soon made compromise impossible.

At the mouth of Charleston's harbor sits a tiny artificial island, Fort Sumter, constructed after the War of 1812 as part of the United States' system of coastal defenses. Sumter's artillery, along with guns positioned at Fort Moultrie, a point of land on Sullivan's Island across the harbor from Fort Sumter, guarded the approaches to Charleston. The Charleston forts and one Florida fort were the only federal installations in the self-proclaimed Confederate states that had not been quickly abandoned by federal authorities. On December 26, 1860, the federal commander in Charleston, Maj. Robert Anderson, evacuated his troops from the indefensible Fort Moultrie to the more secure Fort Sumter and waited for orders from Washington. An attempt by the U.S. Navy to resupply Fort Sumter in January failed when South Carolina artillery, in response to an order issued by Governor Pickens and penned by Frank Moses, opened fire on the supply ship *Star of the West* and drove it away.

The standoff at Fort Sumter continued through Lincoln's inauguration in March 1861. At that point, Confederate commissioners traveled to Washington to demand the surrender of the fort. They were officially rebuffed but received tacit assurances from Secretary of State Seward that the government would not attempt to reinforce the fort while discussions and deliberations continued. Both in Washington and in the temporary Confederate capital, Montgomery, Alabama, many influential politicians argued for a cautious approach. A number of Confederate officials thought secession could be accomplished without war. A number of federal officials hoped a peaceful resolution to the Sumter question would help persuade Virginia to remain in the Union. By April, though, Sumter's supplies were running out and President Lincoln ordered a relief expedition to leave for Charleston. Confederate president Davis, in turn, ordered southern artillery to open fire on the fort. Sumter's guns replied and for two days the citizens of Charleston cheered the artillery barrages from the waterfront.[50] Finally, Major Anderson indicated that he was ready to surrender and a triumphant flotilla of soldiers and civilians headed for the little island. Franklin Moses, who had watched the bombardment with excitement, was one of the first to reach Sumter, and along with several other men, he replaced the Stars and Stripes with South Carolina's green and white palmetto flag.

News of the fighting at Fort Sumter spread quickly via telegraph. President Lincoln asked the loyal states for seventy-five thousand troops to suppress the rebellion. With Lincoln's call for troops, voices of moderation in Virginia, Arkansas, North Carolina, and Tennessee were drowned out and these states left the Union for the Confederacy.

The War

For many of South Carolina's Jews, including several members of the Moses family, the war brought injury and death. For others, like E. W. Moise, the war brought honor and glory. For Frank Moses, the war brought neither. Moses survived the war physically unscathed but without the honors or renown that might have paved the way for a postwar political career. Initially, Frank Moses seemed to be blessed by his father's support, the governor's patronage, and his role at Fort Sumter. But in due course, his star began to lose its luster.

In the first year of the war, Moses continued to serve as Governor Pickens's assistant. His close association with Pickens, however, soon became a liability. After a year in office, Pickens was generally regarded as an incompetent executive and was blamed for the military and civil disasters that soon befell the state. In November 1861 Union forces captured Hilton Head Island. From the island's excellent harbor, federal warships could sail upriver and attack interior areas of the state. In December of the same year, much of Charleston was burned to the ground in what is still known today as the Great Charleston Fire. The cause of the fire was never determined, but Pickens was widely censured for the city's lack of preparation and the scope of the disaster. Early in 1862 Union forces captured the harbor at Georgetown, providing federal warships even greater access to the state's interior. In a panic, the state's Secession Convention reconvened and created a five-member executive council to oversee South Carolina's affairs. Though the governor would be one of the five councillors, the body's purpose was clearly to oversee the governor's actions. In 1862 Pickens's term ended and the state legislature elected a new governor, Gen. Milledge Bonham, a military man who had commanded an infantry brigade at the First Battle of Manassas. The legislature hoped that Bonham's military experience would help him bolster the state's defenses. The new governor replaced many of Pickens's staffers with his own men. Young Franklin Moses was asked to leave the governor's mansion and seek other ways of serving the Confederate cause.

As an able-bodied young man, Moses would have little choice but to serve in some branch of the Confederate military. Fortunately, before leaving office, Governor Pickens had been able to arrange a commission for Moses in the regular South Carolina forces. In January 1863 the honorary colonel became a regular lieutenant assigned to Company F of the First South Carolina artillery regiment defending Charleston's harbor. All through 1863 the First South Carolina saw considerable action. Its artillery helped repel a strong effort by federal forces to capture Fort Sumter in April 1863. In July, Union infantry, including the black soldiers of the 54th Massachusetts depicted in the film Glory, sought to capture Morris Island, which housed Battery Wagner, an artillery position that was an important component of Charleston's defensive perimeter. The initial attack was repelled with heavy losses on both sides. But after fifty days of heavy bombardment, Confederate forces evacuated Battery Wagner and Morris Island during the first week in September 1863.

Moses apparently acquitted himself well when his company came under fire from Union war ships. One observer said Moses had an excellent record in the Confederate army and claimed that when the Confederate flag over Fort Sumter was shot away, the young lieutenant climbed the fort's flagstaff under heavy fire to replace it.[51] Nevertheless, at the beginning of 1864, Frank Moses took himself out of the fight by securing reassignment to a rear echelon position.

By 1864 disaffection with the Confederacy and a sense of impending doom were rampant throughout South Carolina. After Union forces captured Morris Island and replaced Battery Wagner's guns with their own, heavy federal artillery on the island could rain shells on the city of Charleston. Much of the city was destroyed and its residents evacuated during more than five hundred days of unrelenting shelling. The majority of South Carolina's leading politicians, including Andrew McGrath, who would be elected governor at the end of the year, were sharply critical of the Confederate government's policies and virtually every newspaper in the state was vehemently opposed to Confederate president Jefferson Davis, who was blamed for the South's military defeats and economic distress.[52] Carolinians were convinced that their state had not been adequately defended while South Carolina troops were being sent to fight in Virginia and Georgia. Indeed, as Sherman's army drew nearer to South Carolina in 1864 only a handful of troops defended the state.

Within the army, morale was low and desertion rates were high among South Carolina's soldiers, as was increasingly true throughout the Confederate army.[53] South Carolinians had thought the war would be short and glorious. Initially, men eagerly volunteered for service in the army.[54] But, in three years of fighting, South Carolina's forces had suffered heavy casualties. Indeed, by the end of the war, roughly twenty thousand of the state's soldiers had perished. This figure represents approximately one-third of the men of military age living in the state at the beginning of the war. No other state suffered such a high casualty rate.[55] As an almost inevitable result of this carnage, by 1864, conscripts were failing to report for duty and South Carolina veterans were deserting their posts. No troops were coming in, even though, as Col. John S. Preston put it, "Carolina's soil is desecrated."[56] In some parts of the state, armed bands of deserters roamed freely, offering violent resistance to conscription officers and provost marshals. Regiments on their way to the front lines were often riddled with desertion and absenteeism.[57] Even more importantly, a number of South Carolina's politicians began to advocate an armistice and reconciliation with the North.[58]

Against this backdrop of malaise and defeatism, Franklin Moses left the war. Unlike many others, Moses did not walk away from his post or feign an injury that might relieve him of duty. He did, however, secure a transfer away from Charleston and incessant attacks by federal forces. Moses's transfer took him to Edgefield, a district on the North Carolina border, far from the troubled coast. Lieutenant Moses was assigned to serve as an enrolling officer. His job consisted of supervising the district's conscription efforts, certifying disability claims, and keeping a watchful eye open for deserters. In the closing months of the war, Moses was assigned the thankless task of scraping together a force of whatever men could be found, including the very young, the very old, and the disabled, to slow Sherman's march through the South. By the end of the war, Moses had no job. Early in 1865, the Confederacy gave up trying to conscript soldiers. So few reported for duty that the Conscript Bureau was abolished and the army relied on volunteers and militiamen.[59]

At war's end Moses was still in Edgefield shuffling papers. He made the hundred-mile trip to his home in Sumter across a bleak landscape transformed by fighting, arson, and looting. Sumter itself was relatively unscathed as were the homes belonging to Moses and his father. Yet both men found themselves impoverished. The younger Moses had no source of income. The older Moses had held important positions in a government that no longer existed and had invested much of his prewar fortune in now worthless Confederate bonds. And if the Moses family's economic prospects seemed tenuous, young Franklin Moses's once-bright political prospects appeared to be nearly extinguished. Even assuming that South Carolina would eventually be permitted to resume its place in the Union and to select public officials of its own choosing, it seemed unlikely that the state would ever see young Franklin Moses as a suitable candidate for leadership.

To begin with, Moses's war record was undistinguished, to say the least. He had not disgraced himself, but in a state with many who could claim to have been war heroes, a rear-echelon Confederate officer would hardly be a hot political commodity in a region where military service had become a "prime ladder" to prominence.[60] Carolinians had come to hate the war but they held their warriors in high esteem. Moses, it was said, had "lost caste" with his fellow Carolinians.[61] The fact that Moses had transferred from the front lines to a post far from the battle would certainly be held against him, even by those who had, themselves, developed a lack of enthusiasm for the fight. In fact, during Reconstruction, the Democratic press often averred that Moses had been a coward. As one newspaper put it in 1874, "The first fight he got into, he discovered the fact that his nerves were not specially adapted to the music of battle; in other words, a march to the rear to the sound of the enemy's cannon was a most agreeable proceeding."[62]

Frank Moses's postwar prospects were also constrained by his Jewish background. Before the war, Jews had been better accepted and had had more political opportunity in the South than in the North. After the war, the position of the Jews changed. Though Jews had served and were patronized by the southern elite, they had never been fully accepted by the common white populace of the region. Many southerners questioned whether Jews should be considered as members of the white race, the black race, or a separate racial category.[63] This distaste for Jews became evident when the hardships of the war weakened the Jews' planter patrons and emboldened the normally quiescent white populace to speak its mind. Toward the end of the war, a wave of agrarian radicalism swept the South. One observer in South Carolina noted that as the war drew to its conclusion many of "our citizens who have been accustomed to all the luxuries, have been compelled to live on government rations," while, at the same time, the common white country people demonstrated increased "assertiveness" and stood ready to "terrorize" their enemies. In South Carolina, common folk expressed resentment when they heard about Charleston's active social scene, and on several occasions, members of the Secession Convention were attacked on the street by common folk who accused them of dragging the state into a war for the benefit of the rich.[64]

Despite the class distinctions that had been endemic in the region, the common whites of the South were extraordinarily loyal to the Confederacy and proved themselves willing to endure great hardship and privation as the war continued, despite the absence of any direct material stake in a war fought to preserve slavery and the power of the slaveholding planter elite. For example, in North Carolina before the war more than 70 percent of the populace owned no slaves at all. Yet large numbers of North Carolinians served in the Confederate army and more than forty thousand gave their lives for the Confederate cause. The presence of millions of black slaves at the bottom of southern society encouraged poor southern whites to regard themselves as members of the white ruling class. So, unlike the Ukrainian peasantry that it superficially resembled, the southern white lower class had little animosity toward the region's landlords. Indeed, the poor willingly followed the rich into battle.

Nevertheless as the war dragged on, price inflation and shortages of goods produced extensive resentment. Planters were accused of hoarding, speculating, evading military service, and even trading with the enemy. In many parts of the South, popular resistance to conscription and military requisition of food and supplies began to develop. In some areas, this resistance was expressed in the language of class warfare, and the slave owners were denounced for seeking to benefit from the "poor-man's war."

Opposition did not end with rhetoric. In several of the southern states, armed bands of poor whites resisting conscription and impressments fought Confederate authorities and attacked plantations. Even the newspapers that staunchly supported the war effort declared that impressment of provisions had led to "gross abuses, oppressing the people, and menacing the towns and villages of the state with starvation."[65] Some poor whites began to believe that a northern victory would benefit their class. A Confederate colonel sent to suppress bands of armed draft resisters in the Appalachian Mountains reported that some of his prisoners believed that the Union army would come to help them and that when it did "the property of Southern men was to be confiscated and divided amongst those who would take up arms for Lincoln." In South

Carolina, as Sherman's forces approached the capital of Columbia, Col. A. R. Taylor issued orders for the 23rd South Carolina militia to muster at the courthouse. Militiamen refused to report for duty and responded, instead, with death threats against the colonel.[66]

As the South began to collapse militarily, civil authority weakened as well, and state and local governments were no longer able to offer much protection for the property or privileges of the southern elite. By 1865 lawlessness had reached the point that, in some regions, the military and civil authorities were compelled to look to the "better class" among the armed bands of resisters and deserters to provide security against the others.

One element of this agrarian radicalism was an attack on the planters' Jewish allies and agents. In the later stages of the war, on a number of occasions, Confederate troops refused to serve under Jewish officers. When, for example, a Jewish colonel was assigned to a Texas regiment, the enlisted men rebelled. Soldiers made derisive comments and engaged in such forms of harassment as cutting off the tail of the officer's horse. The colonel was soon reassigned, sparking a celebration by the troops.[67]

Throughout the South, Jews were denounced as profiteers, who enriched themselves at the expense of their countrymen. Several members of the Confederate House of Representatives, including Henry Foote of Tennessee, William Chilton of Alabama, William Miles of South Carolina, and Robert Hilton of Florida, voiced such sentiments. Foote charged from the floor of Congress that Jews had taken over 90 percent of the business activity of the South and were engaged in illegal trade with the Union. The end of the war, said Foote, would find "nearly all the property of the Confederacy in the hands of Jewish Shylocks."[68]

Chilton, for his part, blamed wartime shortages and inflated prices directly on the Jews who, in his view, hoarded goods and drove up costs. Chilton cited an instance in which this Jewish scheme had been foiled. A vessel seeking to run the Union blockade had run aground on a desolate part of the Florida coast and its cargo had been confiscated by the authorities. Jews somehow learned the location of the confiscated cargo and "at least one hundred flocked there, led even to this remote point by the scent of gain, and they had to be driven back actually at the point of the bayonet."[69]

This theme of Jewish profiteering was echoed in newspapers, private correspondence, and diaries throughout the South. The well-known wartime diaries of John Beauchamps Jones, a clerk in the Confederate War Department, are filled with complaints against Jewish merchants. Instead of contributing to the war effort, the Jews, reports Jones, "are busy speculating on the street corners." Indeed, muses Jones, "they have injured the cause more than the armies of Lincoln. If we gain our independence, instead of being the vassals of the Yankees, we shall find all our wealth in the hands of the Jews. . . . They care not which side gains the day, so they gain the profits."[70]

Jews were accused not only of profiteering but also of shirking military service. One writer charged that "the Israelites laid in stocks [of merchandise] which, in almost every instance, were retailed at rates from five hundred to one thousand per cent above ordinary prices." Moreover, "having husbanded their goods for one or two years and converted them into coin, if they did not decamp from the Confederacy altogether, they found a thousand and one excuses for not bearing arms."[71]

In several instances, such sentiments led to direct action against the Jews. In Thomasville, Georgia, a public meeting was called to discuss the conduct of Jewish merchants who were accused of being unpatriotic for charging high prices for their goods. The town meeting adopted a series of resolutions denouncing Jews, prohibiting them from visiting the town, and ordering all those presently living there to leave. In Talbotton, another Georgia community, a grand jury denounced Jewish merchants for "evil and unpatriotic conduct." In still another Georgia village, a group of women, including the wives of soldiers, raided Jewish stores and seized merchandise at gunpoint, accusing the Jews of enriching themselves while their men were at war.[72]

Jews were frequently charged with showing too much sympathy

for and being willing to deal with blacks. There was some truth to the latter accusation. Jewish traders usually occupied the lowest rungs of the southern commercial ladder and were, therefore, the most likely merchants and the most willing to sell used clothes and other articles to free blacks and slaves. Commercial dealings between whites and slaves were closely regulated and could entail some risk to the white merchant. Only the most marginal merchants—often Jews—were involved in this trade.

A special target for anti-Semitic rhetoric was Judah P. Benjamin, who had been a U.S. Senator from Louisiana, served first as Confederate secretary of war and then secretary of state, and was probably the most able public official in the Confederate government. Nevertheless, he was vilified as "Judas Iscariot Benjamin" and blamed for every misfortune that befell the Confederacy. He was accused of undermining the South's military effort, sabotaging its diplomacy, and protecting the Jewish speculators who were said to be ruining the South's economy. Some, indeed, went so far as to suggest that because of the high position held by a Jew, God was reluctant to listen to the prayers of the Confederacy's citizens.[73]

The North was certainly not free of anti-Semitic rhetoric during the Civil War era. Newspapers often charged that Jews shirked military service or even actively supported the rebellion. As in the South, Jewish merchants and speculators were frequently blamed for high prices and shortages. As much as southerners maligned the Confederacy's Jewish secretary of state Judah Benjamin, the northern press was even more vicious toward the "little Jew" who showed the same mercy toward the union "that his ancestors had shown toward Jesus Christ." In 1862 General Grant issued the order that expelled Jews from his Tennessee military district on the grounds that they were engaged in trade with the enemy. Lincoln rescinded the order. Grant himself apparently saw nothing anti-Semitic about his order. To this uncouth westerner, who later counted the Seligmans among his chief political backers, Jew was merely a synonym for peddler.

But anti-Semitic sentiment came as a greater surprise to southern

Jews because anti-Semitic rhetoric had been far less common in the antebellum South than in the North. Attacks on Catholics, foreigners, and Jews were a staple of northern journalism in the period before the Civil War. In the South, by contrast, Jews had been relatively unmolested.

The Jews had thought they were accepted in southern society and were shocked to discover what their neighbors really thought of them as the decline and the fall of the Confederacy unleashed a wave of anti-Semitism. During this period some Jews, such as the Strauss family that founded Macy's, left the South to escape the anti-Jewish sentiments of their neighbors.[74] The Strauss family had owned a store in Talbotton, one of the towns where Jews had come under attack.

In the Old South, Jews had occasionally risen to positions of power, though generally as "court Jews," trusted agents of the planter aristocracy. They were governors, senators, members of Congress, judges, and state legislators. Jews would not be so close to power in the post-Reconstruction South. During the years between Reconstruction and 2008, the states of the former Confederacy produced one Jewish senator, no Jewish governors, and, outside the Florida coastal enclaves populated by Jewish retirees, only five members of Congress.

At the end of the war, Frank Moses seemed unlikely to achieve his prewar ambitions. He was without funds; his war record was mediocre; and he had a Jewish background. This congeries of disabilities did not portend a bright future for young Frank Moses, Jewnier.

CHAPTER TWO

The Making of a Scalawag

B Y THE END OF THE WAR, South Carolina had suffered enormous human and economic losses. Nearly twenty thousand of the state's young men had been killed and thousands more wounded. The state's economy had been devastated. Homes, stables, factories, and warehouses had been looted and burned. The slaves, a species of property worth hundreds of millions of dollars before the war, had been freed. Additional hundreds of millions invested in now-worthless Confederate bonds and paper money were lost. The state's two largest cities, Charleston and Columbia, were in ruins, their streets clogged with debris and garbage. Miles of roads and railroad tracks had been destroyed by Union forces, leaving the state's transportation system in shambles. Food was in short supply and thousands of Carolinians were starving. Military and civil authority had collapsed everywhere. The lawlessness that had begun in the closing months of the war grew worse as groups of armed deserters, undisciplined soldiers, common criminals, freedmen, and miscellaneous displaced people roamed about looking for food and sometimes engaging in robbery and looting. Many of the planters who had long ruled the state and had led it into war now faced economic ruin. Indeed, members of the planter class, including some who had only recently commanded regiments and brigades of troops, now found themselves working as porters and day laborers hoping to earn enough money to feed their families.[1]

But South Carolina and its antebellum rulers were not entirely without resources. More than 170,000 bales of cotton, worth millions of dollars, had been hidden during the war. With the end of the naval blockade, they were quickly shipped abroad and sold. Most of the state's cotton factories were still intact and ready to resume production. And while some planters had patriotically invested their money in Confederate paper, others had more prudently sent funds abroad or hoarded gold and silver.[2] Economic recovery might be possible if some semblance of order could be restored in the state.

The only agency capable of bringing an end to the state's turmoil was the federal government, in particular, the U.S. Army. In the aftermath of the war, Carolinians were compelled to look to their former foes for relief and sustenance. Gov. A. G. McGrath attempted to restore some semblance of order, but the U.S. military declared his orders null and void.[3] In May 1865, a month after Robert E. Lee's surrender, the U.S. government declared martial law in South Carolina, arrested the governor and a number of other state officials, and divided the state into nine military districts, each garrisoned by a contingent of federal troops. The army moved quickly to restore order and established a system of military tribunals, partly staffed by local lawyers and judges, to deal with accused criminals as well as civil complaints. Laborers were employed to clear the streets of Charleston and Columbia of trash and debris, and to begin the work of repairing the state's roads and railroad facilities. Agents of the just-established Freedmen's Bureau were dispatched to deal with the problems of the newly freed slaves. The bureau's first task was food relief, and during the next year, its agents distributed tens of thousands of packages of army rations to starving blacks—and whites—throughout the state.[4] General (later governor) Robert K. Scott wrote, "On issuing days might be seen the white lady of respectability standing side by side with the African, both awaiting their turn to receive their weekly supply of rations."[5]

Consistent with a pattern seen throughout the South, local federal army commanders generally had much more sympathy for white Carolinians than for the blacks whom they had been sent to free from slavery. Now that the war was over, army officers could imagine white southerners as friends and neighbors which, in some cases, they had been before 1861. Often too, the racial attitudes of white northern soldiers were not so different from those of the defeated southerners. In many instances, the Union army displayed magnanimity toward South Carolina's whites while exhibiting disdain for its blacks. In Charleston, for example, the local army commander ordered freedmen who had left their owners' plantations in search of food and work to return to their farms. Those who remained in the city were put to work cleaning the streets. And when local whites rioted in protest of black troops in the city, the black units were disarmed and white troops, armed with clubs, were assigned to keep watch over them.[6] Not surprisingly, whites applauded the Yankee soldiers as "gentlemanly and courteous."[7]

Though white Carolinians had few complaints about the U.S. Army, they were less pleased by other aspects of the federal occupation. Congress had imposed a number of taxes on the defeated southern states and had authorized the seizure of property deemed to be abandoned because its owner was away in the service of the Confederacy. Congress had also authorized the seizure of cotton and other property that had belonged to the Confederate government. Since the agents employed to effect these seizures earned a commission of 25 percent, they were happy to seize cotton, horses, wagons, tobacco, and other goods that belonged to private citizens, declaring these to be Confederate property.[8] Property owners had little recourse in such cases. These property seizures came on top of General Sherman's famous Field Order 15, confiscating many of the sea islands and adjoining lands for the use of the freedmen who had followed his army as it cut a swath of destruction across the South.

South Carolina's whites were also concerned about the activities of the Freedmen's Bureau. The bureau had been established by Congress in March 1865 to aid former slaves by providing health care, education, and employment. The bureau, which was an agency within the Department of War, was headed by Gen. Oliver O. Howard. The bureau's agents, however, were mainly civilians, including many former abolitionists and others with a strong commitment to ameliorating the economic, social, and political condition of the freedmen. The bureau established numerous schools and hospitals, taught blacks to read and write, and to the dismay of the state's whites, encouraged blacks to view themselves as the political and social equals of their former masters. The bureau also sought to develop labor contracts to govern the new relationship between now-free black farm workers and their former masters. White land owners, of course, had hoped to dictate the terms of their relationships with black workers and took strong exception to the bureau's attempts to interfere in this realm. A number of bureau officials, General Scott is the prime example, used their contacts with blacks to launch political careers in the state.

Against the backdrop of property seizures and the activities of the Freedmen's Bureau, South Carolina's traditional political leaders made an attempt to resume control of their state's affairs. In mid-May, a delegation of notables traveled to Washington to meet with President Johnson and request that he turn the state over to a provisional civil government. Johnson agreed to the request, and in June he appointed Benjamin F. Perry to serve as South Carolina's provisional governor until a state Constitutional Convention could be called to formally abolish slavery, nullify the ordinance of secession, and provide for popular elections to be held. These steps were expected to restore South Carolina's place in the Union.

Before the war, Benjamin Perry had been a staunch Unionist. After South Carolina seceded, however, Perry held several important Confederate offices and his son, William, served with distinction in the Confederate cavalry.[9] Perry's combination of Unionist sympathies and Confederate service made him acceptable to both the government in Washington and the people of South Carolina. He was appointed provisional governor at the end of June 1861. Perry moved to reestablish civil authority in the state and to restore the old order in South Carolina. He began by reinstating the authority of the state's civil courts and persuading the military to confine the work of its tribunals to cases in which freedmen were involved.

He then authorized the state's magistrates to begin administering oaths of allegiance to thousands of Carolinians. Under the terms of a presidential proclamation, former Confederates who swore to support the Constitution and the Union would be pardoned for their participation in the rebellion and would again be eligible to vote and hold public office. The president's amnesty proclamation had exempted certain classes of Confederates, including certain wealthy individuals and important government officials. These, however, were eligible for presidential pardons on a case by case basis. Perry recommended hundreds of individuals—essentially the state's entire antebellum leadership stratum—for pardons and President Johnson obliged in almost every instance. Once these people received pardons, Perry reappointed many to their old state offices and recommended others for federal offices in the state. When Perry's appointments were questioned, he defended them in a letter to the president. "In selecting my appointments from those who were equally guilty in the rebellion, I did think and still think, that they who had the courage and manhood to imperil their lives in battle, and were maimed and helpless, were more deserving than their compeers, who had meanly skulked from danger and kept out of the war."[10] In other words, ardent supporters of the Confederacy were to be preferred to Unionists.

Perry also addressed the issue of black troops garrisoned in the state. Among the federal units stationed in South Carolina were several companies of black soldiers. The presence of these troops enraged white Carolinians. Black soldiers from the North, moreover, mingled with the freedmen and encouraged them to insist on respectful treatment from whites and, above all, to demand that the government turn over to them the lands and property of their former masters. Whites claimed that black troops incited a rebellious and violent spirit among the freedmen and discouraged them from working. Former general Wade Hampton complained to President Johnson that "the very first act of peace consisted of pouring into our whole country a horde of barbarians—your brutal negro troops under their no less brutal and more degraded Yankee officers. Every license was allowed to these wretches and the grossest outrages were committed by them with impunity."[11]

In August, Perry brought these concerns to Gen. Quincy Gillmore, commander of Union forces in South Carolina, and to Gillmore's immediate superior, Gen. George Meade. He found, in the two generals, a receptive audience for white protestations. Both were sympathetic to South Carolina's whites and disdainful of blacks, including those under their command. General Meade said he was altogether opposed to having black troops in the army and was constrained only by political considerations in the North from getting rid of them. General Gillmore echoed Meade's sentiments and promised to immediately withdraw his black units to the seacoast forts where they could be watched and would have minimal contact with the civilian population.[12] The generals also agreed to allow Perry to organize volunteer white militia companies to help keep the peace in areas where the withdrawal of black troops would deplete the army's forces. Where the presence of black troops had encouraged freedmen to press their grievances and attempt to make the most of their newfound liberty, armed white militiamen would make certain that blacks returned to work on their former owners' plantations. "It is a source of congratulations," said Perry, "to know that the colored troops whose atrocious conduct has disgraced the service and filled the public mind with the most horrible apprehensions . . . are to be placed in garrisons on the coast where they can do no further mischief."[13]

Evacuation of the black troops would also help ensure that the statewide elections scheduled for early September to choose delegates for the state's Constitutional Convention would not be disrupted by freedmen protesting their exclusion from the process. By state law, the suffrage was limited to white males. Former Confederates who had taken the oath of loyalty or received presidential pardons were eligible to vote and stand for election but blacks were not. Governor Perry said, "This is a white man's government and intended for white men only." Exclusion of blacks from the state's effort to produce a new constitution brought sharp rebukes in the northern press and might have stirred up expressions of discontent within the state. But without the black troops to incite and protect them, the freedmen remained quiescent as the state's antebellum rulers sought to reassert their political authority and autonomy.

Blacks were not the only Carolinians who could not vote in September 1865. Whether by design or by chance, loyalty oaths had not yet been administered in most up-country districts where many of the state's poor whites lived. Hence, the electorate was small and consisted disproportionately of the better classes of South Carolina's whites. These voters were more than happy to support the return of the old political order. The 113 Constitutional Convention delegates who assembled in Columbia in September 1861 included many of the most important member's of South Carolina's prewar political elite. Perry called them "the ablest, wisest and most distinguished men of South Carolina."[14] Delegates included former judges, former governors, former members of the Confederate Congress, and four generals and six colonels late of the Confederate army. Among the delegates were a number of individuals who had attended the 1860 Secession Convention, which had met in the same church that now hosted the state's Constitutional Convention. Former governor Francis Pickens, the man who had led the state into secession, was a delegate. John Inglis, the individual who had introduced the resolution of secession in 1860 was a delegate. And duly elected from Sumter District was none other than the elder Franklin Moses.

In the first month after the war, the Moses family had been forced to live on government rations. By the time of the convention, however, the family had begun to repair its fortunes. Franklin Moses Jr. had been able to secure a position as a civilian magistrate on the military tribunal assigned to Sumter. Typically, these military courts consisted of two army officers and a locally recruited civilian. The military officers generally had no legal training. They tended to rely on their civilian colleague, typically a lawyer or judge, for advice on legal and procedural matters. This position not only provided Moses with an income and some influence in the district but also helped his father revive his own legal practice. Clients calculated, not without reason, that the younger Moses would tip the scales of justice in favor of those represented by his father.[15]

As required by the federal government, the 1865 convention nullified the 1861 Ordinance of Secession. It also abolished slavery in the state but not without demands that slaveholders be compensated for their losses. Several delegates averred that means were needed to control "the vast throng of ignorant blacks, so suddenly released from servitude" and called for the appointment of a commission to look into the matter. The report of this commission led later to adoption of the infamous Black Codes that outraged opinion in the North.

The convention also changed the state's system of voting and representation to provide for direct popular election of the governor and presidential electors and to reduce the advantage in legislative apportionment that had traditionally been afforded low-country districts over their up-country counterparts. The issue of legislative apportionment had divided the state throughout its history. Wealthy, low-country planters had established the "parish" system of apportionment. Under this scheme, low-country judicial districts were divided into parishes. Each parish was entitled to one state senator though it might have only twenty or thirty voters. Up-country districts, with as many as two or three thousand voters, were not divided into parishes. Hence the entire district elected only one senator. This was one of the instruments through which the large planters had dominated state politics. In the debate over apportionment, Moses sided with the up-country delegates. Traditionally, Moses had spoken for the low-country planters, but many of these had lost their fortunes during the war and political power within the state seemed to be shifting. Moses reflected this shift by taking a stand that made him popular with the representatives of the up-country whites.[16]

A group of black Charlestonians also petitioned the convention to address the matter of black suffrage but most delegates regarded the idea as too radical and outlandish to be worthy of consideration. Apparently a small number of South Carolina land owners would have been happy to use property rather than race as the basis for the suffrage, thereby enfranchising a tiny number of blacks and disenfranchising many poor whites, but this idea was not broached publicly.[17] A more common view at the convention was that emancipation was a bad idea forced on the state by the federal government. A number of delegates argued that the state should not recognize emancipation unless slaveholders were compensated for their lost property, and they sought a stipulation in the new state constitution prohibiting blacks from engaging in any occupation other than manual labor. Governor Perry blocked this proposal on the grounds that the federal government would never accept it. The precise status of blacks under the new constitution was unclear. They were no longer slaves, but they would not be citizens. The convention adopted a resolution providing for the creation of a commission that would recommend laws defining the political and economic status of the freedmen.[18] The convention also affirmed that blacks would not be allowed to testify in court cases involving whites and established a special system of courts to deal with cases involving blacks. After providing for legislative and gubernatorial elections to be held during the second week in October, the convention adjourned, satisfied that it had taken an enormous step toward the restoration of self-rule by the white citizens of South Carolina.

Legislative and gubernatorial elections were held in October as scheduled. Under Governor Perry's guidance, the convention had taken the unusual step of nominating a gubernatorial candidate and placing his name on the ballot. The chosen candidate was James L. Orr, one of Perry's longtime political allies. Orr had been a Democratic member of the U.S. House of Representatives from 1849 to 1859 and served as Speaker during the last two years. Like Perry, Orr had for most of his career strongly opposed those who called for secession from the Union. After Lincoln's election, however, Orr jumped on the secessionist bandwagon and was subsequently elected to the Confederate Senate.

Though Orr's was the only name on the ballot, he won by only seven or eight hundred of the nearly twenty thousand votes cast. The remaining votes were cast for Gen. Wade Hampton III, South Carolina's most prominent citizen and greatest civil war hero. Hampton's grandfather had been a colonel in the Revolutionary War and his father had been a colonel in Jackson's army at the Battle of New Orleans.[19] Over the years the Hamptons had become the wealthiest land owners and largest slaveholders in South Carolina. When the state seceded from the Union, Hampton organized and financed a regiment consisting of infantry, cavalry, and artillery that came to be called Hampton's Legion. During the war, Hampton was a much-decorated soldier contributing mightily to the Confederate effort despite suffering severe wounds at the First Manassas, at Seven Pines, and at Gettysburg. He lost both his sons to Union fire on the same day in 1864. Hampton ended the war as a lieutenant general in command of Lee's cavalry corps.

Hampton's standing in South Carolina was such that had he indicated in 1865 that he wanted to be governor, no other candidate would have opposed him. Hampton, however, feared that the North would not tolerate the election of a prominent Confederate general so soon after the war. Hampton also needed time to repair his plantations and recover from his physical wounds. Accordingly, the general declared firmly that he was not a candidate. So many Carolinians, nevertheless, wanted to elect Hampton that the general wound up campaigning to discourage his supporters. General Hampton might still have been elected if he had not made certain that the voters in his home district voted unanimously for Orr.[20]

Even before Orr took office, the newly elected legislature met in special session for the purpose of ratifying the Thirteenth Amendment, which would indicate that South Carolinians had accepted the abolition of slavery. Returning to his prewar state senate seat from Sumter District was Franklin Moses Sr. With the support of his new up-country allies, Moses was elected the senate's president pro tempore. Though some disdained him as an "Israelite," the elder Moses's manners and opinions were always impeccably correct and he was clearly an exception to the poor characters of many of his fellow Jews. When the legislature reconvened for its regular session in

November, it also chose the elder Moses to serve as circuit judge for the Sumter District. It appeared that the fortunes of the Moses family were definitely on the mend, as were those of most of the white citizens of South Carolina. The state, to be sure, remained formally under martial law and its government's actions could be overturned by federal authorities. Nevertheless, South Carolina seemed well on the way to regaining the self-rule it had enjoyed before the war.

When the legislature met in regular session in November 1865, its main order of business was an effort to regulate the new relationship between blacks and whites created by the abolition of slavery. The result was the promulgation of South Carolina's Black Codes. These codes, similar to the ordinances enacted in a number of other southern states, defined a "person of color" as anyone more than one-eighth black. This definition meant that anyone with more than one black great-grandparent was defined as "colored." All others were classified as white. Colored people were granted the right to own land and to enter into contracts. At the same time, they were prohibited from engaging in any occupation besides farming or domestic service without a special license; the contractual relations between colored servants and white masters were spelled out; travel by colored people was restricted; they were prohibited from owning firearms; they were prohibited from marrying whites; and severe penalties were prescribed for any crimes they might commit. Sheriffs were authorized to hire out homeless colored people to white farmers. The codes were to be enforced by a system of special courts and forty-five newly authorized white militia regiments. In essence, the codes established a rigid system of control designed to ensure the social and economic subordination of the freedmen. Colored people were no longer slaves, but they would not be free.

Not long after South Carolina's Black Codes were enacted, they were nullified by the federal military commander Gen. Daniel Sickles. Nevertheless, publication of the codes caused howls of protest in the North. Republican newspapers throughout the North saw the Black Codes as nothing less than an effort by the defeated South to reimpose slavery. The Black Codes were declared to be an affront to those who had died fighting for freedom and another expression of the South's continuing hostility to the Union. South Carolina's 1865 constitution was denounced by the northern press as "a scandalous repudiation of democratic principles" and "a document enacted by men who have come red-handed from the battle field, and to whose garments the blood of our brothers and sons still clings."[21] Some influential northerners averred that the South's loyalty and the safety of the freedmen could only be ensured if blacks were enfranchised. Representatives of South Carolina's small educated black population meeting in the November 1865 Colored People's Convention, asked Congress to place "the strong arm of the law over the entire population of the state," to grant "equal suffrage," and to abolish the "black codes."[22]

Southern whites, of course, regarded the idea of black suffrage as an outrage. But northern Republicans realized that black suffrage could ensure Republican electoral control of the entire region. In a number of southern states, including Mississippi, Alabama, Louisiana, and South Carolina, blacks outnumbered whites by a considerable margin, and even where they were not a majority, blacks constituted a substantial minority of the population. The so-called Radical Republicans, led by Thaddeus Stevens of Pennsylvania in the House of Representatives and Charles Sumner of Massachusetts in the Senate, had long argued in favor of voting rights for blacks. And even those northern Republicans who had no particular sympathy for blacks understood the electoral arithmetic. Enfranchised and politically organized blacks could form a solid Republican base in the South, virtually guaranteeing that the Republican party would control the nation for years to come. Thus, even as President Andrew Johnson declared himself satisfied with events in the South and averred that it was time to fully restore civil authority in the former Confederacy, Congress responded to the Black Codes by refusing to seat the members elected from South Carolina and the other southern states and creating a joint Reconstruction Committee to inquire into the question of whether the South was as yet entitled to congressional representation.

By the beginning of 1866 President Johnson and congressional Republicans were locked in an all-out struggle over Reconstruction. Johnson favored a conciliatory policy toward the defeated South and sought to restore the southern states to the Union as soon as was practicable. Between January and November 1866, Johnson ignored congressional objections, reduced the number of federal troops stationed in the South—only twenty-seven hundred in the entire state of South Carolina—and prepared for the complete elimination of the federal government's military presence in the former Confederacy. Congressional Republican leaders Stevens and Sumner, on the other hand, were adamantly opposed to restoring the power of the South's prewar leadership and had already begun to develop their own plan for the region. Congress's plan would require a drastic reorganization of the governments of the southern states as well as enfranchisement of the freedmen.

Early in 1866 Congress overrode Johnson's veto of the Civil Rights Act, which declared that all people born in the United States had equal rights with regard to employment, property ownership, and judicial procedure. This act was Congress's direct response to the Black Codes, superseding and nullifying their provisions by federal law. In June 1866, Congress submitted the Fourteenth Amendment to the states. The Fourteenth Amendment prohibited the states from depriving citizens of rights to which they would be entitled by the federal Constitution, barred most former Confederate officials from holding public office without congressional approval, disallowed any debts owed by the former Confederacy, declared that slaveholders would not be compensated for the loss of their slaves, and affirmed Congress's power to enforce all these provisions whether the states liked it or not. Reaction in the South was immediate and unanimous. To southerners, the Fourteenth Amendment meant black suffrage, and every southern legislature emphatically rejected the proposed constitutional change. South Carolina's governor thundered, "History furnishes few examples of a people who have been required to concede more to the will of their conquerors than the people of the South." South Carolina, he declared, had already agreed to "obliterate the constitution which had been made and hallowed by such hands as Rutledge, Pinckney, Marion and Sumter." Now, given its black majority, the state was being asked to submit to black rule. "Do sensible, fair and just men of the North," Orr asked in his address to the legislature, "desire that these people . . . steeped in ignorance, crime and vice, should go to the polls and elect men to Congress who are to pass laws taxing and governing them?"[23] The legislature's answer was an emphatic no. In December 1866 South Carolina's house rejected the amendment by a vote of ninety-five to one; its senate followed suit.[24]

Even as South Carolinians were fuming over the Civil Rights Act and the proposed Fourteenth Amendment, events in the North were quickly rendering their views moot. The congressional Reconstruction Committee had filed its report in June 1866. The report was a damning indictment of the southern states and Johnson's Reconstruction policies. "In no instance in the southern states was any regard paid to any other consideration than obtaining immediate admission to Congress under the barren form of any election in which no precaution was taken to secure the regulatory of proceedings or the ascent of the people," the report began. "Instead," the report continued, "all feeling of conciliation on the part of the North has been treated with contempt. . . . The burden rests upon the Southern people . . . to show that they ought to resume their federal relations. . . . They must prove that they have established a republican form of government in harmony with the Constitution and laws of the United States—that all hostile purposes have ceased, and that they have given adequate guarantees against future treason."[25] The report went on to assert that the southern states lacked proper governments or constitutions, had forfeited all political rights and privileges, and could be reestablished as governments only through congressional action.

The Reconstruction report and its implications became a major focus of the 1866 congressional campaign. President Johnson traveled about the country speaking against the Radical Republicans and defending his own conciliatory policies toward the defeated southern states. Republican congressional leaders pointed to the joint committee report and to the southern states' unanimous rejection of the Fourteenth Amendment as evidence of continued southern defiance of national authority. This was to be the first of many electoral campaigns in which Republicans "waved the bloody shirt" of secession and war to retain the allegiance of northern voters. "Vote the way you shot," Republicans would remind voters. The result of the 1866 election was a clear victory for congressional Republicans and a repudiation of the president. With overwhelming majorities in both houses, Congress's Radical leadership could be confident of overturning presidential vetoes and implementing whatever Reconstruction program it might choose.

Congressional Republicans lost no time in taking advantage of their new numbers. In March 1867 Congress passed the First and Second Reconstruction Acts, which declared that no legal government existed in any southern state except Tennessee. The remaining ten southern states were divided into five military districts, each commanded by a general with the authority to remove local officials, overturn state court proceedings, nullify state laws, and ignore state constitutions. South and North Carolina were to constitute the Second Military District under the command of General Sickles. President Johnson vetoed the legislation, but his veto was quickly overridden. Under the terms of the acts, a state might be readmitted to the Union if and only if it held a new Constitutional Convention whose delegates were chosen on the basis of universal male suffrage. The convention, in turn, was required to write a new constitution that, among other matters, provided for universal male suffrage in all state elections. The new state legislature created under this constitution was required to ratify the Fourteenth Amendment. President Johnson argued that these congressional actions were unconstitutional but the president's continuing efforts to thwart Congress's design only led to his impeachment by the House and near-conviction in the Senate.

As these events were unfolding, the younger Franklin Moses was embarking on a new career. In May 1866, H. L. Darr, a Charleston journalist, moved to Sumter to start a weekly paper. He called it the *Sumter News* and hired Frank Moses to serve as its editor. The *News* would compete with the long-established *Sumter Watchman*. Frank Moses had no experience in the newspaper business. Nevertheless, under Moses's leadership, the new paper soon achieved a measure of success. Moses possessed a flair for publicity and soon the new paper's name was spread far and wide through its sponsorship of local carnivals and festivals.[26] The *News,* as is typical of small-town newspapers, offered extensive coverage of local events—everything from district business matters to school picnics.

When it came to national and international coverage, the *Sumter News* broke new ground. The telegraph had come to Sumter just before the war, brought to the district by none other than the elder Franklin Moses.[27] Now, under Moses's leadership, the *News* made extensive use of the telegraph and the Associated Press wire service to bring up-to-date national and international stories to its subscribers. In 1866 the *News'* national coverage focused on the story that would be most important to its readers, the ongoing battle between President Johnson and congressional Republicans over the policies to be pursued with regard to Reconstruction. Readers were kept informed of the president's conciliatory gestures, the report of the congressional Reconstruction Committee, the president's veto of the Civil Rights Act, and the Radical Republicans' subsequent override of the veto. Through frequent summaries of the northern news, readers also learned of the almost unremitting hostility of the northern press toward the defeated South.

Accompanying this news coverage, were Moses's commentaries and editorials. Many of Moses's weekly exhortations called for the development of a new and prosperous industrial South. The region, said Moses, should harness its water power and abundant natural resources to build an industrial economy that would rival that of the North. This idea was a common one in the postwar South and was not likely to offend many readers.

Moses's editorials also expressed outrage at the activities of carpetbaggers—"poor wretched fanatics, miserable deluded madmen, lost to shame, lost to remorse, lost to virtue, lost to reason, lost to God, they stand alone in the amazing enormity of their guilt." He predicted ominously that they would "perish alone in their horrible certainty of that dreadful future which they have created for themselves."[28] Among the carpetbaggers, the worst, in Moses's view, were the northern missionaries who had come to work with the freedmen. Rather than bringing the word of God to their new flock, wrote Moses, these missionaries organized Union League clubs to incite the freedmen to turn against southern whites and to train them to engage in Radical politics. The missionaries called together large meetings of freedmen and addressed them in incendiary language. Throughout the South, said Moses, "wherever the United States flag is unfurled and United States soldiers are stationed," one found "these wicked, mischievous, malignant and prying wretches wandering about with the bible in one hand and the contribution box in the other cautiously planning such ways and means as they think best adapted to impose upon the ignorance and credulity of the poor unfortunate Blacks and to wring from them by force or fraud the hard-earned wages of manual toil." At every garrisoned town "we are certain to meet with at least one or two of these itinerant wretches." These missionaries, "with their high-crowned hats, their closely buttoned semi-military coats, their Uriah-Heepish hands and their saturnine smiles . . . prowled through the countryside . . . with the keen scented rapacity of wild beasts seeking whom they may devour."[29] Moses was expressing sentiments with which his readers were certain to agree. Carpetbaggers and northern missionaries were hated by white southerners, who saw them as agents of political radicalism, social revolution, and miscegenation.

In a similar vein, when it came to the great struggle under way in Washington, Moses generally expressed views that would find a sympathetic audience among his readers. He condemned the Radical Republicans as "fanatics" and "madmen." "Bereft of all sentiment of manhood—of honor, and of magnanimity, they are now gathering together all of their prodigious strength . . . in preparation for . . . an even more savage and barbarous campaign than the first

. . . against the peace and welfare of a distressed and most unhappy population."[30] Since the Thirty-ninth Congress had refused to seat representatives from the former Confederate states, Moses, like other southerners, referred to it as the Rump Congress. The actions of this Rump Congress, according to Moses's editorials, violated the constitutional rights of the southern states and amounted to a "revolution" against the constitutionally prescribed powers of the executive branch. These developments should be seen, said Moses, as a "storm which is now brewing on the political horizon" that was "destined to be one of the most dangerous and hazardous through which the country, or any section of the country has passed."[31]

Moses saw Sen. Charles Sumner and Rep. Thaddeus Stevens as particular villains. Sumner and Stevens were, indeed, the most vehement of the Radical Republicans and were among the principal authors of the Reconstruction Acts that would effectively abolish the southern state governments. Denouncing Sumner, Moses referred to him as "the dainty and perfumed Sumner—the same Sumner whose back and head once had the distinguished honor of receiving marks upon them . . . inflicted by the hand of a South Carolina gentleman in punishment for an insult that had been offered his State."[32] Before the war, Sumner had been the victim of a vicious beating at the hands of South Carolina congressman Preston Brooks. Sumner had been unable to return to his Senate seat for nearly three years as he recovered from the severe head wounds inflicted by Brooks's heavy wooden cane. Southerners generally, and South Carolinians in particular, regarded Brooks as a hero and thought Sumner deserved the beating he had received for his speeches vilifying the South. As for Stevens, his sympathy for blacks must, according to Moses, have an unsavory origin. "We can only account for his bitter, unbending and unreasoning prejudice, by supposing that the innate malignity of the cold-blooded Yankee was kindled to unwonted intensity by a very close intimacy with the Negro race."[33]

Like most southerners, Moses had reacted to the Republican party's 1866 victories with dismay. "The election returns," he wrote, "begin to establish what has heretofore been accepted by us as a foregone conclusion, that those advocating radical policy in the treatment of the conquered states and their ultimate restoration to the Union will triumph over those influenced by more conservative views."[34] And as he examined the proposed Fourteenth Amendment, Moses professed shock and dismay. If adopted, the Fourteenth Amendment would mean that "another degradation would be forced upon us for our acceptance, and that the necessity of giving the colored population a vote and a seat in the jury box. We are told that if voluntarily we do not adopt the Amendment, then it will be forced upon us, and that more than that will follow, namely, Negro suffrage—Negro jurymen—Negro judges, confiscation, military despotism—irresponsible rulers."[35]

What was to be done? Moses looked to President Andrew Johnson for salvation. "Mr. Johnson is a 'tower of strength,'" Moses wrote. Johnson is "the great bulwark that stands between the South and the North, and the great yawning chasm of political evil which threatens to engulf us."[36] Moses urged Johnson, the "Constitutional president," to play the role of a Cromwell and eject the Rump Congress from Washington. "He must make a coup d'etat and like Cromwell with Barebone's Parliament dissolve it by the soldiery and say like the Protector at parting, 'God be the judge between you and me.'"[37] If Johnson called for help, Moses declared, the South would come to his aid. "Five hundred thousand gleaming Southern swords will leap from the scabbards in which they have been merely resting for a season and under the leadership of this man of nerve, the Southern states will cleanse from the records of the nation all stains and foul excrescences of Radical supremacy, and, when their task is done, will lay their armor down, amid the thanks and praises of a free and independent—of a strong and united government."[38]

These editorial positions seem rather naive. Five hundred thousand southern swords had already been ground into the dust of a hundred battlefields, no longer gleamed, and were in no condition to answer a call from President Johnson. But Moses's readers were hardly likely to be offended by the young editor's sentiments. Indeed, his editorial positions made Moses quite popular in Sumter

District. Within a few months he was appointed assistant tax assessor, elected as a vestryman of the Church of the Holy Comforter, and became an officer in the Sumter Masonic lodge. In July he was elected to represent Sumter at a state convention called by the governor to demonstrate South Carolina's support for President Johnson. The younger Moses was said to be a true son of his father.

A New Regime

With passage of the Reconstruction Acts in March and July 1867, Moses's editorial fulminations and, indeed, the opinions of white Carolinians, became irrelevant. Congress had effectively dissolved the state of South Carolina and placed its citizenry under the authority of the regional federal army commander, General Sickles. Neither Sickles nor his successor, Gen. Edward Canby, evinced any hostility toward South Carolinians. Sickles declared that the state's civil authorities could continue to exercise their functions so long as they did not interfere with the military. Both generals consulted closely with Governor Orr on most matters of civil administration. At the governor's suggestion, Sickles issued orders halting foreclosures and protecting personal property from foreclosure sales. This was an extremely popular action that saved the lands of many of the state's impoverished farmers that spring. Canby, for his part, followed the governor's counsel with regard to tax policy, adhering to the low-tax program that had been adopted by the state legislature the previous year. Under military rule, the state's finances were put on a firm footing and public order maintained. South Carolina's white citizens were happy to observe that the military dealt firmly with "bellicose Negroes."[39]

South Carolinians, though, were not happy to see the military carrying out congressional demands that the freedmen be afforded equal rights. General Sickles ordered an end to racial discrimination in public conveyances, going so far as to fine a steamboat captain for refusing to allow a black woman to ride in the first-class section with whites.[40] General Canby ordered that freedmen be allowed to serve on juries. One state judge refused to obey the general's order and was summarily suspended from office by the military authorities. South Carolinians hailed the judge as a hero defending the independence of the judiciary against tyrannical military rule.[41]

Most important, the military authorities prepared the state to elect delegates to a new Constitutional Convention. To the chagrin of the state's white citizens, for the first time in South Carolina history, blacks would have the right to vote. General Canby divided the state into 109 precincts and appointed a board of three men within each precinct to supervise voter registration. As stipulated by the Reconstruction Acts, prospective supervisors were required to take an oath to the effect that they had never borne arms against the United States or held office under an authority hostile to the United States. These requirements excluded virtually all southern-born whites from the registration boards, thus ensuring that their membership would consist mainly of blacks and northerners.[42] When it came to registration itself, a prospective voter was required to take the "test oath," that is, to swear that he had never held any local state or federal office and then rebelled against the federal government or given aid and comfort to its enemies. This requirement was designed to exclude the South's antebellum political leadership from the political arena. Finally, the law provided penalties for anyone attempting to interfere with the registration process.

Initially, South Carolina's whites determined to show their contempt for the process imposed on them from Washington by refusing to register. Whites held their own convention in Columbia in November to protest Congress's program. This convention declared that "the Negro is utterly unfitted to exercise the highest function of a citizen. We protest against this subversion of the social order, whereby an ignorant and depraved race is placed in power and influence above the virtuous, the educated and the refined."[43] Under the leadership of General Hampton, a strategy was developed. On election day, voters would be asked two questions—whether they favored holding a convention and, if so, which of the candidates for delegate in their own district they supported. Whites, a minority in the state, were not likely to fare well in the voting. However, the Reconstruction Acts stipulated that a Constitutional Convention might only be held if a majority of the state's registered voters went to the polls. The Hampton plan called for whites to register and then to boycott the election in order to derail the process. Between August and November 1867, virtually all the state's eligible white men—a total of nearly fifty thousand—took the hated test oath and registered, albeit with no intention of going to the polls. During the same period, however, nearly all the state's eligible black voters— more than eighty thousand—also registered. Thus the newly constituted electorate would be approximately one-third white and two-thirds black, with blacks comprising the majority in twenty-one of the state's thirty-one districts.

At first glance, perhaps, these percentages do not seem surprising. Blacks constituted about 60 percent of the state's population in 1867 and so might have been expected to constitute roughly the same proportion of the state's electorate. But it is important to realize that, with only a handful of exceptions, the state's black citizens had just recently been freed from slavery. Few could read or write; fewer still had any understanding of politics or the electoral process. No black person had ever voted in South Carolina before 1867. Bringing tens of thousands of blacks to their voter registration boards required a prodigious organizational effort. This effort was, in the main, coordinated by the state's Union League clubs.

The Union League of America had been organized in the North as a patriotic society during the war.[44] After the war, the league functioned as an arm of the Republican party in the defeated southern states. Leadership of the league was typically provided initially by northerners, both black and white, but in due course, southern blacks and even a small number of southern whites gave it their support. The league endeavored to create strong statewide organizations of black voters who would support the Republican ticket. Often, indeed, the Union League served as the base upon which state Republican party organizations were built.

The league was organized as a secret society, with nocturnal meetings and elaborate ceremonies designed to provide blacks with a sense of membership in a powerful and mysterious organization that would elevate their status and protect them from intimidation at the hands of whites. In most states, the league's statewide leaders and chief organizers were white Republicans, sometimes associated with the Freedmen's Bureau. But local league councils were often led by blacks. League meetings began with elaborate ceremonies and oaths and continued with political speeches and songs. Members formed a circle around the "fire of liberty" and swore to support the Constitution and to work in support of educating black people in the duties of citizenship. League members swore to give their political support to league leaders and others who advocated the principles of the Republican party. The political issues of the day were discussed and the freedmen taught to understand their own stake in these seemingly abstract matters. League members learned something of parliamentary law and debating and were encouraged to attend trials as spectators.[45] Meetings ended with all present reciting the four Ls: Liberty, Lincoln, Loyal, and League, as they completed a series of secret arm signals known only to members.

The league created a chapter in every precinct in the state, held weekly meetings, and worked to make certain that blacks registered to vote. Freedmen who did not support the call for a convention and the Republican party were often subjected to league intimidation and even threats of violence.[46] To the shock and dismay of white southerners, league meetings were often guarded by armed black sentries.[47] Without the strong leadership and organization provided by the league, black suffrage could never have been a reality, whatever the privilege nominally provided by the law. After the state constitution was adopted, the league worked closely with South Carolina's newly organized Republican party to elect Republican candidates to local, state, and national office.[48]

In the weeks preceding the election itself, the league organized feverishly. The *Charleston Daily News* complained that "the blacks are kept in a constant state of camp meeting excitement. Meetings are held everywhere. Traveling 'disorganizers' . . . visit all points, . . .

and the wildest and most reckless whip the disaffected [into] line."[49] League members attended meetings, rallies, speeches, and picnics at which they were drilled in their electoral duties. The Republican party also funded black orators who traveled from town to town addressing groups of freedmen and reminding them of their political duties. The election was held over a two-day period, November 19 and 20, 1867. League organizers brought company after company, regiment after regiment of black voters to cast their ballots. By the time the polls closed, more than sixty-six thousand blacks had voted—a number that constituted more than a majority of all registered voters.

Even though all but a handful of whites boycotted the election, the Hampton strategy had been defeated. A convention would be held. To make matters worse from the perspective of the state's whites, their electoral boycott had allowed black candidates to win the majority of convention seats. Of the 124 delegates elected to the convention, 76 were black, including a large number of recently freed South Carolina slaves.[50] To the further dismay of white South Carolinians, among the 48 white delegates were twenty-three native South Carolinians—scalawags. These native sons were reviled throughout the state for their apostasy. Some of these scalawags had been prewar Unionists. Others, however, had appeared to be loyal southerners. Among this latter group of renegades, duly elected to represent Sumter district, was one-time fire-eater and Confederate officer, the former conservative pundit Franklin J. Moses.

A Change of Heart?

When the U.S. Congress dissolved South Carolina's government and made it clear that blacks would soon be granted voting rights, two schools of thought developed among white Carolinians and, indeed, among southerners more generally. Members of the first school, led in South Carolina by former governor Perry and a former Confederate officer named Thomas Woodward, argued that white Carolinians should refuse to accept the idea of black political rights. Perhaps South Carolina could not prevent the federal government from carrying out its will, this group argued, but the state should never acquiesce. "If we are to wear manacles," cried Perry, "let them be put on by our tyrants, not ourselves."[51] A second group of politicians, initially associated with Governor Orr and Gen. Wade Hampton, asserted that this sort of rejectionism would only serve to guarantee that the state's white citizens would be stripped of all their political power. Instead, Orr, Hampton, and other "compromisers" argued, white Carolinians should make an effort to befriend and control the freedmen. Hampton proposed to "direct the Negro vote." To this end, he and Orr sponsored huge rallies in which freedmen were treated to barbecued lamb while they listened to speakers who extolled the virtues of cooperation between black and white Carolinians.[52] The freedmen were urged to follow the leadership of native whites and to "harmonize" with them rather than put their trust in strangers. Hampton addressed blacks as "southern men" and told them to beware of the promises of "strangers."[53]

Perhaps if the state's white politicians had launched their campaign of kindness immediately after emancipation it might have borne fruit. By 1867, however, South Carolina's freedmen had been organized by the Union League and effectively inoculated against white propaganda. League members had sworn to support the Republican party and the call for a Constitutional Convention. Blacks who deviated from the league's instructions were denounced within the black community as "Iscariots" and subjected to trials at league meetings. The newly proffered offers of friendship from their former masters could hardly compete with the demands of social and racial solidarity asserted by the league. The Hamptons and Orrs, moreover, offered only goodwill and scraps of barbecue thrown from the master's table. The league and the Republicans held out the promise of land, public office, and actual seats at the table for the freedmen.

Franklin Moses's editorial columns in the *Sumter News* carefully followed these debates. When he assumed his editorial post in May

1866, Moses was as much a rejectionist as any other South Carolinian. He decried black suffrage as a form of "degradation" for the state and urged the legislature to spurn the Fourteenth Amendment. He asked for God's help against the North's "barbarous" campaign. During the course of the year, however, Moses's opinions evolved. In the summer and fall, Moses's editorials came to echo the views articulated by Orr, Hampton, and other prominent individuals who advised their fellow southerners to make the best of a situation that they were powerless to change. He denounced the rejectionists as lacking foresight and prudence.

Like it or not, Moses observed, black suffrage would soon be a reality and southerners must make a vigorous and active effort to win the support of the freedmen. It would not be enough to count on the gratitude and affection of blacks with whom white Carolinians might have grown up as playmates. "Universal suffrage is here," Moses wrote, "and the man who deems it dishonorable to participate in public affairs is recreant to his duty." Indeed, Moses averred, "the first step to be taken, by which we are to manifest our desire to shield our country from the ultimate designs of the radicals—is that those of us who are not disenfranchised shall at once determine to continue to exercise the right of suffrage, and to exert our influence, in the proper manner, upon those who have been lately invested with this important and tremendous privilege." In Moses's view, the rejectionists who urged their fellow whites to boycott the polls to protest black suffrage were shortsighted. "Those who talk of willfully casting aside this precious and treasured right are unmindful of the ends which are to be accomplished in the future by its peaceful means. Throw away the right to suffrage? In a Republican form of government we might as well throw away the right to live."[54]

The carpetbaggers and missionaries, Moses wrote, were making a determined effort to delude the naive freedmen and to seduce them with promises of land and political influence. To compete with what he called these "wild beasts prowling through the country," Moses urged white Carolinians to put aside their constitutional and moral principles and focus on "practicality" just as General Lee had "yielded to circumstances he could no longer control, and surrendered his sword in the moment of defeat."[55] Only by winning the friendship of the freedmen and controlling their votes could Carolinians hope to regain their independence from military rule and forestall an even worse possibility—rule by a government of carpetbaggers and blacks that would confiscate white lands and distribute them to the former slaves.

Moses thought it would be a simple matter to gain the support of the freedmen. Already, he said,

> the intelligent freedmen are beginning to realize the truth—
> which we have been so long attempting to teach them—that
> their practical and industrial interests are involved in a line of
> policy and action altogether distinct from that of Radicalism.
> For two long years their interested enemies have been endeavoring to delude them with the false and unfounded idea that the
> desires and interests of their former masters are obstacles in
> the way of their advancement and improvement thereafter. No
> fouler libel than this has ever been promulgated in reference to
> the citizens of the South.[56]

"It must be our task," he wrote later, "to teach and enlighten the uninstructed freedmen as to the real aims and purpose of their hypocritical friends, and adopt those measures in reference to their welfare and interests which will cause them to lend us their aid in rehabilitating the South."[57]

Moses was confident that the freedmen would be happy to follow the leadership of the South's native whites if only the latter would reach out to them. "As a class," he wrote,

> the whites of our section—we mean the native whites—have
> seemed to suppose that it is useless to attempt to exert any
> influence upon the minds of the freedmen. We have kept aloof
> from them and their meetings, and have left them free—either
> to choose for themselves the positions which they are to oc-

cupy, or to ask from others such instructions or advice as we ourselves have failed to impart. . . . It is time that we should exhibit our interest in the freedmen—that interest which we really feel in them and their future, and which it is part of every true and honest man to endeavor to establish throughout the South. They were born and raised under our tutelage and influence, and they now, in great measure, rely upon us to advise and encourage them in their duties as citizens. We have but to tell them the *truth* and they will work *for us and with us*. We have but to teach them who their enemies are, and they will avoid them and cling to us.[58]

Throughout the spring and summer of 1867, Moses worked vigorously to court the support of the freedmen in Sumter district. He used the position of assistant provost judge, which he continued to hold, to "flatter and befriend" the freedmen who came before his court.[59] He used the pages of his newspaper to single out black citizens in the district for their good work and special abilities. He seized an opportunity to make the acquaintance of the Reverend Richard Harvey Cain, an African Methodist Episcopal (AME) minister born free in Virginia and educated in the North who had come to South Carolina as a missionary in 1865.[60] Cain edited a newspaper, the *South Carolina Leader* (later renamed he *Missionary Record*), which was read aloud in black churches across the state.[61] Throughout Reconstruction, newspapers and political tracts were read at AME churches for the benefit of often-illiterate congregants.[62] Because of Cain's newspaper and his growing stature in the AME church—he eventually became a bishop—he had enormous influence within the black community.[63] During the course of several meetings, Moses established a relationship with Cain that was to serve both men well over the next several years. Cain's newspaper supported Moses's political campaigns and Moses, for his part, helped Cain secure election to the South Carolina state senate and then the U.S. Congress, where he served two terms. Moses declared in print, "On three several [*sic*] occasions during his visit we cheerfully and with pleasure sat under his ministration and listened to his teachings, and we were gratified to find in him an intimate, intelligent and accurate acquaintanceship with, and a learned knowledge of, the tenets and doctrines of the religion which he preached."[64] This statement undoubtedly pleased black audiences when it was repeated in their churches.

During this same time, Moses addressed numerous political rallies and public meetings organized to influence black opinion. During this era, in both the North and South, lively political rallies were a standard form of popular diversion. In the absence of sports and other mass entertainment, hundreds, even thousands, of individuals might attend a political event to cheer their heroes and heap invective on their political opponents. At larger rallies, often sponsored by candidates for public office or by the political parties, spectators would watch parades and listen to lengthy orations while eating barbecue and drinking hard cider or other alcoholic beverages courtesy of the rally's sponsors. Typically, a carnival atmosphere prevailed and vendors hawked their wares at the edges of the crowd. Smaller rallies, sponsored by churches or civic associations, might offer a more sober atmosphere but remained popular ways to pass the time on a warm summer evening or Sunday afternoon.

Moses attended political meetings large and small to get the truth—as he saw it—to the freedmen. These included church gatherings, civic meetings, and even Republican rallies. Often, Moses was accompanied by Samuel Lee, who had been a slave in the elder Moses's household. Lee and Franklin Moses had been childhood playmates and their current association helped Moses illustrate his theme of the longstanding and close friendship between the black and white citizens of the state. Moses continually told his listeners that black and white Carolinians had much in common with one another. The freedmen, he said, should look to native whites for leadership and reject the blandishments of the carpetbaggers. White Carolinians, Moses averred, would protect the rights of the freedmen and look after their interests.

In June 1867 Moses addressed more than twenty-five hundred

freedmen at a Grand Union Republican meeting on the grounds of a black church. According to press accounts, Moses

> drew several beautiful and touching pictures of the early as-
> sociation between the whites and blacks. He counseled his
> hearers, in persuasive and evidently heartfelt terms, to cultivate
> friendly feelings with those around them; to be careful and cau-
> tious in making a proper use of the elective franchise granted
> by Congress—besought them to beware of all persons who
> might seek to influence them in their exercise of this privilege
> and who might, with selfish ends, attempt to abridge their right
> to decide. . . . [He] begged them to sell their votes to no man
> or set of men, but to vote only for gentlemen of honor, of intel-
> ligence, and of integrity. . . . [Moses] was ready to tell them of
> their rights, and to protect them in their enjoyment of them,
> and could not be induced by any temptation to swerve from his
> path of duty to his State and country. [He swore that he would
> always work to protect the rights of the freedmen and their
> enjoyment of] all the privileges which had been bestowed upon
> them.[65]

For a time, Moses was able to convince a number of Sumter district's prominent white politicians to accompany him to freed-men's meetings. In his editorials, Moses averred that native whites must work together to beat the carpetbaggers at their own game. "We should meet these men, and defeat them with their own argu-ments," he declared. "Our orators of the South should gird on their armor of justice, of truth, and of genius, and enter the arena to con-quer or to fall."[66] He persuaded his father to address the freedmen on a number of occasions. Moses even convinced Confederate hero E. W. Moise to advise the freedmen of their true interest in follow-ing the leadership of the state's native whites. Moses and his friends urged the freedmen to oppose the idea of a new Constitutional Con-vention and to reject the Union League and the Republican party.

Moses was convinced that these efforts were bearing fruit. After one freedmen's meeting addressed by General Scott, Moses wrote,

Sensible and friendly speeches were also made by Revs. Benj. Lawson, Jack Witherspoon and Jim White (freedmen). They expressed kind feelings toward whites, and indicated unmistakably their perfect willingness to do all in their power to bring about harmony and friendship between the two races. Altogether, the occasion was one of great interest and pleasure to all who were present. The offer—from our white citizens—to instruct and advise the blacks in reference to their rights and their duties, was met on the part of the latter, with seeming alacrity and good will and nothing was said or done to excite distrust, or to destroy confidence.[67]

By the fall of 1867, most of Moses's friends in Sumter district, like other whites in the state who had advocated reaching out to the freedmen, saw that their efforts were in vain. For the most part, the freedmen did not trust their former masters. At rally after rally freedmen listened politely to the pleas of the native whites and then, following the lessons they had learned from the Union League, pledged en masse to vote for the convention and to support the Republican party. Gradually, in Sumter district as in the rest of the state, the compromisers abandoned their efforts and joined the rejectionist camp determined to boycott the coming election. Throughout the spring and summer Moses continued to urge his fellow whites to participate in the electoral process and to use whatever influence they might have to sway the votes of the freedmen. He declared:

The experiment we are about to make is entirely a new one. Suffrage has been extended to those who, we have always considered, were unworthy and unfitted to enjoy it. It is useless now to descant upon the means which have been used to effect this result. The plain stubborn fact stares us in the face, and it is our bounden duty so to accept and dispose of the same as will deprive our enemies of the power to harm us. We are firm in our conviction that the new element of political influence can be managed in such a way as will divide and distract the forces of the Radicals, and render united and confident the Conservative party—North and South.[68]

Native whites must come to see leadership of the freedmen as an important responsibility. It was the "first duty" of the native whites who had been "fortunate enough to have attained the intelligence which is imparted by education, to properly instruct and inform their neighbors as to the prerogatives conferred upon them by the Constitution of their State."[69]

In the end, few whites came to the polls, and the freedmen ignored their former masters and honored their pledges to the Union League. When ballots were cast in November, of the 66,418 blacks who participated, every single one voted in favor of holding a convention.[70] This result was a tribute to the prodigious organizational work of the Union League. Among whites, 42,354 of the 46,882 who were registered did not vote. This white boycott, however, did not derail the convention. In fact, it ensured that most of the elected delegates would be black and Republican. The boycott's organizers had achieved a tactical success but a strategic disaster.

In the months before the vote, as his fellow compromisers turned to rejectionism, Franklin Moses chose a different path. As other prominent local whites gave up their efforts to address the freedmen, Moses continued to attend black church services and to address black assemblies and rallies in Sumter district. More and more often, Moses was the only native white man in attendance, and his speeches and remarks shifted to reflect the makeup of his audience. Moses continued to review the long history of affection between the state's blacks and whites, but he also began to castigate those whites who opposed universal suffrage and equal rights for all. He began to denounce President Johnson rather than the Radical Congress as the betrayer of the South. He praised the freedmen for their courage and sagacity.

Moses soon discovered that he, among all native whites, was accepted by his black audiences. His words, his mode of address, his manner all seemed to captivate the freedmen. Black audiences followed his every word and applauded his every point. When they knew he was present, blacks called for Moses to speak even if he was not on the program. After several months trying to convince the freedmen to trust their former masters, Moses had apparently succeeded in persuading them of the virtues of only one native white—himself.

This was heady stuff for young Moses. Within the white community, Moses had some standing but he was hardly among the state's or even the district's most prominent figures. He was the editor of an upstart small-town newspaper, the assistant tax assessor, and a local magistrate. He was not a Hampton, an Orr, or even a local war hero like E. W. Moise. Given his family background and lack of appropriate military service, moreover, it seemed unlikely that Moses would ever be a major figure in white South Carolina. He was likely condemned to remain at the fringes of the state's white elite.

Among the freedmen, though, Moses was a star. They hung on his every word. They shouted his name. They called for him to speak. And in the new South Carolina, the freedmen would be a potent force. Armed with the right to vote, the freedmen might vault a clever individual to a previously unattainable position of prominence and power. Of course, a native white man who sought to make himself a leader of the freedmen would be ostracized by the white community. Such a person would become a pariah among his neighbors, perhaps even within his own family. Such a man would gain power and prominence but at enormous cost. Such a man would have to ally himself with Radical Republicans, among whom, Moses had formerly proclaimed, "we look in vain for any exhibition of statesmanship or diplomacy. . . . Strife but causes them to flourish and prosper. Anger and discord are the 'working tools' of their leaders. . . . [They] keep alive the smoldering embers of passion and the dying wish for revenge in the councils and offices of the American nation."[71]

Moses was filled with indecision. Should he take the safe course of action and join the white community in rejecting congressional

Reconstruction or should he surrender to the whispers of ambition that told him to strike out on a new course? Moses used the editorial pages of the *Sumter News* to consider his options. His editorials were filled with veiled references and cryptic questions. On the one hand, he wrote, "the destiny of the state was in the hands of those who, by education and intelligence, could lead all others who had not the wisdom to judge for themselves." Providing such leadership, on the other hand, required "courage to breast the storm," which could be unleashed on an individual who dared to provide such leadership.[72]

He wrote an editorial on the topic of ambition. The "desire for glory" was among the "most natural of passions," Moses declared. He asked, editorially, whether an individual should allow his actions to be influenced by public opinion. His answer was that a wise man listened to his own counsel and was not afraid to pursue an independent course of action. He praised the man who did not allow himself to be swayed by community sentiment but was, instead, "in love with that praise alone which is a natural attendant of virtue, and does not value those public acclamations which are not seconded by the impartial testimony of his own mind." Should an ambitious man be troubled by his fear of failure and his unease at the thought of antagonizing his fellows? His answer was no. An ambitious man should not shrink from decisive action. Indeed, if properly directed, ambition was a virtue. "If we look upon the great multitude of mankind," Moses observed, "and endeavor to trace out the principles of action in every individual, it will, we think, be found highly probable that ambition in some form or other, runs through the whole species, and that every man, in proportion to the vigor which belongs to his race, is more or less actuated thereby," and if channeled by proper ideas of "justice and honor," could be the mark of "brilliant genius and sound sense."[73]

After wrestling with his ambitions and fears throughout the summer of 1867, Moses was ready to act. In September, he wrote his last editorial for the *Sumter News*. He had previously told his readers that every man must think and speak for himself regardless of the opinions of others. "Every man must be in himself a sovereign," Moses said, despite the "rebukes and calumny" that unpopular stances often elicited.[74] Indeed, he observed a little later, "It requires some courage in these perilous times, to be honest or even to ape honesty, yet at a period of great danger to the country, the citizen should use no other language but that of truth. It is as much his duty to be candid as it is the duty of the physician to prescribe the remedies which his judgement approves, without reference to the caprices of his patients." Should his readers object to his views, Moses reminded them that "in 1860 not a single paper in South Carolina would consent to publish an article against the prevailing insanity—it was entire[ly] too unpopular. Yet we now see that it would have been far better that the subject had been discussed, patiently and carefully. But everyone shrank from the daring attempt, and we now know too well the consequences."[75]

That being said, Moses urged his readers to support the congressional plan of Reconstruction as the only course available to the state. In the wake of a storm of protest, Moses resigned his editorship the following week. "For some time past," he said in a public statement, "I have seen that my political sentiments have not been in accord with the large majority of the patrons of the *News*. These sentiments having been the legitimate result of honest conviction, I could not change them to suit the popular feeling."[76] The owners of the *News* quickly accepted their editor's resignation.

Having cast off his editorial and psychological restraints, Moses joined the Union League. With the support of R. H. Cain's *South Carolina Leader*, Moses received the Republican nomination for one of the four delegate slots allocated to Sumter district. Since the Democrats put forward no candidates and all but twenty-four of Sumter's white voters boycotted the election, Moses was swept to victory with the other members of the Republican ticket. Moses had now embarked on a political path from which he could never turn back. He could only hope that he had the courage to ride out the storm that his actions would unleash.

CHAPTER THREE

Reinventing South Carolina's Government

O N JANUARY 14, 1868, the members of South Carolina's Constitutional Convention assembled in Charleston. The delegates consisted of fifty-one whites and seventy-three blacks, making South Carolina's one of only two Reconstruction-era state conventions (Louisiana's was the other) in which blacks were in the majority. Given the fact that blacks had constituted over 95 percent of those voting in 1867, they might have comprised an even more overwhelming majority of the convention's delegates had not nominations been controlled by the state's white Union League members and white Republican leaders, who thought an all-black convention would lack credence even to most northerners. Accordingly, Republican political bosses assigned a number of delegate slots to northern whites and eagerly recruited sympathetic southern whites whose participation, it was hoped, would help induce their relatives and neighbors to cooperate with congressional Reconstruction. Republicans were particularly anxious to attract members of the antebellum elite, which represented "the wealth, experience and intelligence of the South." Some Republicans were convinced that without at least some white support, Reconstruction could not hope to succeed.[1]

Of the white delegates, twenty-three were native South Carolinians. Many had been prewar Unionists or had, in other ways, been at odds with state or Confederate authorities. One of these individuals, A. G. Mackey, an outspoken prewar Unionist, was elected to chair the convention. A handful of the native whites were, like Moses, former Confederates who had decided to throw in their lot with the new regime. These included interim convention chair T. J. Robertson, a businessman and land speculator who had made a fortune buying up property at foreclosure sales, and Joseph Crews and C. C. Bowen, who had been accused of Unionist sympathies and various crimes during the war. Bowen had been convicted of murdering a Confederate officer and had spent the last months of the war in prison.[2] The remaining whites were carpetbaggers, which included missionaries, Freedman's Bureau and Union League officials, and former Union army officers such as future governor Daniel Chamberlain.

Sixteen of the black delegates were also from the North; the remaining fifty-seven were native South Carolinians. The black delegates were drawn from the uppermost stratum of antebellum black society. Fourteen had a common school education; five were graduates of normal schools; and ten had graduated from college or a professional school—in an era when most southerners, black or white, had no formal education.[3] Nearly half the black delegates had been free before the war, most were literate, and a number owned property.

Several of the black delegates were individuals of exceptional ability. Francis Cardozo, like Moses, was half-Jewish—one of three sons of a Jewish civil servant, Isaac N. Cardozo (brother of the prominent economist Jacob Cardozo), and a free black mother.[4] Cardozo was raised by his mother as a Presbyterian, and in an extraordinary step in antebellum South Carolina, Cardozo's father had sent him abroad for an education. Cardozo studied at the University of Glasgow and subsequently trained for the Presbyterian ministry at seminaries in Edinburgh.[5] Upon his return to South Carolina, Cardozo became a leader in Charleston's long-established mulatto community and a spokesperson for its political interests. He also founded a black teachers college, Avery Normal Institute, in Charleston immediately after the war and would later serve as president of the state's Union League, a trustee of the state university, and South Carolina's secretary of state and state treasurer. Another prominent and extraordinarily able black delegate was Robert B. Elliott, a future member of Congress and famed debater. Elliott had been educated in England and claimed to have attended Eton. He was associate editor of the *South Carolina Leader,* chairman of the state Republican executive committee, and later became a major congressional foe of the Ku Klux Klan.[6] The *Charleston Daily News* was referring to Elliott as well as Cardozo when it observed that "the best men in the convention are the colored members."[7]

Despite the endorsement of the *Daily News,* most of the state's white press, led by the Democratic *Charleston Mercury,* lost no time in ridiculing the assemblage as the "ringed streaked-striped-convention," the "black and tan," the "Great Unlawful," or the "Congo Convention." Black delegates were continually mocked. Motions were said to have been offered by "the munching delegate," the "scrunching delegate," and the "bending delegate." One black delegate, S. A. Swails, was characterized by the *Mercury* as someone who, "when sober, would make a good-looking bandit." Harry McDaniels was said to be "one of those very common animal-like Negroes."[8] Francis Cardozo was described as having "neither abilities nor accomplishments that would distinguish him among white men," yet appearing "to great advantage among the more ignorant people of his own race."[9] Richard Cain, who was later to be elected to the U.S. House of Representatives, was described as "black, ugly and shabby," and "because of these exceptional qualities," was said to be enjoying "considerable influence among the darkies."[10] Robert DeLarge, according to the *Mercury,* "might have lived and died without having his name in print, except in an advertisement, if it had not been for the great social revolution which like boiling water has thrown scum on the surface."[11] For a time, white Carolinians hummed a ditty penned by the editors of the Mercury to describe the delegates:

Some are black.
Some are blacker.
And some are the color of a chaw of tobaccer.[12]

The *Mercury* heaped even more scorn on the white delegates than on their black colleagues. The black delegates, despite their many defects, presented "a decidedly more respectable appearance than the whites," because they at least "represented the highest type of their race." The renegade whites, on the other hand "represented the lowest type of theirs."[13] The *Mercury* averred that the destinies of South Carolinians were safer in the hands of blacks than they would be "if confided to the more unscrupulous care of the white men in the body."[14] Convention president Albert Mackey, a prominent physician, was said to be a drunk and a fraud who was interested only in the per diem he could earn for presiding over the convention. "We now behold him receiving a salary . . . for performing the duties of chairman of the great negro convention."[15] The *Mercury* also claimed that some of the white delegates were not actually white. The paper characterized William Collins as "a white man so-called . . . white in complexion and blood, but in his associations and character he is a negro." Another white delegate, John K. Terry, "was said to be a white man but could easily be mistaken at a short distance for a cross between a grizzly and a hyena."[16] As to Moses, the *Mercury* declared that this white delegate to the "Sambo Convention" was a renegade who had supported the Confederacy in every way "except in the fight."[17] Moses's old paper, the *Sumter News,* echoed the *Mercury,* declaring that the convention was filled with "barbarians from the jungles of Dahomey" and a "menagerie of Carolina gorillas." The *News* reviewed accounts published in other South Carolina papers and reported general agreement in the state that the convention was a sham, and a travesty of self-government.

> This body of misrepresentatives of the people known in South
> Carolina as a curious menagerie, according to the Marion
> *Star*—a great sham and humbug according to the Edgefield
> *Advertiser*—the far-famed Ringed-Streaked-and-Striped, ac-
> cording to the indomitable Charleston *Mercury*—the Carolina
> Gorillas according to the patriotic Wilmington *Journal*, and
> known by all as a compound mixture of Disorganizers, has still

[been] holding its disgusting saturnalia in the city of the heroic RUTLEDGE—the chivalrous PINCKNEY and the gifted LAURENS.[18]

At one point, E. W. M. Mackey, a son of the convention's president, became so incensed by the *Mercury*'s attacks on his father that he physically assaulted the newspaper's reporter in the corridor outside the convention hall.[19] Mackey had to be restrained by other delegates. Subsequently, the convention adopted a resolution condemning the *Mercury* as a scurrilous and libelous sheet and banning its editors and reporters from the convention hall. The resolution was adopted almost unanimously with only Moses, a former newspaper editor himself, dissenting.

Libelous accounts in the *Mercury* and other conservative newspapers were more than just annoyances. Their steady drumbeat ridiculing the convention and, later, the state government, was soon echoed by northern Democratic newspapers whose reports did much to convince northern readers that blacks were incapable of self-government. Indeed, sensational stories in the national media written by prominent northern journalists like James Pike made South Carolina such a symbol of governmental ineptitude that most Americans viewed the Palmetto state as a cesspool of civic depravity.[20] The Democratic press attacked all the Reconstruction-era southern governments.[21] South Carolina, however, was a particular target for hostile reporters because a substantial majority of its voters were black; most of its convention delegates were black; and later, its legislature and executive agencies boasted a larger and more influential contingent of black politicians and officials than any other southern government at the time. The presence of so many black faces in positions that had until recently been reserved for whites provided journalists with a splendid opportunity to vent whatever contempt for blacks they might have felt while, at the same time, appealing to their readers' racist preconceptions.

Pike described a South Carolina legislature at whose desks "sit colored men whose types it would be hard to find outside of the

Congo."[22] Such savages could hardly be expected to understand the niceties of self-government as practiced by the "orators and statesmen" of South Carolina's past. These "dregs of the population habilitated in the robes of their intelligent predecessors" and were capable only of "gush and babble" and a variety of depraved and corrupt practices.[23] "Sambo takes naturally to stealing, for he is used to it," Pike assured his northern readers as he described the many forms of petty thievery in which black politicians allegedly engaged.[24] After a decade of news stories in which blacks were matter-of-factly described as "thick-lipped, wooly-headed, small-brained" brutes whose only political skill was theft of public funds, northern whites could hardly object to southerners' efforts to extrude blacks from the political process.[25] Even President Grant was eventually moved to declare that the Fifteenth Amendment, granting voting rights to freedmen, had been a mistake. "It had done the Negro no good, and had been a hindrance to the South, and by no means a political advantage to the North."[26]

As the *Charleston Mercury* and other conservative newspapers fulminated against it, the convention, nevertheless, sought to address many of the pressing issues facing the state and the South as a whole. These included voting rights, black hopes for social equality, problems of taxation and public finance, and above all, demands for land redistribution. Watching from the sidelines were the tens of thousands of fearful whites who had boycotted the recent referendum. These white Carolinians feared that blacks would use the Constitutional Convention to impose continuing political disabilities on former Confederates and to mandate "race mixing" in public institutions. White planters were concerned that blacks would seek to craft constitutional provisions that would result in the confiscation or substantial redistribution of private lands. Whites had reason to be concerned. Throughout the South, black political orators were telling the freedmen that they were entitled to lands belonging to rich whites. At one Alabama rally, an orator asked, "Didn't you clear the white folks' land?" "Yes," voices from the crowd answered, "and we are entitled to it."[27] In a number of states, armed groups of freedmen sought to take possession of land by force.[28] In South Carolina itself, black delegates to an 1867 Republican convention demanded the abolition of large estates and heavy taxation of uncultivated land to force its division and sale to the "poorer classes."[29] And in the Sea Islands, blacks had organized and armed themselves to resist efforts to remove them from land they had occupied since General Sherman had set it aside for their use during the war.

In the end, most of the fears of South Carolina's white citizens proved groundless. Some convention delegates, to be sure, hoped to develop a confiscatory land policy, but most did not, in part because they knew that such a step would not be tolerated in the North. Some delegates sought to prolong the political disabilities that Congress had imposed upon former Confederates. Most delegates, however, were conciliatory in their attitudes. They favored equal rights for blacks and whites, but few thought it would be wise to devise policies that might be seen as forcing undue mixing of the races.

While the conservative press presented a picture of a monolithic "Congo Convention," delegates actually came to the convention from a variety of backgrounds and with various motives. Delegates included northern and southern whites as well as northern and southern blacks. Some of the southern blacks were impoverished freedmen, but a large and racially self-conscious group were members of the relatively prosperous Charleston mulatto community who had been born free. Each group had its own perspectives and interests. Most of the northern whites and some of the southern whites had been drawn into South Carolina politics by the unprecedented political and business opportunities that the state's postwar condition seemed to offer. The collapse of the Confederacy had undermined South Carolina's political and economic leadership. Entrepreneurs and speculators saw in this an opportunity to seize and use the machinery of the state's government to promote their pecuniary interests. This group included native-born whites like Robertson and carpetbaggers like future governor Daniel Chamberlain. A Massachusetts native who served in South Carolina during the war, Chamberlain remained in the state in hopes of making his fortune as a planter. These delegates generally supported constitutional provisions that would promote the breakup of large estates. Their goal, however, was not the redistribution of land to the freedmen. Rather they hoped millions of acres would be sold at public auction where white speculators would easily outbid poor blacks. Other whites, like Moses and Robert Scott (a former union army officer and Freedmen's Bureau official from Ohio who would become the first governor under the new constitution), were more interested in political careers that had been made possible by the enfeeblement of South Carolina's traditional ruling class. This mix of motives was common among white Republicans throughout the South.[30]

The chief concerns for many black delegates were guarantees of political and social equality, and opportunities to improve their condition through access to education and land ownership. William Nash and Robert Elliott often spoke for this group. Many mulatto delegates, however—including some of the most active members of the convention such as Robert DeLarge, Alonzo Ransier, Henry Hayne, William McKinlay, Stephen Swails, and William Whipper— were themselves owners of land and other property. They were opposed to demands from northerners and freedmen for the redistribution of private lands. DeLarge and the others were prominent members of the Brown Fellowship Society, a Charleston mulatto fraternal organization founded in 1790 that barred blacks from membership.[31] DeLarge, Rainey, and Ransier were also important officials in the state's Republican party and were active in the ongoing effort to build a strong Republican organization in South Carolina. Though not a formal member of the Brown Fellowship Society, Richard Cain had for several years been associated with this group. As the freeborn son of an African father and Cherokee mother, Cain was difficult to classify in South Carolina's racial terms. He was, however, a substantial land owner and had considerable commonality of interest with the Charleston group.[32]

As for political rights, not all South Carolinians with dark skins espoused the principle of one man, one vote. Hayne and McKinlay, for example, were dubious about universal suffrage if this meant that uneducated and propertyless blacks, or for that matter whites, would have the right to vote. Similar divisions manifested themselves over taxation and economic development. Most black and northern white delegates supported the idea of expanding the state's revenue base to provide funding for education, social services, and industrial development. Native-born whites and Charleston mulattos, however, were more concerned about the effects that state support for such programs might have on their own taxes.

These divisions, coupled with personal, regional, and even sectarian differences, presaged the factional conflicts within the Republican party that would eventually help undermine Republican rule in South Carolina and throughout the South. In his revolutionary manifesto *What Is to Be Done?* Lenin famously explained that a revolutionary party that tolerated internal dissension was almost certain to fail. Revolutionaries, said Lenin, could not permit factional strife because "we are marching in a compact group along a precipitous and difficult path, firmly holding each other by the hand. We are surrounded on all sides by enemies, and are under their almost constant fire."[33] Or as another well-known revolutionary theorist observed to his comrades, "We must all hang together, or assuredly we shall all hang separately." In some respects, Reconstruction-era Republicans, seeking to bring about a social revolution in the face of southern white hostility and northern vacillation, were marching along an even more dangerous path than Lenin's Bolsheviks. And, indeed, unrestrained factional struggle would eventually carry them over the precipice. Over the course of two months, the members of the convention debated a number of topics. The most important were political rights, education and social equality, public finance, and the issue of land. In the end, they drafted a document that, as South Carolina's leading historians put it, "was as good as any other constitution the state has ever had."[34] No constitution drafted by the Congo Convention, could placate the state's angry whites. Nor, in the end, could the parchment guarantees of a constitution safeguard the hard-won liberties of South Carolina's black citizens.

Political Rights

In antebellum South Carolina the right to vote and the privilege of holding political office had been restricted to white males, as was true in most other states throughout the Union. Blacks were not citizens and had no political rights. But even possession of white skin had been no guarantee of political rights in South Carolina. The planter aristocracy that had ruled the state had been no more willing to share power with poor whites than with blacks. The franchise had been limited; legislative apportionment favored the planter class; and property requirements restricted public office to the privileged few.

The idea that freed blacks would possess the right to vote was not a given at the end of the Civil War. Most northerners doubted whether recently freed black slaves had sufficient intelligence or education to merit the franchise. Even many abolitionists opposed black voting. In his famous periodical the *Liberator*, William Lloyd Garrison declared in 1864, "When was it ever known that liberation from bondage was accompanied by a recognition of political equality? Chattels personal may be instantly translated from the auction-block into freemen; but when were they ever taken at the same time to the ballot box, and invested with all political rights and immunities?"[35] In 1868 most northerners remained unconvinced that black suffrage was a good idea. The Republican party, however, was convinced that with black votes it might hope to establish lasting rule in the southern states. Coupled with the Fourteenth and Fifteenth Amendments, the new southern state constitutions were expected to ensure that blacks would have unfettered access to the ballot box.

As in the case of all the other newly enacted southern constitutions, the South Carolina constitution provided for universal manhood suffrage. For the first time, black and poor white Carolinians would have the right to vote in all state and local races. The convention's committee on franchise and elections initially proposed that every male citizen, "without distinction of race, color or former condition," who was a resident of the state at the time the constitution was adopted or, subsequently, a resident of the state for one year and of his county for sixty days, should be entitled to vote. The initial proposal disqualified anyone who, after 1875, reached the age of twenty-one without being able to read or write. The committee's presumption was that this provision would force illiterate South Carolinians to attend school. A number of delegates, including even several leaders of the Brown Fellowship Society, supported the idea of a literacy test. William McKinlay said, "In order to have wise men at the head of our government, it is necessary that the people should be educated and have a full sense of the importance of the ballot."[36] Most delegates, however, asserted that every South Carolinian should have the right to vote, whether he was literate or not. Alonzo Ransier averred that the right to vote "belongs alike to the wise and to the ignorant, to the virtuous and vicious." Ransier hoped that the "music of the 19th century" would move the convention to strike out every word from the proposed constitution that might limit the "manhood" of the citizen with regard to his right to vote.[37]

Similarly, the convention defeated a proposal to disfranchise individuals for nonpayment of their poll tax. Contrary to popular notion, a poll tax is not a tax on voting. It is simply a capitation, as opposed to income or property tax. Such taxes were common in the nineteenth century, and at the convention some delegates argued that a one dollar poll tax could provide ample support for the state's proposed school system. Whatever they thought of the poll tax as a fiscal device, most delegates were concerned that tying this tax to the right to vote could be used in the future to disfranchise poor and black voters. Robert DeLarge said with some prescience, "If there was any system devised by man that could act as a perfect curse upon his fellows, it would be a system of poll tax. . . . Unless we insert in this Constitution an explicit provision that no man shall be disfranchised for nonpayment of poll tax, in a year's time we may see a political party in position who will use it as an instrument against us for partisan purposes and to our injury.[38] Moses called the proposed tax scheme a blow "at the freedmen of South Carolina who are among the poorest of the poor," which would "allow power to go again in the hands of the [white] aristocratic element."[39] The convention did adopt a poll tax for the support of the schools, but nonpayment did not result in the forfeiture of an individual's right to vote.

The new constitution abolished property qualifications for holding office and mandated popular election of presidential electors, the governor, and a number of other state and county officials, including justices of the peace. Ministers were, for the first time, declared to be eligible to hold public office. This was important because the clergy was a major source of political leadership for both blacks and poor whites. Both houses of the legislature were now to be apportioned solely on the basis of population and the old district system was abolished in favor of a more conventional division of the state into geographically compact and contiguous counties. This change was more than a change of name. It introduced a greater degree of local self-government than had existed in the state. The old districts had been judicial districts possessing no legislative or executive power, which were concentrated at the state level. Voters in each new county, by contrast, would elect a three-person board of commissioners with budgetary and taxing authority. The list of crimes that could result in loss of the franchise was also shortened considerably. Imprisonment for debt was abolished. Life tenure for judges was abolished and the terms of justices of the peace and circuit judges set at six and four years, respectively. The only restriction on political rights approved by the convention was aimed at former Confederates. A move to give the state legislature the power to restore the political rights of whites who had been disfranchised by the federal government was defeated. This guaranteed that portions of the prewar political class, at least initially, would be barred from the political arena.

One proposal to expand the suffrage was soundly defeated by the convention. This was William Whipper's plea for women's suffrage. Whipper argued that it was inappropriate to refuse voting rights to a large segment of society to whom the law applied but who would have no power to shape the law. During this same period, Susan B. Anthony and Elizabeth Cady Stanton were making similar arguments in the North. The convention ignored Whipper's plea for women's voting rights, just as the larger society was ignoring Anthony and Stanton.

Education

Prior to the war, South Carolina lacked an effective system of public education. The planter elite that governed the state employed tutors for their children or sent them to private academies. They had little incentive to spend money on the education of their fellow citizens' offspring. Appropriations for public schools and teachers were always meager, and most children received only a bit of schooling before joining the labor force. School attendance was not compulsory. In rural areas small farmers generally thought their children had better things to do than spend time on book learning, though they might teach them to read and write at home if they themselves were literate. All in all, perhaps 10 percent of the state's white children of school age were enrolled in public school in any given year.[40] The public schools were not open to black children. Only a handful of the most fortunate blacks had any chance at all for an education. The new constitution required the state legislature to establish a universal system of education and required attendance by all children between the ages of six and sixteen for a minimum period of two years. The constitution also provided for the position of state superintendent of education and required each county to appoint a school commissioner. Together, the superintendent and commissioners would constitute the state board of education. Each county was to be divided into school districts and at least one school within each district was to be kept open every month of the year. The new educational system was to be financed through property taxes and a poll tax of one dollar. The constitution also required the state legislature to support the state university, a normal school (teachers' college), an agricultural college, and schools for the deaf, dumb, and blind. Schools supported by the state were to be open to all children, regardless of race or color.

No delegates opposed the creation of a public school system. The two issues that divided the convention were whether education should be compulsory and whether black and white children would attend the same schools. Many delegates, particularly those from rural areas, objected to the idea of compulsory education, arguing that farmers, whether black or white, depended on their children to work alongside them in the fields. But a number of the black delegates saw education as essential to the progress of the freedmen and wanted to be sure that black children would receive an education even if their parents did not fully grasp the value of schooling. For both black and white children, compulsory education would also function as a vehicle for citizenship training, teaching them to respect the new institutions established by the nation and the state when, in the case of the whites, their parents might be propounding a somewhat different lesson. Francis Cardozo explained the importance of compulsory civic education. "I appeal to the gentlemen of the convention to know whether they desire to see a state of anarchy or a state of confusion in South Carolina in the future. . . . The child that remains in ignorance until grown up will never learn the first duty that ought to be learned by every man, which is to love his country and love his state. . . . To be a good citizen every one should know what are the duties of a citizen, and the laws of the state and country in which he resides."[41] Several of the white delegates warned that whites would reject the proposed constitution if they believed that they would be forced to send their children to school with blacks. To this, Cardozo replied, "There is an element which is opposed to us, no matter what we do will never be conciliated. It is not that they are opposed so much to the constitution we may frame, but they are opposed to us sitting in convention. Their objection is of such a fundamental and radical nature that any attempt to frame a constitution to please them would be utterly abortive."[42] Cardozo went on to say that both black and white parents might prefer to send their children to same-race schools, and within limits, counties might establish separate black and white educational institutions. However, he warned, "if any colored child wishes to go to a white school, it shall have the privilege to do so."[43] As white delegates had warned, this section of the constitution, more than any other, became a touchstone for white opposition and resistance to the new regime.

Equality before the Law

Opening the public schools to children of all races was just one of the convention's measures designed to legally mandate racial equality. Under the constitution, all racial distinctions were prohibited, with all classes of citizens entitled to "enjoy equally all common, public, legal and political privileges." This provision meant that no category of person could be prohibited from owning property, disqualified as a witness in court, or denied an education. All the prohibitions and exclusions associated with slavery and the more recent Black Codes were outlawed. No class of individuals could be subject to any other legal restraint or disqualification "than such as are laid upon others under like circumstances." Blacks were to be entitled to serve in the state militia. Slavery and imprisonment for debt were prohibited. The rights of women, too, were enhanced and the property of married women declared to be no longer subject to seizure to fulfill their husband's debts.

The convention also made an effort to expunge the symbols of inequality from the state's life. In the context of the times, the distinction between symbol and substance was often complex. White South Carolinians were often more horrified by acts that symbolized the new order than they were by more substantive measures. As Cardozo had observed, the fact that blacks constituted the convention's majority was more important to many of the state's white citizens than anything the convention might decide. Black Carolinians, for their part, were eager for assurances that their status had changed for the better and would continue to do so. Since what was being represented was an enormous political and social revolution, fierce struggles were sometimes waged in the state over symbolic issues.

Before the convention adopted the new constitution, a number of symbolic questions were debated. A proposal was introduced to outlaw the use of such epithets as "nigger" and "Yankee." A proposal denouncing the state's former government was adopted and a recommendation made to the military governor, General Canby, to remove all the state's sitting judges because of their past association with the Confederate cause. And as a slap at former slave traders, all still-outstanding debts incurred for the purchase of slaves were annulled. "A few years ago," said Robert Elliott, "the popular verdict of the country was passed upon the slave seller and the slave buyer, and both were found guilty of the enormous crime of slavery. The buyer of the slave received his sentence, which was the loss of the slave, and now we pass sentence upon the seller."[44] This provision had little practical effect since most of the relevant debtors had long since declared bankruptcy, but it was seen as a "moral rebuke" to those who had formerly trafficked in human beings. Some of the mulatto delegates, men who had no wish to disturb the sanctity of contracts, opposed this symbolic act of debt annulment and predicted that it would never survive a court challenge.[45] Some years later, the South Carolina courts did indeed invalidate this constitutional provision as an impairment of the federal constitution's guarantee of the obligation of contracts.

Public Finance

The 1868 constitution also established a new and more equitable tax system. Before the war, the state had depended heavily on poll taxes, and wealthy planters had all but escaped taxation of their land and property. The new constitution retained a one dollar poll tax but placed the main burden of taxation on real property. Approximately half the projected revenues from state taxes, including property and poll taxes, were earmarked for the support of the new public school system.

The new tax system was designed to generate substantially more revenue than the system it would soon replace. The prewar planter aristocracy had little need of government assistance and favored keeping both government expenditures and taxes to a minimum. In the postwar period, however, blacks hoped that more money in the state's coffers would mean better schools, while a number of the carpetbaggers and scalawags hoped to use state funds to promote industrial and economic development.

Under the new constitution, real property was to be taxed at a rate of 3 percent, a sixfold increase over the prewar rate of 0.5 percent. It was estimated that this would result in state revenues of more than $2 million, a trivial sum by contemporary standards, but an enormous amount at the time. By comparison, South Carolina's prewar public revenues were only $350,000 per year. If anything approaching $2 million could actually be collected, the state government would have more than adequate funding to build and maintain a system of public education while also embarking on an ambitious program of economic development. A land commission composed of blacks and whites, including Moses, Chamberlain, Robertson, and DeLarge, was created to begin the evaluation and assessment of real property within the state. The inauguration of the new tax system also had enormous implications for patterns of land ownership in the state (see below).

In addition to enhanced powers of taxation, the new constitution authorized the state to raise money through bonded indebtedness and placed no limit on the amount of debt that the state legislature could accrue in this way. The constitution also placed no restrictions on the legislature's capacity to authorize private bond issues backed by the credit of the state. Some delegates had argued for a five hundred thousand dollar debt ceiling and against permitting the legislature to guarantee private bond issues. But this measure was defeated by the proponents of state-sponsored economic development who saw, for example, railroad bond issues backed by the credit of the state as a major vehicle for that purpose.

Land

In some respects, the most important topic addressed by the convention was land, and it was here that Frank Moses played a significant role. Generally speaking, Moses was not a major figure at the 1868 Constitutional Convention. For the most part, the body's deliberations were dominated by the able and articulate members of the Brown Fellowship Society, along with Francis Cardozo and Richard Cain. Moses had difficulty finding his footing in the unfamiliar terrain of a Republican conclave dominated by blacks. Moses had assumed that the freedmen would look to him for leadership, but for the most part, leadership was provided by DeLarge, Cain, Cardozo, and Ransier. White Republicans frequently reminded Moses that he was a very recent convert to the Radical cause and should hold his tongue. In a debate over land policy, for example, B. F. Whittemore, a white delegate from Darlington, sarcastically said to Moses, "We are very glad to hear the affirmations of the newly fledged, and we are very glad to know where they are going to stand. We are very glad to hear of their honesty, their purity of motives and their character." Moses replied angrily that Whittemore had been "shirking" his duties to his black constituents. To this Whittemore said, "I shall not require any new comers in the flock to tell me that I shirk my duty."[46]

Moses frequently asserted that he had come to the convention with no goal or ambition beyond the welfare of the people of South Carolina. He claimed that he did not plan to seek any public office after the convention and that he intended to stick to his principles "undeterred alike by the frowns of open enemies, or the innuendos of pretended friends."[47] Asked if he was a candidate for Congress, Moses replied, "I stand here a candidate for no office. I came here to do my duty for my people." "Bully for Moses," was his interlocutor's caustic reply.[48] His protestations to the contrary notwithstanding, Moses did aspire to public office. But in the unfamiliar context of the convention Moses had difficulty identifying an issue or position that would solidify his credentials as a committed Republican, much less catapult him to a place of leadership among the delegates.

In several instances Moses took positions that seemed better calculated to please his former white Democratic associates than his new Republican friends. He argued, for example, that for reasons of economy he opposed hiring a convention chaplain on the grounds that the several preachers among the delegates should provide the service on a voluntary basis. Blacks saw the chaplaincy as a useful patronage position and only the state's white Democrats might have been interested in Moses's desire to economize. Moses argued vehemently that an invitation to address the convention be extended to provisional governor Orr, a Democrat, hated by most Republicans because of his strong opposition to the effort to frame a new state constitution.

Moses launched a quixotic defense of freedom of the press. The vicious attacks mounted by the *Charleston Mercury* on both black and white convention delegates had led Daniel Chamberlain, a carpetbagger who would become governor of the state in 1874, to introduce a motion banning the *Mercury*'s reporters from the hall. Moses vehemently but unsuccessfully opposed this measure saying, "Good God . . . shall we abuse a newspaper on account of its mere opposition or burlesque of our course?"[49] This was an unpopular stance among Republicans, particularly among the black delegates who reacted bitterly to the *Mercury*'s efforts to portray them as subhuman savages. And if Moses's goal in these matters was to retain some ties to the state's disaffected whites, his actions were of no avail. The state's white press either ignored Moses or treated him with contempt as a man who had, by his participation in the Congo Convention, betrayed the "untainted" white men of the state.

The land issue gave Moses the opportunity he needed to affirm his Republican bona fides and assert a claim to leadership. Land was the most important issue facing the convention. Indeed, land was the most important issue facing the South. The most radical northern Republicans, Charles Sumner and Thad Stevens, saw land redistribution as the linchpin of Reconstruction. The prewar South had been a landlord-peasant society in which an elite stratum of wealthy landowners controlled the region's economy and political affairs. Millions of blacks and poor whites toiled on the land—the former as slaves, the latter as tenant farmers or smallholders. So long as a small number of proprietors held much of the South's productive land, their economic power guaranteed that political and social equality for blacks or, for that matter, poor whites would be a sham. Land redistribution was essential to reconstructing the South's politics and society. As Stevens put it in an 1865 speech, "The whole fabric of Southern society must be changed. . . . How can republican institutions, free schools, free churches, free social intercourse, exist in a mingled community of nabobs and serfs? If the South is ever to be made a safe republic, let her lands be cultivated by the toil of the owners."[50]

In 1867 Stevens introduced legislation that would confiscate millions of acres of land from southern planters and divide it up among the freedmen in forty-acre plots.[51] Stevens calculated that the former Confederate states contained 465 million acres of land. Almost 85 percent of this total was owned by seventy thousand individuals. Stevens proposed that this land—about 395 million acres—should be confiscated by the federal government. From this total, each adult male freedman would be presented with forty acres at no charge. This would account for approximately 40 million acres. The remaining land would be divided into farms and sold to the highest bidder. Stevens further proposed that the proceeds from those sales should be used to pay pensions to veterans and their widows and orphans, to reimburse loyal individuals whose property had been destroyed during the war, and to pay off the national debt. Stevens admitted that land confiscation was a harsh measure that might drive the South's former aristocrats into exile in South America or elsewhere. But what of it? "If they go, all the better," he declared." These seventy thousand land owners were, on the whole, the "arch traitors," and "since they had caused an unjust war they must be made to suffer the consequences."[52]

Stevens's proposal had no real chance of adoption. Few northern Republicans supported land confiscation. Sen. John Sherman, brother of the famous general, feared that land confiscation would "disorganize and revolutionize society in the Southern states."[53] The *New York Times* said that "fear of confiscation" had paralyzed southern business and prevented investment in that region.[54] The *Times* was even more concerned that if confiscation began it would not be limited to the South. The North's industrial aristocracy began to worry that the implications of a policy of confiscation went beyond the South's landed aristocracy.[55] And indeed Sen. Benjamin Wade had declared that a more equal distribution of property should be sought throughout the nation. The *Times* warned that some Radical Republicans sought a war on all forms of property to succeed the war on slavery.[56]

The slim chance that the federal government would adopt a confiscatory land policy was all but eliminated by the result of the 1867 congressional elections. Throughout the North, Republicans suffered an electoral drubbing and measures associated with the Radical Republicans, such as black suffrage referenda in Minnesota, Ohio, and Kansas, went down to defeat. The Republican party's previously overwhelming majority in the Congress was substantially reduced, leaving the Radical group with far less power than it had wielded the previous year.[57] Though many factors contributed to the Republican decline and Democratic resurgence, it was widely believed that the party's identification with black rights, especially with radical demands for land redistribution, had proven to be disastrous at the northern polls. Henceforward, "let confiscation be an unspoken word in your state," advised one Republican leader.[58]

Stevens's proposal, though, had touched off a wave of land hunger throughout the South. Hundreds of thousands of freedmen believed that the federal government had promised them forty acres of land and would not believe those who tried to tell them that this was simply a myth. The freedmen were so certain that they would soon be receiving land that a group of Republican speakers toured the South in the spring of 1867 to inform gatherings of freedmen that no such commitment had been made by the federal government.[59] Horace Greeley told one gathering that they were "more likely to earn a home than get one by any form of confiscation."[60]

From the perspective of South Carolina freedmen, the idea that the federal government would confiscate white-owned land and give it to them seemed neither mythical nor surprising. During the war, federal troops had occupied Hilton Head, Saint Helena, and other islands along the South Carolina coast. Large numbers of blacks had sought refuge on these islands and for several years were employed as farm workers on abandoned plantations under the supervision of federal authorities. Charitable groups in Boston and Philadelphia sent teachers and ministers to the islands as well. These northern volunteers encouraged blacks to dream of land ownership and also brought pressure to bear on the federal government to make land available for this purpose.

In 1864, in what came to be known as the "Sea Island experiment," the U.S. government offered several thousand acres of this land in twenty- and forty-acre tracts to the heads of black families at $1.25 an acre. This price was within the reach of some blacks who had been working for wages on the federally operated plantations, and by 1865, more than five hundred plots had been sold to African Americans. Many more plots, however, were sold to white speculators. That same year, Gen. William T. Sherman issued his famous Field Order 15, which stipulated that nearly half a million acres of abandoned plantations and farms, along with the loan of army mules, be given to approximately forty thousand freed slaves then living on them. Sherman viewed his actions as an expedient means of relieving his command from the responsibility of feeding and caring for an enormous group of blacks. No legal title was conferred by the order. The freedmen, however, thought the land was theirs in perpetuity. They were encouraged in their belief by Sherman's land administrator, Gen. Rufus Sexton, who told the freedmen "that they were to be put in possession of lands, upon which they might locate their families and work out for themselves a living and respectability."[61] By 1869 most of the original landowners had resumed possession of their property with the assistance of federal troops,[62] but in 1868 at least some South Carolina freedmen had reason to hope that the government would allow them to keep the land upon which they had been encouraged to settle.

Of course, even in their heyday, the Sea Island experiment and Field Order 15 provided land for only a small fraction of South Carolina's black families. But tens of thousands of freedmen throughout the state hoped that they, too, could acquire homes and small farms for their families. Delegates to the 1868 convention were well aware that their constituents wanted land. "I have gone through the country," reported Richard Cain, "and on every side I was besieged with questions: How are we to get homesteads?"[63]

Delegates were deeply divided over the issue of how land might be provided for the freedmen. Virtually all the state's arable land belonged to white farmers and planters, and some delegates believed that Stevens's idea of confiscation had been a good one. But even without the outright confiscation of "rebel" lands proposed by Stevens, an enormous amount of land owned by white Carolinians was already or might soon be available for purchase at foreclosure sales. Many of the state's land owners were in desperate financial straits in the winter and spring of 1868. Collectively, they owed millions of dollars to banks, suppliers, and other creditors, certainly more than they could hope to pay until their crops were harvested and sold in the fall. Most had pledged their land as collateral for their loans. The fearsome Radical Republican Thad Stevens might not be able to confiscate the planters' property, but their unctuous and mild-mannered local banker surely could.

Several of the black delegates were not displeased with this state of affairs. They believed that foreclosure sales might afford blacks an opportunity to acquire land at a substantially discounted price. As a result they were opposed to efforts to assist the beleaguered planters through the enactment of "stay laws" and other instruments designed to forestall foreclosures. Francis Cardozo spoke for many of the black delegates when he declared,

> This is the only way by which we will break up [the plantation] system, and I maintain that our freedom will be of no effect if we allow it to continue. What is the main cause of the prosperity of the North? It is because every man has his own farm and is free and independent. Let the lands of the South be similarly divided. If [the plantations] are sold . . . the chances are that the colored man and the poor man would be the purchasers. . . . Now [while the planters are weak] is the time to take the advantage. . . . I say then just as General Grant said when he had Lee hemmed in around Petersburg; now is the time to strike, and in so doing we will strike for our people and posterity.[64]

Another group of delegates also welcomed foreclosure sales. These were the land speculators, the carpetbaggers and the wealthy scalawag Thomas J. Robertson. "I for one," said Robertson, "am willing to see the property of the country change hands, and if lands are sold cheap, so much better for working men. It will enable poor men to provide themselves with a home, and identify each one more closely with the soil." Robertson appealed to the black delegates' anger at the abuse they were suffering every day in the white press. "The men asking relief," he charged, "call this convention a menagerie, a collection of wild animals. Is this menagerie to protect their property at the expense of the loyal citizens, and the working men of the country?"[65]

Many delegates agreed with Cardozo and with Robertson's radical discourse. The state's Republican leadership, however, was concerned that a wave of foreclosures would give the impression that South Carolina Republicans had adopted a confiscatory land program in opposition to the policy mandated by the national Republican leadership. Accordingly, the convention's leaders, Robert DeLarge, Joseph Rainey, and Alonzo Ransier, argued vehemently in favor of offering relief to distressed land owners. "Is there a man upon this floor," asked DeLarge, "who does not feel it incumbent upon him to do everything possible to relieve the sufferings of his fellow men?"[66] Most of the land that might be sold after foreclosure, said DeLarge, would fall into the hands of speculators rather than freedmen. "[The lands] will pass into the hands of the merciless speculator, who will never allow a poor man to get an inch unless he can draw his life blood from him in return. The poor freedmen are the poorest of the poor, and unprepared to purchase lands."[67] And as to the argument that the endangered white landowners were former Confederates who deserved to lose their land, DeLarge claimed that many had been loyal to the Union and had been "forced into the Confederate army."[68]

DeLarge undoubtedly knew that few of South Carolina's farmers or planters had been forced to fight for the Confederacy. Most were willing, indeed, enthusiastic soldiers. Current political considerations, though, compelled him to make the case for relief. Besides, DeLarge added, adoption of the proposed tax code would have the effect of forcing planters to sell a good deal of land over the next several years.[69] A "stay" on current foreclosures might offer poor freedmen sufficient time to accumulate capital with which to buy land that would almost surely fall into the hands of speculators if it was immediately thrown on to the market. Later, too, the uproar over confiscation might diminish and land redistribution in South Carolina be undertaken without threatening the national fortunes of the Republican party. Indeed, during Reconstruction, as DeLarge predicted, many large South Carolina estates were broken up and portions sold off to pay taxes. With the return of white rule in 1876, though, much of this land was restored to the original owners.[70]

On the vitally important issue of land redistribution, Moses moved to align himself with the convention's black Republican leaders. Moses offered the resolution, which would be supported by DeLarge and the others, asking General Canby to impose a three-month moratorium on property foreclosures. During the debate on the resolution, Moses echoed DeLarge's claim that the freedmen were too poor to benefit from forced land sales. "I venture to say that not one in two thousand laboring men can buy an acre of land. I say they have not the money," he declared.[71] And, like DeLarge, Moses averred that many of the endangered landholders had been loyal Union men.[72] After a lengthy debate, this motion carried by a narrow margin, as did a homestead provision exempting a landowner's first one hundred acres from foreclosure by creditors.

Through these actions, the convention's leaders protected themselves from being accused of adopting a program of land confiscation. But stay and homestead provisions did not respond to the demands of the freedmen for an opportunity to own land. To this end, Richard Cain introduced a resolution petitioning Congress to appropriate the sum of $1 million from the budget of the Freedmen's Bureau in the form of a loan to the state. That money would be used to provide loans to freedmen to purchase homesteads of ten to one hundred acres. It was to be repaid within five years from the sale of crops produced by the landholders.[73]

Cain's scheme was immediately denounced as a fraud by most of the convention's carpetbaggers and native land speculators. A *New York Tribune* reporter covering the convention saw Cain's proposal as a political ruse and declared in an article opposing federal subsidies that the freedmen needed to learn how to fend for themselves. They should "root hog or die," the reporter said.[74] Cain replied, "The abolition of slavery has thrown these people upon their own resources. How are they to live? I know the philosopher of the *New York Tribune* says, 'root hog or die,' but in the meantime we ought to have some place to root. My proposition is simply to give the hog some place to root."[75] Cain's proposal was strongly supported by DeLarge and Ransier. And Moses quickly became one of its staunchest advocates. In a lengthy speech supporting the land purchase plan, Moses proclaimed that "you cannot make citizens out of these people [former slaves] unless you give them those things which make men citizens. . . . Give them land; give them houses. They deserve it from the people of South Carolina."[76]

After the proposal was adopted, the convention received word from Washington that the federal government would not agree to loan the necessary funds to the state. Cain, DeLarge, and Moses presented an alternative plan to the convention. Rather than depend on the federal government for funding, they proposed that the state of South Carolina should create a land commission known as the Board of Public Lands. This commission would be authorized to issue bonds and, thereby, raise money with which to purchase land at public sale. The land would be divided into tracts to be sold on credit to "actual settlers," not land speculators. Purchasers would be required to farm the land and to pay taxes and pay interest until the loan from the state was repaid.[77]

This provision, patterned after the national Homestead Act of 1862, was adopted virtually without debate as a substitute for the now-abandoned notion of petitioning Congress for assistance. The land commission turned out to be an extremely important institution. Over the next several years, even as the state's economy improved, the new tax structure created by the convention forced land owners to sell thousands of acres of farmland every year. A portion of this land was purchased by the commission and resold, mainly to black farmers. By the end of Reconstruction, approximately fourteen thousand black families had been able to acquire land from the commission.[78] After 1876, most of this land was regained by whites, but a small number of black families continued to hold title to what had once been "commission land" well into the twentieth century.[79]

Taken as a whole, South Carolina's new constitution mandated a political and social revolution in the state. The former ruling stratum was, at least for the time being, barred from taking part in political life. The former slaves were enfranchised and placed in a position of legal equality with their former masters. Hypothetically, at least, poor whites, too, would benefit from the elimination of the property restrictions, poll taxes, and literacy tests that had delimited political participation.

Of course, whites bitterly denounced the new constitution as "radical," "bogus," "monstrous," and "unjust." It was, said the *Charleston Mercury,* "a subversion of the American republic," de-

signed to "establish Negro rule." The worst part of the new constitution, thundered the *Mercury*, was that whites were to be forced
to send their children, both male and female, to school with blacks
where they would be "debased and corrupted." The *Sumter Watchman* declared that the convention was "the work of sixty-odd Negroes, many of them ignorant and depraved, together with fifty
white men, outcasts of Northern society, and Southern renegades,
betrayers of their race and country."[80] Despite this heated rhetoric,
whites eventually came to accept most elements of the new constitution including the public school system. Whether they would admit
it or not, most of the state's white citizens benefited from the democratic reforms embodied in the document. Interestingly, in 1895,
some years after white rule had been restored in South Carolina,
a new constitution was written. This new document incorporated
most of the 1868 constitution. Only those sections that provided
rights for blacks were completely eliminated. Apparently, the work
of the "ringed streaked-striped convention" turned out not to have
been so terrible, after all.

Nevertheless, in the immediate aftermath of the 1868 convention, whites organized to fight against the adoption of the new constitution. White objections, of course, centered on the provisions for
racial equality. The constitution was called "an instrument for negro rule and supremacy at the point of the sword and the bayonet."
Many whites also objected to the new, racially integrated public
school system, as well as the taxes needed to pay for it.

White Democratic clubs began to organize vigorously, and on
April 2, white Democrats held their own convention in Columbia
to protest the proposed constitution as well as to nominate candidates for the 1868 statewide elections to be held in conjunction with
the popular referendum on the new constitution. This Democratic
convention issued a lengthy set of objections to the constitution and
even called on the black citizens of the state to reject the new constitution as an alien document imposed by force. White Democrats promised that they would eventually grant blacks "qualified by property
and intelligence" the right to vote and other privileges, as well.[81]

This promise made little impression on black voters, and in a special statewide vote held in April 1868, the proposed constitution was adopted by about seventy thousand to twenty-seven thousand.

Whites were not yet ready to give up hope. The Democratic party's executive committee addressed a formal protest to the U.S. Congress, which had the authority to accept or reject the new constitution. The protest included a number of exhibits and attachments detailing the constitution's defects, ranging from the new political rights granted to blacks and the continued disfranchisement of whites who supported the rebellion, to the taxes that were to be imposed to support the public school system. As a result of black suffrage, "intelligence, virtue and patriotism" would give way to "ignorance, stupidity and vice. The superior race is to be made subservient to the inferior." The constitution was denounced as "the work of Northern adventurers, Southern renegades, and ignorant Negroes." It was said that "not one per cent of the white population of the state approves it, and not two percent of the negroes who voted for its adoption understand what the act of voting implied."[82] Congress, however, was unimpressed by these objections. Indeed, Rep. Thaddeus Stevens of Pennsylvania was moved to reply: "What the protest claimed as grievances . . . [we regard] as virtues."[83] South Carolina's new system of government was now a fact.

During the last week of the Constitutional Convention, the state Republican party held its convention in Charleston to nominate candidates for the 1868 statewide elections, which would be held in conjunction with the popular referendum on the proposed Constitution. Many of the Constitutional Convention delegates also served as delegates to this nominating convention. Robert Scott was named the Republican gubernatorial candidate, and Lemuel Boozer, a scalawag, was nominated for the position of lieutenant governor. Republican leaders continued to believe that it was politically expedient to show a mainly white face to the nation. Hence, the only black man nominated for statewide office was Francis Cardozo, slated for the position of secretary of state (1868–72). Moses, who had shown his loyalty and demonstrated his worth at the convention, was named the party's candidate for the powerful post of adjutant and inspector general. This position would give him control over the state militia, an important source of patronage as well as an important instrument for defending Republican rule. In addition, Moses was named a candidate for the state legislature.

With the continued disfranchisement of much of the white political class, Republican statewide candidates were certain to be victorious. Nevertheless, the Union League vigorously organized its black constituents while Democratic clubs made an effort both to rally those whites who had the right to vote and to inhibit voting by blacks. Through the three days of voting, efforts to intimidate black voters and candidates were common. A number of blacks were murdered, including two candidates for the state legislature whose murders were ordered by the Ku Klux Klan acting in concert with Democratic party leaders.[84] At least one white Republican was shot to death after a campaign rally. Only determined efforts by federal troops prevented armed bands of white thugs connected to the Democratic party from completely disrupting the voting process. White Democrats charged that blacks had been secretly arming themselves in preparation for a statewide attack against the white populace, but nothing of the sort ever materialized. Virtually all the violence connected with the 1868 election was directed by white Democrats against blacks and against white Republicans.[85]

With the ratification of the new state constitution and the election of state officers, the stage was set for the readmission of South Carolina to the Union. The new legislature was convened in July and quickly ratified the Fourteenth Amendment to the U.S. Constitution, the key condition set by Congress for the readmission of any southern state. Congress responded by duly swearing in South Carolina's new senators and representatives, and declaring the reconstruction of the state to be complete. Moses easily won election. Republican campaigners told credulous voters that he was the Moses from the Bible, returned to earth to lead them from bondage to the promised land just as he had led the children of Israel so many millennia earlier.[86]

CHAPTER FOUR

Speaker Moses

SOUTH CAROLINA'S NEWLY elected Republican government convened for the first time in July 1868. The state's white press lost
no time in launching a vigorous attack against the entire administration, not waiting to see what it would do. Merely watching the new
officials and legislators assemble was enough to convince the *Fair-
field Herald* that South Carolina had been "trampled beneath the
unholy hoofs of African savages and shoulder-strapped brigands"
and subjected to the rule of "gibbering louse-eaten, devil worship-
ing barbarians, from the jungles of Dahomey, and peripatetic buc-
caneers from Cape Cod, Memphremagog, Hell, and Boston."[1]

White observers professed to be shocked by the number of black
faces they saw in the new government. In actuality, though, blacks
did not hold nearly as many offices as they wanted. Though nearly
two-thirds of South Carolina's registered voters were of African descent, this distribution was reflected only in the state's House of
Representatives where blacks held a seventy-eight to forty-six majority. The new state Senate consisted of twenty-one whites and ten
blacks. The new state administration was virtually all white. The
state treasurer, Francis Cardozo, was the only black statewide official.

This paucity of black officials reflected, to some extent, the fact
that the overwhelming majority of South Carolina's blacks were
newly freed slaves who lacked education or any experience that
might have prepared them to assume leading positions in public

life. A handful of educated African Americans, most of whom had attended the Constitutional Convention, sought to provide leadership for the black community. This group included the members of the Brown Fellowship Society, as well as Francis Cardozo, Richard Cain, Robert Elliott, and a handful of others. Gradually, the pool of black leaders was enlarged as more blacks became literate and familiar with the intricacies of democratic politics. The Union League played an important role in introducing former slaves to the rules of parliamentary procedure and, by encouraging members to attend trials as spectators, to the rules of court procedure as well. Samuel Lee and Beverly Nash were former slaves who became influential black politicians and ultimately even earned the grudging respect of some of the state's conservative whites. Within a few years, experienced black politicians would seek to supplant their white allies in South Carolina and in other states with substantial black electorates such as Florida, Louisiana, and Arkansas.[2] In 1868, however, the potential black leadership cadre was so small that African Americans had no choice but to look to whites for leadership.

At the same time, national and state Republican leaders continued to worry that an all-black government in South Carolina would hurt the party's image nationally. Francis Cardozo cautioned against naming a black man even to the largely ceremonial post of lieutenant governor, saying that this would be a step "beyond the limits of true victory."[3] Among northern Republicans, only Sen. Charles Sumner argued that the southern states should seize the opportunity to elect blacks to the U.S. Congress. The Democratic press replied by urging the Massachusetts legislature to select a black senator to replace Sumner if more blacks were needed in the Congress.[4]

Most numerous among the new government's white officials were the carpetbaggers. Many of these immigrants had arrived in the region as soldiers in the Union army or officials in the Freedmen's Bureau and had remained to try their hands at business, politics, or farming. Freedmen's Bureau officials, in particular, were drawn into politics because they believed that their contacts with the freed slaves would give them an advantage in an electoral arena in which blacks generally constituted the majority. Robert Scott, the newly elected governor, was an Ohioan who had come to South Carolina to head the Freedmen's Bureau. Daniel Chamberlain, the new attorney general, was a native of Massachusetts who, as an officer in the Union army, had been stationed in South Carolina. Chamberlain purchased a plantation and became active in politics. Ultimately, he was elected governor, serving from 1874 to 1876 when the state was "redeemed" by white Democrats. Niles Parker, the new state treasurer, had been a captain in the Union army and, like Chamberlain, had purchased a plantation and remained in South Carolina. B. F. Whittemore, elected to represent South Carolina's first district in the U.S. Congress, was a Massachusetts native who had been sent to South Carolina by the Freedmen's Bureau to organize schools. Frederick Sawyer, also from Massachusetts, was elected to the U.S. Senate. He had come to Charleston to take charge of the Normal School. Several years later, the legislature elected "Honest John" Patterson, a Pennsylvania native noted for his shadiness, to replace Sawyer as U.S. senator.

A second and smaller group of white officials consisted of native Carolinians. Several prominent scalawags had roles in the new regime. Frank Moses had been elected to the state's House of Representatives and would soon be chosen its first Speaker. With the support of the Brown Fellowship Society, Moses had defeated northern black Republican Robert Elliott for the post. Moses was also appointed to serve as adjutant and inspector general of the state militia and as a trustee of the state university. To mend fences with Elliott, Moses appointed him assistant adjutant of the militia. Later, Moses supported Elliott's successful bid for a seat in the U.S. House of Representatives where he served with distinction. Joseph Crews was another highly visible scalawag who held office under the new regime. Before the war, Crews had been a "Negro trader," that is, a white businessman who catered to a black clientele. Crews served on a number of important committees, where he came to be known as one of the most radical members of the state legislature. Moses appointed Crews to serve as the ranking officer of the state militia.

Though Crews had minimal military experience, he was an effective enough leader to induce Democratic party paramilitary forces to assassinate him in preparation for the 1876 election campaign. "It was understood that they intended to put an end to his leadership," one Democrat reported.[5] Former provisional governor James Orr, the state's most prominent Unionist during the prewar and war years, was not elected to serve in the new administration. In September 1868, however, the legislature elected Orr judge of the Eighth Judicial Circuit. Thomas Robertson, a scalawag who had played an important role at the Constitutional Convention, was elected by the legislature to represent the state in the U.S. Senate.

Another group of whites who played a role in the new government were more numerous but initially far less important than the scalawags. These were the white conservatives elected under the Democratic party's banner. Seven white Democrats had been elected to the Senate and sixteen to the House, most from up-country counties where there were few blacks. In both houses of the state legislature, the Democrats generally sat together and took little or no part in the proceedings, except occasionally to protest Republican plans or to question the motives and integrity of a speaker. This small group of white Democrats was in the peculiar position of representing the views of the bulk of the state's white populace, including those who continued to be barred from politics under the terms of the Reconstruction Acts.

At the beginning of the Reconstruction era, some white Democrats had toyed with the idea of competing with the Republicans for the support of blacks. In 1865 no less a figure than Gen. Wade Hampton, the state's most powerful Democrat, was prepared to support a qualified black suffrage. Hampton declared that the white people of South Carolina must develop "amicable relations" with blacks in order to teach them to trust their white fellow citizens. Toward this end, Hampton opposed the most onerous portions of the Black Codes enacted after the state's 1865 Constitutional Convention, and favored giving blacks the right to vote on precisely the same terms and conditions that the franchise was exercised by whites. In both cases, Hampton favored a "slight" educational and property restriction. Hampton and others believed that with some encouragement, blacks would accept the leadership of native whites as they had long been accustomed to doing. Were this to occur, the antebellum political structure of South Carolina would soon be restored.

A number of factors had prevented the Hamptonian policy of conservative reconciliation from taking effect. First, Democrats had no real hope of outbidding the Republicans for black support. While the Democrats spoke of offering a qualified suffrage to African Americans, the Republicans asserted that blacks should govern, or at least play a major role in governing, the state. Second, the Union League clubs and the Freedmen's Bureau were urging blacks to support the Republican cause. One Democratic observer complained that the Union League taught blacks that voting for the Republican side was virtually a religious obligation. "He was not only taught that it was his truest policy to vote against his former master on every occasion, but a solemn obligation to God who emancipated him—always remembering that God had used the Radical [Republican] party as his chosen instrument for this great end." As the Union League clubs strengthened their hold on black political involvement during the mid-1860s, there was less and less likelihood that blacks could be lured away from the Republican camp.

Finally, the Hampton plan was rejected by a significant group of whites. In particular, up-country whites viewed the idea of black enfranchisement as a plot on the part of low-country planters who would control the black vote. Before the war, up-country whites, who were mainly small farmers working the land without the use of slaves, bitterly resented the dominance of the wealthy low-country planters. The war had done nothing to erase this class division from state politics. Up-country whites assumed that black voters would be controlled by the planters, who would use them to reassert their grip on state government. Hampton's proposal was rejected by many of the state's whites, and as a result, the notion of a political alliance between native whites and native blacks that would have restored white conservative rule to the state was stillborn.

The impossibility of an alliance between blacks and whites under the auspices of the Democratic party left the field clear for the Republicans. For white Republicans, be they carpetbaggers or scalawags, an alliance with blacks was the ticket to political power in South Carolina. White Republicans assumed that they would provide the leadership and direction, with blacks providing the votes that would give the Republican party control of the state's affairs. Certainly, if political power is measured by electoral success, this alliance was triumphant in 1868 and in the ensuing three elections, before going down to defeat in 1876. Electoral success, however, was only part of the story of political power in South Carolina.

Though some were disfranchised and they lacked full representation in the government, the state's white Democrats were hardly powerless. They owned much of the state's land. Thus, in a rural economy, they were the state's principal employers; their welfare could not be entirely ignored. They controlled the press, whose vicious attacks and critical accounts of the government eventually began to reach and influence northern audiences. Finally, they were heavily armed and more than willing to use their military training to defend their interests. On many occasions, Democratic militias composed of veteran Confederate officers and soldiers easily routed the half-trained and inexperienced black state militia controlled by the Republican government and could only be checked by federal troops, which were not always reliable. Some federal commanders sympathized with the white populace and were scornful of the Republican government. Federal troops, moreover, would not remain in the South forever. Conservative whites, therefore, were very much a factor in the political life of South Carolina despite their conspicuous absence in the new government. During the 1868 election, whites had given notice that they were fully capable of using violence to achieve their political goals. In that election, a campaign of political violence organized by the Democrats claimed the lives of at least eight blacks including James Martin who had been elected to the state House of Representatives and B. F. Randolph who had run successfully for the state Senate.[6]

Many blacks regarded their alliance with white Republicans as a necessary but temporary expedient, and most white Republicans also saw their relationship with blacks as a marriage of convenience.[7] White Republicans believed that to place their control of the state on a firm footing, they must ultimately come to terms with South Carolina's whites. One possibility was to try to build an alliance with the poorer up-country whites. This group shared many of the political goals of blacks, such as the expansion of public education, a progressive system of taxation, and a suffrage unburdened by property or education requirements. If Republicans endorsed such programs, they might attract the support of at least some up-country whites. Such support, however, was not forthcoming. The closely related issues of race and regionalism presented enormous obstacles. Very few up-country whites were willing to link themselves to a northern party that catered to blacks.

As a result, instead of seeking the support of poorer, up-country whites, most white Republicans sought to build ties to members of the wealthy low-country class made up of planters and businessmen. Many of the carpetbaggers, in particular, were more comfortable with this stratum than with poor whites or blacks. Gov. Robert Scott preferred to socialize with South Carolina's aristocrats, including Wade Hampton.[8] Indeed, he did not invite any blacks to his first annual governor's ball.[9] Attorney general and future governor Daniel Chamberlain had been educated at Yale and Harvard and constantly sought to be accepted at the highest levels of South Carolina society. Years later, Chamberlain confessed that during his entire period of involvement in South Carolina politics, he had barely been able to overcome his aversion to working with blacks.[10] Scott, Chamberlain, and other carpetbaggers encouraged the state's elite to participate in and profit from the program of railroad construction and economic development championed by the Republican party, and allowed them to benefit from the corruption attendant on these

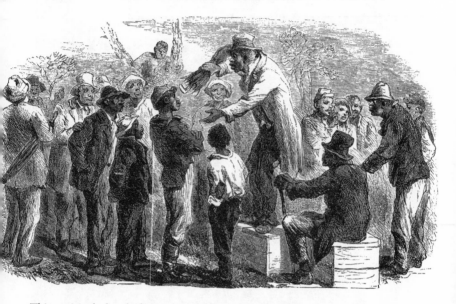

This satirical sketch first appeared in John Townsend Trowbridge, *The South: A Tour of Its Battle-fields and Ruined Cities, A Journey through the Desolated States, and Talks with the People* (Hartford, 1866). It captured both the freedmen's excitement as they contemplated the new political order and the patronizing perspective white observers typically adopted—portraying them as childlike and uncomprehending. Francis Butler Simkins and Robert Hilliard Woody, *South Carolina during Reconstruction* (Chapel Hill: The University of North Carolina Press, 1932).

RADICAL MEMBERS
OF THE S⁰. Cᴬ. LEGISLATURE.

Collective portrait of Radical legislature. In 1868 South Carolina elected a majority-black legislature. Democrats characterized the black legislators as a group of louse-eaten barbarians and averred that the white Republican legislators were even worse. Franklin Moses's picture is labeled "Judas Moses who raised the Confederate Flag on Fort Sumter!!" The portrait was taken by Col. James G. Gibbes of Columbia. Courtesy of South Caroliniana Library, University of South Carolina, Columbia.

Franklin Moses Jr. Courtesy of South Caroliniana Library, University of South Carolina, Columbia.

The Present Stage. This 1868 cartoon depicts Franklin Moses whiling away his time in the embrace of black women while his allies, including Governor Scott and State Treasurer Parker, lead South Carolina to the edge of a financial precipice. Moses was hated more for his willingness to socialize with blacks than for his financial misdeeds. Courtesy of South Caroliniana Library, University of South Carolina, Columbia.

Freedom and Pardon from Governor Moses. This 1873 *Harper's Weekly* cartoon depicts Governor Moses handing out pardons to black convicts, who are portrayed with glowering, simian features. The point, as in George H. W. Bush's infamous "Willy Horton" ad, was to frighten whites by suggesting that Moses was freeing dangerous black convicts who would prey upon them. For the most part, Moses used his pardons for political purposes, rewarding loyal Republican workers. Francis Butler Simkins and Robert Hilliard Woody, *South Carolina during Reconstruction* (Chapel Hill: University of North Carolina Press, 1932).

Governor Moses Viewing the Promised Land from Mount Ruin. By the
end of his gubernatorial term, Moses was frequently pilloried in the press
for his alleged corruption. The biblical Moses looked across the River Jordan to a land of milk and honey. Franklin Moses, standing atop a mountain of debt, peers across the river to the land his opponents have promised
to him—the state prison. From *Harper's Weekly,* 1873. Francis Butler
Simkins and Robert Hilliard Woody, *South Carolina during Reconstruction* (Chapel Hill: University of North Carolina Press, 1932).

Moses with Broken Tablets. One of the black convicts pardoned by Governor Moses seems to have broken most of the Ten Commandments after his release. The governor looks on indulgently as the black man, portrayed as an apelike figure, stands over the shattered tablets. Unlike his biblical namesake, the Moses depicted in this cartoon appears to have little concern for God's law. The willingness of Radical Republicans to tolerate the inherent criminality of their savage black followers was a common journalistic theme that the northern press copied from its southern counterpart. The cartoon also reminds readers of Moses's Jewish background. Circa 1873. Robert N. Rosen, *The Jewish Confederates* (Columbia: University of South Carolina Press, 2000).

Aping Bad Examples. The southern white press typically depicted black politicians as apes from the jungle. Eventually, southerners won the propaganda war and the "respectable" northern press began to express similar prejudices. This Thomas Nast cartoon is from *Harper's Weekly*, March 14, 1874. Francis Butler Simkins and Robert Hilliard Woody, *South Carolina during Reconstruction* (Chapel Hill: University of North Carolina Press, 1932).

ventures. Businessmen and planters were happy to take advantage of the opportunities presented to them. Few, however, joined the Republican camp. Most waited, instead, for an opportunity to rid themselves entirely of Republican rule and reestablish their antebellum power and position.

A Black Republican

As recently as 1867 Frank Moses, like General Hampton and other conservatives, had believed the freedmen could be convinced to follow the leadership of prominent native whites and reject the blandishments of the Republicans. When this notion turned out not to be true, Hampton and most of the others temporarily abandoned electoral politics to consider new strategies. Moses took a different course. When the freedmen would not follow him into the Democratic party, he followed them into the Radical Republican camp. This led to Moses's almost immediate ostracism from white society. Former friends and associates shunned hm. The new editors of his former newspaper, the *Sumter News*, wrote that they could not understand "how any intelligent white man, born and raised in South Carolina, can consent to become a part of the negro government which it is now proposed to be set up in this state."[11] Moses, along with another scalawag, Thomas J. Robertson, were expelled from the state university's Euphradian Society. Only a few years before, Moses had been proud of his election to this literary honor society but now, at a special meeting, the society declared that Moses, along with Robertson, had "proved false to their own race, unloosed every tie of honor, every golden chord of virtue, and left the remaining fragments to trail in the dust underfoot." Moses was said to have "lowered his dignity and station" and to have become a "black stain" on the society's roll.[12] This was strong language even for a literary society.

Shunned by white society, Moses took a truly extraordinary step for a white Carolinian—he joined black society. Most of the well-known South Carolina scalawags, including Robertson, Thomas J.

Mackey, Elliott Hayes, and James M. Smith, were involved in political and business dealings with blacks mainly as a temporary matter of expedience. For the time being, at least, the bottom rail was on the top and shrewd operators sought to make the most of the situation. After 1876, when the state had been "redeemed" by white Democrats, Robertson, Mackey, and others made haste to rejoin the Democratic fold.[13] Their relationship with blacks was purely a marriage of convenience, generally unconsummated by social intercourse. Almost all of the white carpetbaggers preferred white society and avoided the company of blacks. As historian Joel Williamson has observed, racial separation "marked the formal social life of the official community in Columbia."[14]

Moses, however, felt comfortable with blacks generally and with his new black colleagues—Cain, Cardozo, Elliott, William Whipper, and the others—in particular. During sessions of the legislature, Moses entertained black representatives with "cigars, champagne and sundries at the fine saloon in the State House."[15] Moses was fond of gambling with his black colleagues. One instance involving a thousand dollar bet between Moses and Whipper on a horse race became nationally famous when journalist James Pike cited it in his newspaper articles as evidence of the state's corruption.[16]

Moses insisted that blacks be treated with appropriate respect. He complained loudly and bitterly when Governor Scott did not invite blacks to his official Christmas ball. Moses infuriated his white neighbors by actually inviting blacks to his home—at a time when only black domestics were permitted in white homes.[17] "Gossiping tongues began wagging, especially when the gleeful howl over a good billiard shot came in the Gullah dialect," Buxton reports. "When African accents rose in feminine tones, when [his wife] Emma was out of town, the flow of words across neighbors' fences reached flood proportions."[18] Moses was often seen in the company of the Rollin sisters, four beautiful daughters of a French father and mulatto mother. The Rollin sisters were prominent in Charleston mulatto society, and the sisters were especially well known for their advocacy of women's suffrage. Moses allowed Louisa Rollin to deliver a speech on the topic from the floor of the House and later spoke at a prosuffrage rally organized by Lottie Rollin.[19] Social relationships between white men and women of color were, of course, hardly unknown in South Carolina, but to be seen together in public was a major affront to southern white mores.

Moses also visited the homes and churches of his black constituents. Except for an occasional campaign rally, most of the state's white elected officials—from the governor on down—had little or no personal contact with the black families they nominally represented. South Carolina's white politicians relied on the Union League to round up votes, and if they thought about their mainly black constituents at all, it was in purely abstract terms. Most had no idea where or how the impoverished freedmen who kept them in office actually lived. But Moses was quite familiar with the freedmen and their living conditions. Some northern newspapers, unable to think of any other explanation for his conduct, actually reported that Moses was black.[20] In his classic 1929 attack on Reconstruction, historian Claude Bowers angrily accused Moses of "frequenting Negro cabins, kissing Negro babies, swirling through the dance with dusky maidens in his arms in Negro dance halls." Like other men of his era, black and white, Moses was not above using racist terms in his everyday speech. Presumably a Thad Stevens or Charles Sumner would have condemned such behavior. Yet Moses, said Bowers citing Reconstruction-era journalist James Pike, had "none of [Sen. Charles] Sumner's academic notions of social equality." Instead, "[Moses] lives what Sumner preaches."[21]

Speaker Moses

Living what Sumner preached required Moses not only to socialize freely with blacks but also to develop a set of programs and policies to improve the condition of black Carolinians. Under Moses's leadership, the state legislature sought to develop such programs in the realms of civil rights, education, land redistribution, and economic development. To protect these programs, and their own positions, the Republican leadership sought to build institutions that would maintain the party's power. Here, Moses played a vitally important role. As he assumed the Speaker's chair for the first time, Moses chided his fellow white Carolinians for boycotting the polls and refusing to cooperate with the new government. He called on his black colleagues, unprepared as they might be for public office, to rise to the occasion. "Since those whose especial duty it was," he averred, "to resurrect from her recumbent posture our fallen and unfortunate State have failed in the performance of [their] task . . . let us address ourselves to the work before us as men who are alive to the necessities of the hour."[22] The "hour" seemed to require programs in the realms of civil rights, education, land redistribution, and economic development.

CIVIL RIGHTS

The legislature's first goal was to guarantee the newly won civil rights of the state's black citizens. To this end, the legislature enacted a civil rights act designed to provide for state enforcement of the 1866 federal Civil Rights Act. The state act proclaimed all persons to be equal before the law and prohibited all public and private agencies from discriminating on the basis of "race, color or previous condition of servitude." Discrimination was prohibited in public accommodations, places of amusement and recreation, on common carriers, and in hotels and restaurants. The act provided harsh penalties for anyone convicted of violating its provisions. Ostensibly, violators could be sentenced to as much as five years at hard labor plus a one thousand dollar fine. To ensure that the state's courts would enforce the civil rights act, Moses persuaded the legislature to appoint his father as the state's chief justice. The elder Moses was required to claim Radical Republican sympathies; in turn, the governor petitioned the Congress to remove the political disabilities that disqualified Moses, an antebellum state official who had been part of the Confederate government, from participating in politics. Moses's disabilities were removed in December 1868, and he took his seat on the bench.[23] Though the elder Moses was loyal to his son, Chief Justice Moses turned out not to be a reliable friend to the new regime and was often lauded by whites for his decisions.[24] A more reliable Republican justice was Jonathan Jasper Wright, a black lawyer originally from Pennsylvania. With Richard Cain's backing, Moses pushed Wright's appointment through the legislature in 1870 over the opposition of most white Republicans who were not friendly to the idea of a black state supreme court justice. The third justice was a carpetbagger from New York, A. J. Willard. Democrats disparaged the new court as consisting of "a scalawagger, a carpetbagger and a nigger," but most of the court's critics eventually came to see its decisions as reasonable, especially in 1876 when the court played a role in the electoral crisis that followed the disputed voting of that year.

The Civil Rights Act was more important for what it symbolized than for what it actually accomplished. Only one individual was ever convicted for violating the act. The director of Charleston's academy of music, John Ford, was fined for refusing to admit a group of blacks to the main floor of the academy's auditorium for a performance. For the most part, however, South Carolina's blacks and whites lived in such different social worlds that laws mandating equality of social treatment were irrelevant. Blacks generally did not endeavor to attend the opera or symphony. Whites and blacks did not frequent the same restaurants. And when blacks did win access to a public institution, whites withdrew from it. For example, when blacks were finally granted use of Charleston's streetcars, whites stopped riding them.[25] Of course, blacks enjoyed equality before the law in South Carolina for only a brief time. Blacks were assured legal equality so long as Republicans controlled the legislature and many of the courts. When that ceased to be true after 1876, equality before the law diminished and then disappeared altogether. The act was repealed in 1889.

EDUCATION

The second of the legislature's goals, the creation of a system of public education, was extremely important to South Carolina's African Americans. Education had been denied to slaves, and black leaders strongly believed that education was a necessary condition for black equality and progress. Billing itself as the first formal conclave of African Americans in the state, the Colored People's Convention, held in Charleston in 1865, proclaimed that the highest priority of the freedmen should be "good schools for the education of our children." This was essential because "an educated and intelligent people can neither be held in nor reduced to slavery." Throughout the state, blacks had seized every possible opportunity to learn to read and write, and they looked to the Republican government to establish a statewide set of institutions to ensure the education of their children. Prior to the Civil War, the state's educational system had been quite backward, even by the standards of the time. South Carolina was dominated by the low-country planter elite, which had little interest in spending money on schools for the common folk. Few rural whites and no blacks had access to public education. Public schools existed in some towns, but in most rural areas education was a private matter. This meant that, for the most part, only the children of well-to-do whites received even rudimentary schooling. In Charleston and other towns, free blacks maintained their own schools, and a small number of blacks were taught by friendly whites or educated abroad so that perhaps 5 percent of the black population was literate before the war.[26]

In the war's aftermath, the state government made some effort to expand the educational system. By 1869, however, only 8,255 out of some 68,000 white school age children were enrolled in public elementary schools.[27] Some 650 white boys attended private academies that were the equivalent of modern high schools; 950 attended one or another of the state's colleges. The publicly supported University of South Carolina (formerly South Carolina College) enrolled only 65 students in 1869. White girls whose parents could afford the tuition attended seminaries whose educational efforts were focused on etiquette and decorum.

By 1868 an annual average of 5,800 black children were enrolled in the fifty-six schools the Freedmen's Bureau had established across the state.[28] Several hundred more attended one of the handful of publicly supported schools for blacks created during the 1860s. The best known was the Morris Street School in Charleston. Only one public high school was available to black children. This was the Howard School in Columbia, which had been built by the Freedmen's Bureau in cooperation with a private philanthropic association, the New York Freedmen's Relief Society. In a number of instances, African Americans erected school buildings and raised money for supplies in the hope that teachers would be sent by the Freedmen's Bureau. Typically, the Freedmen's Bureau schools were staffed by northerners since few native whites were willing to teach blacks.

Whites alleged that the Freedmen's Bureau schools focused more on political indoctrination than on reading, writing, and arithmetic. Often, indeed, the schools sought to teach their young charges to love their country and to revere the Republican party that had brought them out of slavery. This effort to build patriotism and partisan attachments, however, hardly distinguished the bureau's schools from public schools in many parts of the nation. What is more significant is that before they were closed by the federal government in 1869, the Freedmen's Bureau schools had taught thousands of black children at least the rudiments of reading and writing and strengthened the conviction of black leaders throughout the state that education was critically important.

The 1868 South Carolina constitution provided a blueprint for a public education system modeled after those found in the New England states. The state constitution called for the creation of a system of universal education with two-year compulsory attendance for all children between the ages of six and sixteen. Schools supported by public funds were prohibited from excluding black students. The constitution called for the division of each county into school districts and provided for the establishment of a state superintendent of education and a school commissioner in each county. The education system was to be supported by a property tax and a poll tax. In addition to elementary schools, the constitution mandated state support for a university, a teacher's college, an agricultural school, and schools for the physically disabled. When it convened in 1869 under Moses's leadership, the new legislature sought to implement these constitutional mandates. Salaries were appropriated for the position of state superintendent of education and for the county education commissioners. Curricular guidelines were developed, school district boundaries drawn, provision made for free textbooks for those unable to afford books, and a school tax put into place. On paper, at least, South Carolina now had one of the nation's finest school systems. Translating paper into reality, however, proved to be quite difficult.

The state's first superintendent of education was appointed in 1868. He was Justus K. Jillson, a Massachusetts native who had come to South Carolina to help supervise the Freedmen's Bureau's school system. Jillson was an energetic and competent administrator who, during his seven years in office, achieved some notable successes. Between 1869 and 1876 the number of public schools in the state increased from 400 to nearly 2,800. The size of the teaching staff increased from 500 to more than 3,000. In a similar vein, the number of students enrolled in some form of schooling rose to nearly 125,000—an increase of more than 100,000—during the first five years of the system's operation.[29]

The new public schools were not integrated in the contemporary sense. Black and white children generally attended separate schools, though in some instances they might attend separate classes within the same building. Nevertheless, from the beginning, many white Carolinians viewed the new school system as an institution aimed mainly at promoting black education. This view was strengthened in 1873 when, as governor, Franklin Moses opened the state university to blacks. Since most whites were bitterly opposed to the education of blacks, the education system had little or no support in the white community.

White suspicion of the school system was fanned by the state's Democratic leadership, which characterized the public schools as little more than an institutional base for the Republican party. Republicans, it was feared, would use this base as a source of patronage positions for their activists and as a channel for pumping state money into the party's coffers. Through the school system, Republicans might not only indoctrinate and mobilize blacks but also begin to bring some poor whites into their orbit. This was not to be tolerated. The state's Democratic leadership attacked the school system and encouraged whites to evade the poll tax, which was an important school funding source. Within a short period of time, poll tax evasion became the norm among whites.

The state's entire revenue base eventually collapsed under white attack, leaving the schools, along with most other state institutions, chronically short of funds. Most schools, particularly in rural areas, could afford to stay open only one or two months per year. There were no funds for combating truancy and absenteeism. Textbooks could not be furnished to poor students. The dream of a public education was never fully realized by South Carolina's black citizens or, for that matter, most of its white citizens.

LAND REDISTRIBUTION

The third major undertaking of the new Republican administration had to do with the issue of land. The land issue had two interrelated components. The first of these was how to respond to the desire of thousands of freedmen to own their own land. While land ownership was a dream of freedmen throughout the South, in South Carolina it had been stimulated by the events of the war. The Sea Island experiment, coupled with Sherman's Field Order 15, gave South Carolina's black population a taste of land ownership that it would not soon forget. From the perspective of the new Republican government, finding a formula through which its black supporters might acquire land was a political imperative.

The second component of the issue was the fact that land ownership was the basis of the white elite's power in South Carolina. A relatively small number of families owned most of the state's productive land in the form of large plantations. These families controlled the state's economy and would exercise political power regardless of whether they had the right to vote or hold public office. During much of Reconstruction, wealthy land owners dominated a set of white institutions parallel and separate from the state's official institutions. Indeed, toward the end of the era, the white community, led by Wade Hampton, essentially governed itself outside the official system of government.[30] The wealth of the white land owners also financed a well-organized and well-supplied insurgency that eventually brought down the Republican regime.

In principle, the two components of the land question could have been resolved with one simple policy—confiscation. In the immediate aftermath of the war when, as Senator Stevens averred, the South's landed aristocracy was at its weakest, large plantations might have been seized, subdivided, and turned over to land-hungry freedmen. In one fell swoop, the freedmen would have the land for which they hoped and the power of the southern aristocracy would be broken. But if there had ever been a moment when confiscation had been a realistic possibility, by 1868 that moment had passed. The federal government would not support a policy of confiscation, and state-level Republican politicians were compelled to disassociate themselves from the idea.

Unable to pursue a program of confiscation, Republicans instead adopted a two-pronged policy that promised to achieve at least some of the same results. To provide land for the freedmen, the new Republican legislature turned to the land commission established under the 1868 constitution. To reduce the land holdings and power of the white planters, the legislature developed a new system of taxation designed to "drive them to the wall."[31]

In the first session of the Republican legislature, Moses and his fellow Republicans enacted a bill to fund and implement the constitution's provision for the creation of a state land commission. The commission was charged with purchasing farmland and reselling it to black families at a price and under terms that would make it possible for large numbers of blacks to acquire their own land. Pursuant to the act, land purchased by the state was to be divided into sections ranging in size from twenty-five to one hundred acres. Lots were to be sold to settlers—who might be black or white—at the state's purchase price. Purchases could be made entirely on credit at a 6 percent annual rate of interest. To discourage land speculators, purchasers were required to live on the land for three years before they could pay or begin paying the purchase price. At that point, settlers would have eight years to complete their payments and receive title to the land. The legislature authorized two hundred thousand dollars in bonds to be issued to pay for land purchases. In 1870 the legislature authorized the sale of another five hundred thousand in bonds to fund land acquisitions.

Governor Scott appointed Charles P. Leslie, a carpetbagger from New York, to be the state's first land commissioner. His work was to be overseen by a board consisting of the governor and other prominent Republican politicians, including Attorney General Chamberlain and State Treasurer Parker. Over the next several years, Leslie was replaced by black Republicans, first by Robert DeLarge, then by Francis Cardozo, and finally by Henry Hayne.

The commission began purchasing land in 1869. From the outset, the state's purchasing procedures were beset by problems. Many land owners saw the state's purchasing efforts as an opportunity to rid themselves of undesirable land at an inflated price. Land owners often bribed state surveyors and assessors to approve the purchase of land that was utterly unsuitable for farming. The state was then unable to resell the land to settlers. One example of this practice was the notorious case of a tract of land that went by the unappealing but apt name of Hellhole Swamp.[32] This was a thirteen-thousand-acre tract that had belonged to one of Charleston's wealthiest families, the Manigaults. The land commission paid the family eight thousand dollars, but the purchase price was recorded as thirty-eight thousand. The thirty thousand dollar difference went directly into the pockets of the land commission members. The tract was generally uninhabitable, much less suitable for farming. Local wags were fond of saying that even the swamp's snakes and alligators struggled to eke out a living from the inhospitable environment.

Despite the various frauds connected with the land commission, South Carolina's efforts to acquire land for African Americans were at least a partial success. Some fourteen thousand black families were, at one time or another, settled on tracts of land acquired by the state. This meant that during Reconstruction some seventy thousand people, or nearly 15 percent of the state's black population, lived, at least briefly, on their own land. A number of poor whites also acquired land during this period, and on many tracts black and white families farmed side by side.[33]

Over the years, many blacks and poor whites lost possession of the land on which they had settled because of their inability to make the payments mandated by state law or to scrape together enough money to meet their tax obligations. Particularly after the end of Reconstruction, the state government demanded strict adherence to the specified payment schedule and was quick to evict black settlers who fell behind on their taxes or their land payments. After 1890 the state halted the sale of small parcels of land altogether and sold off its remaining lands to wealthy land owners and investors in large tracts that were beyond the financial reach of settlers. Despite this manifest change in the state's attitude toward land settlement, thousands of blacks managed to hold on and acquire full title to their state lands. Some were even able to expand their holdings. This is why black land ownership in South Carolina in the twentieth century was higher than in any other southern state. In 1900 South Carolina blacks owned more than fifteen thousand farms. To a substantial extent, Republican policy in the 1870s did fulfill the freedmen's dream of land ownership.

Frank Moses supported the work of the land commission, but the land policy to which he gave his attention as a legislator, and later as governor, was taxation. Moses was a strong proponent of high taxes on land. Indeed, these taxes reached their peak during his term as governor.[34] Republicans fully understood that heavy taxes could gradually sap the wealth and power of the state's traditional rulers. A tax program could be as effective as confiscation "and yet avoid the strenuous opposition that any scheme of land pillaging would infallibly meet with in the North."[35] Over time, taxes would erode the planters' wealth, force them to sell more and more land, and reduce their power to direct the state's affairs. "Taxes are always a burden, will be assessed yearly upon all lands, and they must be paid. The expenses of the state will be a continual drag upon those who attempt to carry on large landed estates."[36] Over the next several years, tax rates and tax assessments were steadily increased to the point that many land owners were unable to pay, and hundreds of thousands of acres were sold at a discounted price or disposed of by state and county governments at tax sales. "I don't see how we can stay in the country," said one Laurens County land owner, "for our taxes will be increased and we will be under the very heels of the Radicals."[37]

Perhaps through taxation the Republican legislature might eventually have redistributed political power as well as land in South Carolina. However, resistance to taxation soon developed, and it was not limited to the white planter class. White land owners organized a series of taxpayer conventions to publicize their plight.[38] Among the attendees were carpetbaggers and black landowners who, having acquired property, found themselves the victims of the same Republican tax programs that had been justified by the need to provide blacks with an opportunity to purchase land. "Negro voters," said the *New York Times,* "are not exempt from the visits of the tax gatherer."[39]

White land owners petitioned the press and the U.S. Congress; black land owners and carpetbaggers complained to their state legislators. One group of land owners formally presented a petition to the Grant administration pointing out the obvious. "It has been openly avowed by prominent members of the [state] legislature," declared the petition, "that taxes should be increased to a point which will compel the sale of the great body of the land, and take it away from the former owners."[40] Republicans were compelled to briefly reduce taxes in anticipation of the 1872 election. After the election, however, the Moses administration resumed a high tax policy that, had it continued, might have taken away the great body of the land from its former owners. But political developments over-threw the Republicans and saved the white land owners.

ECONOMIC DEVELOPMENT

The fourth major goal of the Republican administration that as-sumed office in 1868 was industrial and commercial development. Such development would serve a number of purposes. Through industrial development, jobs would be created for the freedmen, converting them from backward agricultural laborers into a more progressive industrial working class. Moreover, the transformation of the state's agriculture-based economy to one based on industry would further undermine the power of the antebellum planter ar-istocracy and make way for a new commercial and industrial elite. Finally, industrial development would increase the entire state's prosperity, which would, it was hoped, give all Carolinians and especially the state's business community, a reason to tolerate—if not enthusiastically support—Republican rule. James Harrison, a scalawag and president of the Blue Ridge Railroad, wrote to Gov-ernor Scott that by creating a climate favorable to business and enterprise, the Republican party might win the support of more of "the old citizens of the state."[41] Reliance on black support, wrote Harrison, was ultimately a losing proposition. "The colored people from a vain lust for office and brief power, are going to bring swift destruction on their race. . . . The Negro is played out."

While the state government did take some interest in phosphate mining and iron production, its major emphasis was on the con-struction of railroad lines that would connect South Carolina with the major manufacturing centers of the North, promoting the shipment of cotton and other crops to northern factories. Railroads would also connect the port of Charleston to the agricultural regions of the West, thus expanding Charleston's role as a shipping center. An expanded rail network would also provide the necessary infrastructure for further industrial development, particularly in the realm of cotton manufacture.

Before the war, the city of Charleston had actively encouraged railroads, purchasing nearly $2 million in bonds to promote construction of rail lines to Nashville, Chattanooga, and Memphis. Despite these efforts, railroad construction in South Carolina, as in the South as a whole, had lagged far behind that in the North. At the outbreak of the war, there were only 973 miles of track in the entire state of South Carolina. Much of this was destroyed during the war, along with bridges, stations, locomotives, and railcars.

After the cessation of hostilities, the owners of four lines, the South Carolina, the Charleston and Savannah, the Greenville and Columbia, and the Blue Ridge railways, moved to repair their track and resume service. It was, however extremely difficult for these lines to raise the huge amounts of capital needed, given the general paucity of capital in the region and the reluctance of northern investors to commit funds to what were viewed as extremely risky ventures. As a result, all four lines asked the state legislature to make their bonds more salable in national credit markets by guaranteeing payment in the event of default. Between 1865 and 1868 the state legislature gave limited assistance to all the rail lines, most notably guaranteeing an issue of South Carolina Railroad bonds in 1867. Not until 1868, at the beginning of the Scott administration, did the state government throw its full weight behind railroad repair and construction projects.[42]

Between 1869 and 1871 the state guaranteed nearly $1 million in Charleston and Savannah bonds and allowed the railroad to postpone payment of principal and interest on another $1 million in bonds that the state had guaranteed before the war. In addition, the state purchased outright more than a $250,000 in the line's common stock. During the same period, the state legislature also guaranteed nearly $2 million in Greenville and Columbia bonds, while purchasing almost $500,000 in the company's common stock. The state guaranteed more than $4 million in Blue Ridge securities for the construction of a rail line linking Charleston to Knoxville, Tennessee, and gave the Blue Ridge a loan of $200,000 for repairs and construction. Only the South Carolina Railroad was able to operate without help from the Scott administration.

Despite millions of dollars in state bond guarantees and loans, South Carolina's railroad system did not develop rapidly during the Scott era or, indeed, during the entire period of Republican rule. In 1868 South Carolina had roughly eleven hundred miles of usable track. By 1875 this had increased to little more than thirteen hundred miles, despite millions of dollars in state investment. The Blue Ridge Railroad had been forced into bankruptcy in 1873 without ever completing its line to Knoxville. The Greenville and Columbia was sold in bankruptcy in 1872 to the South Carolina. The Charleston and Savannah went bankrupt in 1874. Only the South Carolina railway, the one railroad that did not receive much in the way of state support, prospered during this period, tripling its freight and passenger business as the other railroads faltered. The administration's dream of creating the infrastructure for industrial development had failed.

Several factors account for this failure. The first was corruption. As was the case throughout the country, state aid for railroad construction created opportunities for massive public fraud. A group of prominent Republican politicians who came to be called the Greenville and Columbia ring looted hundreds of thousands of dollars from the railroad. The members of the ring, including Attorney General Chamberlain, State Treasurer Parker, Secretary of State Cardozo, U.S. senator John J. Patterson, used their powerful positions to acquire control of the railroad. "There is a mint of money in this or I am a fool," Chamberlain wrote to one of his fellow conspirators.[43] Speaker Moses was certainly aware of the ring's activities and may have facilitated its efforts, but despite his reputation as the Robber Governor, Moses was not a direct participant in this or the other major frauds promulgated during Scott's term as governor. Moses was sometimes a "tool" but seldom an associate of the various fraudulent operations during this period.[44]

The Greenville and Columbia ring's method was simple. To assist the railroad, the state had purchased nearly a half million dollars in its stock, paying approximately $20.00 per share. The ring secured the enactment of a state law authorizing the sale of surplus state property, ostensibly to permit the disposal of damaged construction material lying around the grounds of the statehouse. The sale of these and other surplus materials was to be managed by a commission headed by Chamberlain. The remainder of the commission was conveniently made up of the other members of the ring. At its first meeting, the commission declared the state's Greenville and Columbia shares to be surplus property and offered them for sale at $2.75 per share. All the shares were immediately purchased by the commission members who now, in their capacity as private citizens, were able to exercise control of the railroad. They quickly created a new board of directors composed exclusively of members of the commission.

At that point, however, the ring became too ambitious. Chamberlain and the others sought to use their influence to persuade the legislature to guarantee more than $1 million in new Greenville and Columbia bonds. They hoped to pocket the proceeds from the sale. Learning of the plan, however, New York bond traders refused to purchase any Greenville and Columbia securities. The collapse of its bonds forced the line into bankruptcy. The ring had lost its investment and the railroad was ruined. A similar effort to plunder the Blue Ridge Railroad resulted in that corporation's bankruptcy also. The same commission that sold the state's shares in the Greenville and Columbia, also sold the state's holdings in the Blue Ridge at a price of $1.00 per share. This allowed a group headed by Senator Patterson to gain control of the railroad for a little more than $13,000. Since the state had already agreed to back some $4 million in Blue Ridge bonds, Patterson and his associates hoped to reap an enormous profit from their investment. They discovered, unfortunately, that even with the state's endorsement, the bonds could not be sold on the market. The group then turned to the state legislature and secured the enactment of the Revenue Bond Scrip Act.

This ingenious piece of legislation authorized the state treasurer to issue nearly $2 million in "certificates of indebtedness" to be issued in exchange for $4 million in outstanding Blue Ridge bonds. These new securities were to be treated by the state almost like cash, insofar as they were to be receivable in payment of taxes and other obligations. In essence, members of the Patterson group had secured legislation bestowing on themselves a grant of nearly $2 million dollars in state funds in exchange for a set of worthless bonds. Eventually, the Scrip Act was overturned by the state courts. Before that time, however, several hundred thousand dollars in revenue bonds were issued by the state and sold on the financial market. The members of the Patterson group earned a very substantial return on their investment. The Blue Ridge Railroad, unable to borrow money, was forced into bankruptcy without completing its repairs or new construction.

The Politics of Corruption

Accounts of official corruption such as the Greenville and Columbia ring and the debt certificates dominate historical writing on South Carolina during Reconstruction. In both older and more contemporary works, Frank Moses is singled out as the leader of a gang of thieves who devoted themselves to stealing as much as they could from the good people of South Carolina. In his influential 1905 work, the historian Frank S. Reynolds called Moses "notorious, not only in this state, but in the other states of the Union."[45] In their monumental 1932 volume, the historians Francis Butler Simkins and Robert Hilliard Woody aver that Moses was "thoroughly unscrupulous."[46] Simkins and Woody approvingly reprint an editorial cartoon depicting Moses surveying his "promised land" from the pinnacle of a mountain of fraudulent notes labeled "Mt. Ruin."[47] Many of the editorial cartoons of the period link Moses's Jewishness to his alleged cupidity. One Thomas Nast cartoon shows Moses issuing an official pardon to a black man, drawn with Simian features, who has just broken both stone tablets of the Ten Commandments. Even in recent years, volumes such as Robert N. Rosen's *Jewish Confederates* emphasize the notion that Moses presided over "one of the most corrupt state governments in U.S. history."[48]

There is no doubt that Moses and his allies were corrupt, though Boss Tweed and other legendary northern politicos of roughly the same era would have been shocked at the idea that Frank Moses even approached their accomplishments in the realm of thievery.[49] Two points, however, should be made with regard to corruption on the part of South Carolina's Reconstruction government. The first is that charges of corruption were an aspect of political warfare. By charging Republicans with corruption, Democrats were able to appeal to northerners and to white and black Republicans in the South on a basis other than overt racial prejudice. They could, as Mark Wahlgren Summers has observed, "insist that their enemy was not the Negro but the thief."[50]

Throughout the South, the white Democratic press continually charged Republican governments with the most outrageous forms of corruption in an effort to smear and discredit them. Republicans did finance their own newspapers in the South usually through state government patronage.[51] The Republican papers, however, were never as vigorous or numerous as their Democratic counterparts, and rather than presenting a united front against the Democrats, their editorial policies often reflected the factional divisions within the Republican camp.[52] Moreover, when northern journalists like James S. Pike visited the South, they interacted mainly with white people, particularly the "respectable ones," that is, white professionals and propertied persons.[53] From these individuals, journalists learned that the Republican state governments were gangs of thieves and looters and learned very little, if anything, of the social and economic programs these governments had undertaken. Even the then staunchly Republican *New York Times* accepted this version of events, reporting retrospectively that "a recital of [Frank

Moses's] crimes against taxpayers and the state would fatigue the indignation. He had absolutely no shame, there seemed to be no limit to his capacity for squandering, throwing away money." In the same story, the *Times* reporter acknowledged that Moses had been "every day making new friends" in the state, but could think of no reason why this might have been the case.[54]

Northern journalists also allowed their stories to be shaped by their own racist preconceptions. In the northern press, black politicians were generally described in terms designed to suggest that they were ignorant subhumans. A prominent black politician was said to possess "as much intelligence as one would observe in a dead mackerel." A black senator was said to have a physique and brains "that could make more impression in the corn field." Blacks, generally, were said to know as much about political issues "as a pig does of the bible."[55] The *Atlantic Monthly* declared, "It has for years been notorious that the ignorant negro rulers of [South Carolina] had carried into their legislation and administration the spirit of the servile raid upon the plantation hen-roost and smoke house."[56] In its review of Pike's book, the *Nation* said that Pike showed that the intelligence of black South Carolinians was "so low that they are but slightly above the level of animals."[57]

Southern whites, on the other hand, were treated with some deference in the northern press. They were depicted as struggling to maintain their honor and dignity though beset by thieves and black savages. The press typically blamed murderous blacks for the violence that afflicted the South. Many reporters sympathized with what they saw as the desperate efforts of southern whites to defend themselves and persuaded their readers of this point.[58] In short, as historian Walter Edgar observes, by successfully manipulating the northern press, "the white community won the propaganda war."[59]

A second point about Reconstruction-era corruption is that Moses and other southern Republican politicians of the period did not skim from the public treasury simply to line their own pockets. Diversion of public funds, patronage appointments, selling of favors, and official pardons are, as political scientist Martin Shefter notes, typical of political parties seeking to overturn the previously dominant class of notables by building a party organization and mobilizing a mass following.[60] In Europe and the United States—the Jacksonians are a prime example—new political movements seeking to mobilize mass constituencies have usually found it necessary to distribute jobs, money, and favors to secure their hold on power.[61] A good deal of what white southerners and, eventually, the northern press, labeled "corruption" was related to the Republicans' effort to build a party organization based on an impoverished base that would be capable not only of winning elections but also of withstanding the intimidation and violence directed against it by its foes.

For example, Frank Moses was accused by the white press of selling pardons and freely pardoning fellow Jews convicted of criminal activities. Perhaps he did. For the most part, however, Moses issued pardons to local Republican officials who had been caught using their official positions for personal gain—a crime to be sure, but a crime that had to be tolerated in the interest of maintaining a party organization. Moses issued many pardons during his two years as governor, most on the application of interested politicians. Moses pardoned James Gulagher, who had been convicted of kidnapping, when Thomas Mackey, an important Republican, told the governor that Gulagher was "an active politician." Moses pardoned Benjamin Hernandez, a state constable who did political work, who had been convicted of assault with intent to kill.[62] Moses pardoned Samuel Fraser, a black militia officer, convicted of forgery, because he was a "good political nigger."[63] Moses used his pardons, as the white press sometimes pointed out, to help maintain his control over the black vote.

Maintaining Republican Power

From the first days of their rule, Republicans recognized that the task of organizing and mobilizing black voters on an ongoing basis would be a difficult one. The freedmen had no education or political experience, and many whites assumed that once the early political hubbub abated, blacks would lose interest in politics and be easily discouraged or intimidated. Moses acknowledged that "many expected nothing but absolute failure" from the "startling experiment" of enfranchising "a race hitherto enslaved, reared to manhood without the advantage of an education, and trained to a quiet and unquestioning obedience to the will of a dominant people."[64] Republicans struggled to avoid this "absolute failure," while Democrats worked to bring it about. During the entire period of Moses's tenure as Speaker of the House, South Carolina was the site of an intense and frequently violent political battle that required Republicans to fully mobilize their constituency, build a potent armed force, and establish a reliable revenue base. Democrats, for their part, employed a variety of techniques, including violence, to defeat Republican efforts to maintain control of the state.

A combination of federal and state efforts helped bolster the mobilization of black Republicans while undermining the political—or at least electoral—mobilization of white Democrats in South Carolina. Federal policy at least temporarily disfranchised those whites who had held any state or federal office and then engaged in acts of rebellion against the United States. This affected all whites who had been politically active before the war and subsequently served in the Confederate, state, or local government during the war or, of course, in the Confederate army. Only a small percentage of the potential white electorate was disfranchised by this provision. However, those excluded were the leaders of the white community. In essence, the bulk of the prewar political class was excluded from participation in postwar electoral politics. By 1870, most had regained their political rights, but for a time the white electorate was demoralized and disorganized.

Blacks, for their part, were registered under the supervision of federal military authorities in 1867. After this initial registration was complete, the state's electorate consisted of 80,832 blacks versus 46,929 whites. Though registration figures varied over the years, South Carolina's black voters outnumbered their white counterparts by a similar margin throughout the Reconstruction era. Merely registering African Americans, of course, was not the same as actually getting them to the polls and making certain that they continued to support the Republican ticket. In many areas, whites used violence and intimidation to try to prevent blacks from voting. In other areas, white land owners threatened to evict black farm workers who supported the Republicans. Such threats were quite credible. And since the secret ballot had not yet been adopted in the United States, how an individual voted quickly became a matter of public knowledge.

To mobilize black voters, Republicans relied initially on the Union League, which organized throughout the state in the aftermath of the war. For electoral purposes, the league was organized along the lines of an urban political machine with its ward bosses, precinct captains, and state committees. A local league board, or council, was organized in every precinct in the state. The activities of the precinct councils were governed by a state council that, in turn, was directed by its executive committee, a body consisting of two representatives from every county. Members of the precinct councils served in the same capacity as assembly district leaders or precinct captains. Prior to an election, they mobilized campaign workers, organized rallies and meetings, made arrangements to bring voters to the polls, and instructed voters on their responsibilities. Just as the activities of northern machine politicians were a necessary condition for electoral participation by illiterate and politically inexperienced immigrant voters, so were the efforts of the league councils essential for illiterate and politically inexperienced freedmen to take part in politics. In the 1870 election, conservative whites organized a Reform Party whose Union Reform clubs were designed to lure blacks away from the Union League clubs. State Union League president Francis Cardozo spent much of his time warning black voters to avoid being fooled by the similarity of names.[65]

The league was so effective in mobilizing black voters between 1867 and 1870 that its local councils came under violent attack by the Ku Klux Klan and other paramilitary forces associated with the Democratic party during the winter of 1870–71.[66] League officials and activists were beaten, whipped, and even murdered. In York County, a sixty-one-year-old black man and Union League member named Sam Sturgis was beaten by a group of Klansmen who told him that "they come for to break down these damned Union Leagues, and these Radical parties." In another part of the same county, Klansmen whipped and killed Charlie Good, a county league official, in order to "discountenance people from joining the League." According to the courtroom testimony of one Klansman who participated in the killing of Charlie Good, "Those who belonged to the League were to be visited and warned. . . . On the second visit they were to be whipped . . . [and] after this, if they did not leave, they were to be killed." This violent action was regrettable but justified, according to the Democratic press, because of the league's responsibility for "the shameful state of things which now exists." After 1871, the league ceased to be politically important and the state council met only for ceremonial purposes. At this point, the political work of the league was largely taken over by the state constabulary and black militias.

The Constabulary and Militias

Republican rule in South Carolina was, in the first instance, a result of the fact that federal military forces had conquered and occupied the state. Because of the hostility of heavily armed white citizens to the continuation of Republican rule, the continued presence of federal forces was an essential prop. Federal troops alone, however, were not an adequate tool for the state government. First, South Carolina officials did not actually control the movements and conduct of federal troops in the state. The governor might ask for their assistance, but there was no guarantee that federal forces would be deployed at the precise time and in the precise place and manner that state Republican officials wanted.

For example, during the 1870 statewide elections, Governor

Scott asked federal authorities to send troops to Laurens, where whites were rumored to be arming and organizing to disrupt the voting process. The local military commander declined to take the matter seriously. He dispatched only a small force that camped too far away from the town to be of any use in the event of trouble. The result was that federal troops were not available to prevent the violence that disrupted the voting process. Many federal officers and soldiers had little sympathy for blacks and were often disinclined to do much to help them. Some officers, indeed, were Democrats and not especially eager to lend their support to Republican politicians. The attitude of the federal troops was a problem throughout the South. In Mississippi, federal troops sent to protect Albert Morgan, a prominent Republican politician who had been threatened by local whites, savagely beat him while in the middle of the street. Morgan was later involved in gun battles with Democratic paramilitary forces and eventually fled the state.[67] In South Carolina, according to a northern newspaper correspondent, "acts of cruelty and oppression are constantly perpetrated" by federal troops against blacks. In both Edgefield and Charleston, major riots erupted from confrontations between blacks and soldiers. An armed force controlled directly by the state government was an absolute necessity if the regime was to survive.

For this reason, one of the first acts of the new administration was the creation of a state police force, popularly known as the state constabulary. John B. Hubbard, a carpetbagger from New York who had some experience in police work, was appointed chief constable. Hubbard assembled a force of five hundred men armed with Winchester repeating rifles and pistols. A deputy chief constable was appointed in every county. Each deputy chief was authorized to hire as many deputy constables as he deemed necessary to keep the peace. Eventually, the force had some four hundred deputies. In general, the deputy chiefs were white carpetbaggers or scalawags; the deputies were usually black.

The state constabulary functioned primarily to bolster Republican rule by protecting the political and civil rights of blacks, making sure that blacks went to the polls and voted the Republican ticket, intimidating opponents of Republican rule, and maintaining Republican control over the state's electoral machinery. In general, the deputy chiefs were drawn from among the leaders of the Republican party within each county. In addition to their regular salaries, deputy chiefs were in a position to skim from the state's coffers and, from time to time, engage in a bit of extortion. Corruption was part of the price of maintaining a political machine. In this way, the Republican party's electoral machinery and the machinery of law enforcement were integrated. The state constabulary was under the direction of those best able to use it for political purposes, and the deputy chiefs recognized that their government positions depended on their ability to achieve results at the polls. In some measure, the constabulary and the black militias were armed versions of the Union League.

The constabulary also exercised power on a statewide basis. The constables were state—not county—officers, and they executed warrants issued by a magistrate in Columbia, the state's capital. Those arrested by the constabulary were brought to Columbia for trial. In this way, the Republican administration sought to circumvent county and local law enforcement agencies that, in several cases, remained in the hands of white Democrats. Through the constabulary system, the state government's political opponents could be charged, arrested, and tried by a process that was firmly in Republican hands.

The constabulary was a small force and not able to police the entire state of South Carolina. Backing up the constabulary was a much larger force, the state militia, or national guard. Freedmen were organized into militia units throughout the South during this period and, in several instances, were deployed in pitched battles against armed groups of whites calling themselves white citizens leagues or white liners. Louisiana, Arkansas, and South Carolina were the three states whose black Republican militia companies saw the most action.[68]

Beginning in 1869 the Scott administration began to organize and arm black militia companies throughout the state. A militia was needed, said Governor Scott, because the only law white South Carolinians really understood was the Winchester rifle. Prior to this period, militia companies were formed by volunteers who then applied to the state for arms, supplies, and official recognition. Under the 1869 militia law, the state assumed responsibility for initiating the formation of militia companies and reserved the right to reject applications for recognition from units formed on a voluntary basis. The law also prohibited "organizing, drilling or parading by any bodies other than the National Guard of South Carolina." This prohibition was designed to discourage whites from organizing their own paramilitary forces.

Under the leadership of Adjutant General Moses, the state government organized several dozen black militia companies and rejected the applications of all but one white company of volunteers. This one white militia company disbanded after Moses placed it under the command of a black officer.[69] At its height, the black militia consisted of about fourteen regiments, each with about one thousand enlisted men and officers. All of the common soldiers and most of the militia officers were black, though the militia's highest ranking officer, Joseph Crews, was a white scalawag. To support the militia, Moses arranged for the legislature to establish a special "armed services fund." This fund was designed to pay for rations, uniforms, weapons, ammunition, and the like. As was typical, the fund came to be associated with fraud and corruption.[70] Militia officers expected to be able to pocket some portion of the money that came into their possession and this was overlooked so long as they carried out their political and military duties.

Arming the militia proved to be a problem. The state owned a small number of obsolete, single-shot muskets which had been provided by the federal government. In the event of a violent confrontation with whites, black militiamen equipped with muskets would be no match for white veterans armed with rifles. The rifles were easier to load, more accurate, and had a considerably longer range. Some whites owned sixteen-shot Winchester repeating rifles. These had begun to make their appearance toward the end of the war and became the favorite weapon of the cavalry. Some Confederates had managed to retain possession of their weapons after the surrender. Others were able to purchase Winchesters after the war. For the black militia to be effective, something would have to be done to improve the quantity and quality of the arms they carried.

To this end, Moses went to Washington, D.C., where he persuaded the War Department's Militia Bureau to issue South Carolina its full quota of arms for the next ten years. This would provide the state militia with nearly ninety thousand firearms of various sorts.[71] Some of these weapons were new Winchesters; others were older Springfield muskets. Moses contracted with the Roberts Breechloading Company to have the Springfields rebuilt and converted into far more effective breech-loading rifles. The muskets' cartridges were then retrofitted as rifle shells. Republicans hoped that with these new weapons black militia companies might be able to hold their own in the event of trouble. Moses, as was trumpeted by the white press, apparently pocketed a one dollar "commission" per converted rifle, which he spread around to his black followers. What seems to be most important in this story, though, is not the petty graft denounced by the conservative press, but the fact that the militia received more effective weapons than would otherwise have been available. Even the graft was related as much to party building as to personal venality.

Like the constabulary, the militia was integrated into the Republican party's political machinery and its main purpose was to help maintain Republican control over the political process. Black militia officers were often drawn from among the leaders of the Union League, and the militia served, in many respects, as the military complement to the league's political efforts. While the Union League organized blacks and sought to teach them how to exercise their political rights, the militia was designed to make certain that it remained possible for them to do so. The presence of an armed black militia gave African Americans the confidence to go to the polls, while service in the militia gave blacks a sense of empowerment and a feeling that they could control their own political destinies. Militiamen were also subject to intense indoctrination, attending political rallies and lectures as often as they practiced their military drills.[72]

In rural up-country areas or other areas in which white opponents of the Republican regime were particularly active, the militia, working closely with the constabulary, played a critical political role. In rural Laurens County, for example, whites were very well organized. Through a campaign of intimidation designed to discourage blacks from voting in the 1868 election, white Democrats had won control of most county offices, including the county's judicial and police machinery. Both the sheriff and the county judge were Democrats and known to be contemptuous of blacks. With the local government firmly in white Democratic hands, the Republican state administration was intent on organizing constabulary and militia forces in the area.

State militia commander Crews was, as it happened, a native of Laurens. Governor Scott named Crews the leader of the county's Republican party as well as its commissioner of elections. Crews organized and armed more than six hundred black militiamen with Remington and Winchester rifles. He used the constabulary to create a network of informants in the county. Typically, these were black household workers who might be in a position to provide information on the political activities of their white employers. Crews also devoted a great deal of energy and attention to the indoctrination of his troops, who were required to attend "military barbecues," where they listened to political speeches.

Local whites thought the political indoctrination sessions were calculated to make blacks behave in an "insolent" manner toward whites. And, indeed, they were not far off. Republican hopes rested on the ability of inexperienced, half-trained black militiamen—recently slaves—to stand up to their former masters. What whites saw as training in insolence was an essential effort to build the confidence of the militiamen and give them a sense of the importance of their task.

In preparation for the 1870 statewide elections, Crews used his authority as county election commissioner to order all ballot boxes brought to the county seat where they were set up in the public square. This arrangement would, of course, be an inconvenience to residents of outlying areas of the county who normally voted in local polling places. Crews, however, calculated that the Republicans would have a better chance of success if all the balloting took place in a single area where it could be closely supervised by his militia. On election day, militiamen were deployed throughout the county to mobilize black voters and bring them to the county seat to cast their ballots. Crews ringed the public square itself with black militiamen to discourage whites from interfering with the voting process and to reassure blacks that they could exercise their voting rights in relative safety.

These political tactics were quite successful. Black voter turnout increased dramatically. Realizing that their hold on the county would be broken, however, whites armed themselves and attacked the black militia force in the county square. After a short battle, the militiamen were routed and disarmed. Several were wounded and several others captured and murdered during the night. Most of the militia's weapons were confiscated by the county sheriff and stored at the courthouse.

For the remainder of election day, large groups of mounted and heavily armed whites looking suspiciously like companies of Confederate cavalry—patrolled the streets, driving away those blacks who had come to vote and preventing others from entering the town. Armed whites now ringed the courthouse square, permitting only other whites to cast ballots. The electoral situation appeared to have been reversed.

Despite the defeat of the black militia, however, Republicans were able to salvage an electoral victory from the debacle in Laurens County. Federal troops that had been stationed some twenty miles away arrived at the courthouse square at the end of the day. These troops, accompanied by Joseph Crews, took control of the ballot boxes and removed them to the state capital. Here Crews, in his capacity as Laurens County election commissioner, personally counted the ballots and declared that the Republican slate had carried the county. Subsequently, federal and state authorities arrested a number of the whites suspected of having taken part in the attack on the black militiamen, though none was ever convicted.

The black militia and constabulary were central to the Republican party's hopes of maintaining its power in South Carolina. Whites did not hesitate to use violence to prevent blacks from exercising their political rights. Without effective armed forces, the Republican regime could not hope to persevere against the implacable hostility of the white populace. At the same time, through the organization of military forces, Republicans hoped to imbue blacks with the confidence they would need to look their former masters in the eye—impudently, as it were—and challenge them for political power. To some extent they succeeded. As the Laurens case suggests, however, the poorly trained black militiamen ultimately were no match for the veteran Confederate soldiers who could be mustered in support of white Democratic political interests. Only federal troops could successfully confront these forces.

Money

If a military force was one essential for the new government, a source of revenue was another. The 1868 constitution had authorized a tax rate that should have been adequate to support all of the state's expenditures. Initially, the state was able to collect sufficient taxes to cover its expenses. At the end of 1869, Moses reported to the legislature that "the millions of dollars assessed for state taxes by the authority of this General Assembly has been collected with a promptness never before equaled in this state." From these tax revenues, the state was able to pay "the interest upon the entire public debt," as well as "salaries, contingent accounts and claims upon the state."[73]

Soon after Moses delivered this positive assessment, however, the state's economy began to decline and tax collections quickly lagged far behind the state's needs. The state, which relied chiefly on property taxes, augmented to some extent by sales taxes, had estimated that the total value of taxable property in 1868 was about $300 million. The actual value of all the real estate and taxable personal property in the state amounted to only $180 million. Over the next several years, as land prices fell, this assessed value steadily dropped. By 1876 it was barely $100 million.

The government responded to the dwindling tax base by raising taxes. As rates increased, more and more property owners were unable, or in some cases unwilling, to pay. Between 1868 and 1871, the state's property tax rate tripled, from three to nine mills. Tax receipts, however, actually declined, from approximately $1.5 million to barely $1.2 million, which amounted to less than half the state's annual expenditures. As tax collections lagged, foreclosures increased throughout the state and property owners began actively resisting tax payment and foreclosure. Taxpayers banded together and chased tax assessors off at gunpoint. Tax bills were ignored. In the counties controlled by whites, the local authorities often turned a blind eye to tax resisters.

Tax resisters also sought to block foreclosure sales. Groups of armed men often appeared at these sales to intimidate potential bidders. Those bold enough to consider purchasing land at tax auction faced the very real threat of violence from organized tax protestors. A letter to the *Charleston Daily News* signed by "one hundred men who fought under Lee" promised that those purchasing land at auction certainly would not live to enjoy it.[74] Though out-of-state land speculators were beyond the reach of tax resisters, violence was used against locals, especially blacks, who ignored such warnings.

The solution to the state's revenue problem was either to drastically cut expenditures or to borrow against anticipated revenue. Reducing expenditures was not a politically viable option. Expenditures on education, public works, social services, and industrial development were needed to serve the constituencies mobilized by the Republicans. The state's new land commission had promised to spend nearly $1 million to purchase and distribute "homes to the homeless and land to the landless." The government's administrative expenses were considerable, especially the operating costs of the state legislature. In 1868–69, legislative expenses were nearly $700,000 (compared with less than $60,000 the year before the war). The prewar legislature, consisting mainly of wealthy planters who paid their own expenses, had met for short sessions and done little. The new legislature, which was made up mainly of poor blacks who could afford to serve only if their expenses were borne by the state, was in session for most of the year and sought to accomplish much. And high levels of military spending were essential. Without military forces, the regime might be driven from power by armed and hostile foes. The cost of organizing and training militia forces represented nearly 20 percent of the state's budget—a higher level of defense spending than is currently borne by the U.S. government. Unable to cut spending or increase tax revenues, the state government turned to borrowing.

A commission consisting of Governor Scott, Attorney General Chamberlain, and State Treasurer Parker was appointed to supervise bond sales. This commission, in turn, appointed Hiram Kimpton of New York, who was well connected in national Republican politics, to act as the state's agent for the purpose of marketing the securities. Between 1868 and 1871, the legislature authorized the governor and state treasurer to issue more than $10 million in state securities. Because of fraud and financial mismanagement, the total actually issued may have been as high as $25 million. Had such an enormous quantity of money actually reached the state's coffers, the Republican administration would have been able to finance even the most grandiose schemes of industrial development and land redistribution. Unfortunately, nowhere near this amount of money was received by the state for its bonds. Often, the state did not have enough money to pay its employees or fund the programs it had undertaken. There was no money for schools and no money for social services. The superintendent of the state insane asylum mortgaged his own home to raise $15,000 to feed and clothe the inmates. What happened to the revenue from state bond sales? Some money, of course, was skimmed off the top by corrupt state officials.

Corruption, however, was not the principal reason the state's bond issues did not produce the revenues needed to fund state programs. Corruption accounted for hundreds of thousands of dollars in losses, while the difference between the quantity of bonds issued and revenues received was millions of dollars. The fact of the matter was that South Carolina bonds sold at a deep discount—when they could be sold at all. At most, and for only a very brief period, the state's securities sold at 70 to 80 cents on the dollar. More typically, South Carolina securities sold for 20 to 30 cents on the dollar. By the mid 1870s, the state's bonds could hardly be sold in the United States at any price.

The difficulties the state faced in the nation's credit markets mainly reflected the political power of the state's conservative white community. White Democrats did not want the state government to be able to borrow money because they correctly saw this source of revenue as a mechanism for enhancing the power and stability of a regime they were determined to depose. Revenues from bond sales would allow the Republican government to consolidate its power by expanding its military forces, embarking on ambitious social programs, and redistributing land. Conservative whites were determined to prevent this outcome even if it meant the financial ruin of the state.

Whites could not prevent bonds from being issued. They could keep them from being sold. One of their primary allies in this endeavor was the South Carolina press, which was largely, albeit not exclusively, in the hands of white Democrats. The Democratic press launched a concerted effort to undermine investor confidence in South Carolina securities by denouncing them as "bayonet bonds" that would never be paid. "Should New York or Boston touch these bonds, issued by a horde of Negroes, and in the face of the protest of the white people of the state?" asked the *Charleston Daily News* in 1868. "No bonds issued by this legislature will ever be paid," the *News* asserted. These press attacks frightened investors and effectively destroyed the state's credit.[75]

A second set of institutions used by whites to attack the state's credit were the local chambers of commerce, which had been established by white business leaders. In 1871 the Charleston chamber of commerce declared that the state's bonds had been fraudulently issued and would not be binding. The chamber warned potential purchasers that the state's business community considered South Carolina securities to be "null and void." To drive home its point, the chamber organized a "taxpayers convention" in Columbia to investigate the state's debt. This convention was attended by a host of white businessmen and Democratic politicians. One observer called it "the best body that I have seen assembled in South Carolina, except the secession convention of 1860." The concerned taxpayers included eleven former Confederate generals and a host of officials from the prewar government. Not surprisingly, the convention claimed that a host of abuses surrounded state bond sales and warned "all persons not to receive, by way of purchase, loan or otherwise, any bonds or obligation issued by the present state government." The convention received considerable publicity and generally sympathetic treatment in the northern financial press as well as in the *New York World,* one of the national Democratic party's most influential organs.

The campaign to discredit South Carolina's bonds also received help from an unexpected quarter. In 1871 Republican attorney general Chamberlain joined the attack on the state's credit, charging that the state had issued bonds not authorized by the legislature and that fraud and mismanagement permeated the state's financial dealings. Chamberlain became an active participant in the "taxpayers convention" and was elected its third vice president.[76] Republican newspapers allied with Chamberlain praised the convention and declared that it was a fair and nonpartisan enterprise. At the convention, Chamberlain's role was somewhat equivocal. On the one hand, he was a champion of reform. At the same time, however, he was personally involved with Blue Ridge Railroad bonds and worked with several other delegates who owned such securities to prevent their devaluation. Subsequently, Chamberlain supported the creation of a legislative commission to investigate the handling of the state's debt. This commission found considerable evidence of fraud and cited mismanagement on the part of every official connected with bond sales, except Chamberlain.

Chamberlain had two reasons for lending his support to the attack on South Carolina's credit. First, he was hoping to undermine support for some of his rivals within the Republican party. Governor Scott was closely aligned with State Treasurer Parker and Speaker Moses, one of whom was likely to be his successor as the Republican gubernatorial nominee in 1872. If Chamberlain could discredit Scott, he might be able to prevent Scott from influencing the succession. This plan nearly succeeded. The legislative commission looking into fraud connected with securities sales recommended that Chamberlain's colleagues on the financial board, Scott and Parker, be impeached. The motion was blocked in the House by Speaker Moses, who allegedly accepted a substantial bribe for his services.

In addition to seeking to discredit his Republican rivals, Chamberlain was also courting conservative whites. Chamberlain was one of the Republican politicians who foresaw that a Republican regime based exclusively on black support would always be unstable and dependent on the presence of federal troops. Chamberlain, moreover, craved social acceptance in South Carolina's white society and, as he acknowledged years later, had utter contempt for blacks. Accordingly, Chamberlain sought to win the support of conservative whites whenever possible. This is why he participated in the taxpayers convention and several years later, as governor, sought to build a white following in the state. Even as early as 1871 Chamberlain was seeking to distance himself from his fellow Republicans and, above all, from African Americans. In a letter published in the *Charleston Republican,* Chamberlain wrote that Reconstruction had had the unfortunate result of giving political control of the state to "a race [that was] devoid of political experience" and that depended on outsiders "who have drifted here from other states." Though he himself was one of those outsiders, Chamberlain averred that all his interests were now identified with South Carolina. Through his efforts to win the support of white Democrats, Chamberlain unwittingly helped undermine Republican rule in South Carolina and paved the way for the restoration of white Democratic government.

In the meantime, with Chamberlain's active participation, the campaign to undermine South Carolina's securities succeeded in virtually destroying the state's credit. By 1872 South Carolina bonds could not be sold; as a result, the state's revenues were insufficient to meet ordinary expenses. Republican politicians could no longer indulge in grandiose visions of "homes for the homeless and land for the landless." Instead, by 1873, the newly elected governor Franklin Moses was forced to declare, "There is no money in the Treasury with which to meet either the current expenses of the State Government, or its large and outstanding liabilities. The necessities of the several charitable, educational, and penal institutions, which have been so extremely urgent for many months past, still remain unsatisfied."[77] In other words, on the fiscal front at least, white Democrats had succeeded.

Violence

After the Republican government had been in power for one year, Frank Moses told the state legislature that he expected white Carolinians to eventually learn that the state's laws were "enacted for the equal benefit of all." As soon as they did so, "an era of peace will dawn upon us and wholly displace the distemper of feeling which here and there develops itself in scenes of disturbance and violence."[78] This prediction was completely off the mark. Whether or not Reconstruction-era South Carolina was the most corrupt state in the Union, it was certainly among the most violent. South Carolina's whites were heavily armed and thousands had fought in the Confederate army. Soon after the end of the war, members of the state's white citizenry launched a campaign of terror designed to intimidate white Republicans and their black supporters.[79] Initially, acts of violence were the work of local groups calling themselves bushwhackers or patrols, but in the wake of South Carolina's 1868 Constitutional Convention, which whites saw as an effort to institutionalize black rule in the state, local groups merged into more or less coherent statewide organizations including rifle companies and the Ku Klux Klan. Typically, the Klan and other terrorist groups targeted white Republicans and politically active or simply outspoken blacks. Several black members of the state legislature were murdered, leading Speaker Moses to observe that it would not be forgotten "that more than once have the halls in which we assembled been draped in mourning for the memory of those of our number who had fallen by the hands of violence, martyrs to their principles of political freedom." Black federal soldiers were also frequent targets of Klan violence. During the course of the 1870 electoral campaign, more than five hundred instances of Klan violence took place in Spartanburg County, alone. Blacks known to be active Republicans were beaten or shot, and at least two people were murdered.[80]

The Klan made a special effort to disarm and intimidate black militia forces. The organization and arming of the black militias had been seen as an affront and a threat by South Carolina's whites.[81] Some said that the presence of an armed black militia was "an insult too grievous to bear."[82] Klansmen frequently raided the militia's arms depots and singled out militiamen for beatings, whippings, and murder. In Union County, perhaps a dozen black militiamen were lynched.[83]

The Klan and similar groups arose throughout the occupied South in the late 1860s.[84] Klan violence in the Palmetto state, however, was so extreme and so widespread that South Carolina became the only state in which the federal government invoked the military enforcement provision of the 1871 Enforcement Act, generally known as the Ku Klux Klan Act. This piece of legislation, aimed at suppressing Klan activities, authorized the president to designate areas in which the right of habeas corpus would be suspended for individuals arrested for participation in "unlawful bands" that conspired to deprive individuals of their constitutional rights. Such individuals would be subject to arrest by federal authorities and tried in federal rather than state court. This provision reflected Congress's lack of confidence in state authorities and local criminal proceedings.

In response to hundreds of beatings, whippings, shootings, murders, and other Klan atrocities, President Grant applied the Enforcement Act to nine South Carolina counties in 1872. The president declared that the Klan aimed "by force and terror to prevent all political action not in accord with the view of the members; to deprive colored citizens of the right to bear arms and of the right to a free ballot; to suppress schools in which colored children were taught and to reduce the colored people to a condition closely akin to that of slavery."[85] More than five hundred people were arrested by federal authorities and held without charge until all the suspects in the various conspiracies had been apprehended. In a series of trials, surviving victims described heinous acts committed in the dark of night by masked and robed thugs. Klansmen who had confessed in exchange for leniency and were vilified as "pukers" by their fellow citizens also testified in court. The testimony was frequently blood curdling. A black man named Amzi Rainey testified that two dozen masked men burst into his home during the night. "My little daughter . . . run out of the room and says: 'Don't kill my pappy . . . ' He shoved her back and says; 'You go back in the room you God damned little bitch; I will blow your brains out!' and he fired and shot her sure enough."[86] What prompted the Klan's attack on Rainey's family? He had staunchly and publicly supported the Republican ticket in the 1870 statewide elections.

Despite weeks of similar testimony, juries convicted relatively few Klansmen. The majority of federal jurors in South Carolina were black, but the presence of even a small number of white jurors made it extremely difficult for prosecutors to win the unanimous verdicts required for conviction. Moreover, a statewide effort led by South Carolina's most prominent citizen, former Confederate general Wade Hampton, raised ten thousand dollars to pay for the legal defense of the accused Klansmen.[87] The money, a princely sum at the time, was used to hire two of the most famous defense attorneys of the day, Reverdy Johnson and Henry Stanbery. Johnson, a former U.S. attorney general had argued for the defense in the Dred Scott case; Stanbery, also a former U.S. attorney general, had served as Andrew Johnson's counsel in the president's impeachment trial.

Johnson and Stanbery secured a number of acquittals, and these skilled advocates raised enough questions during the trials to allow sympathetic newspapers, including such northern dailies as the *New York Tribune*, to portray the murderous Klansmen as heroes who merely sought to defend southern women against the depredations of black savages.[88] The government's effort to suppress the Klan was also hampered by the fact that the federal charges brought against the Klansmen carried relatively light sentences. Someone who might have been charged with capital murder in state court could only be charged with conspiring to deprive victims of their civil rights in a federal proceeding. As a result, even the handful of Klansmen who were convicted received light sentences considering the brutality of their crimes—the average punishment ranged from six to eighteen months in federal prison.[89]

During the course of the trials, the Klan's campaign of violence diminished somewhat in intensity. But as federal troop strength began to decline after 1872, white South Carolinians reorganized their paramilitary forces. To deflect the attention of the federal authorities, these new groups called themselves rifle, gun, or saber clubs and held parades, picnics, and balls to mask their actual purposes.[90] Between 1873 and 1876, these "clubs" were responsible for numerous acts of violence including beatings, riots, murders, and political assassinations. Joseph Crews, the powerful Republican leader of Laurens County, was killed in 1875 as pro-Democratic paramilitary forces prepared for the 1876 election.[91]

The effect of continuing violence in South Carolina and the other southern states was twofold. To begin with, the constant threat of violence effectively intimidated both black and white Republicans, discouraging the former from voting and compelling many of the latter to cut their ties to the Republican party or even to leave the state. During the 1874 and 1876 elections, violence helped Democrats carry districts in which black voters outnumbered white voters by as much as a five to one ratio. Future U.S. senator Benjamin Ryan "Pitchfork Ben" Tillman called this a process of "manipulation" and a "lesson in the possibilities of what white nerves and brains can accomplish."[92]

Incessant violence also provided northerners with one more reason to regard Reconstruction as a failure. Many northerners came to believe that peace could only be restored to the nation by allowing the South to manage its own affairs, particularly in the realm of race relations.[93] Other northerners took at face value press accounts blaming murderous blacks for the violence that afflicted the South. These individuals sympathized with what they saw as the desperate efforts of southern whites to defend themselves.[94] This view, in fact, became quite prevalent in the North and later was the basis of popular potboilers like *Gone with the Wind* and such mass market films as D. W. Griffith's silent epic *Birth of a Nation*. All in all, incessant violence contributed to northern disenchantment with the idea of Reconstruction in the same way that continuing violence in occupied Iraq eventually persuaded many Americans that it was time to withdraw U.S. forces from that benighted country.

In 1872, as the threat of white violence increased, the state's ability to raise needed revenue diminished, and the likelihood of continuing federal support waned, Franklin J. Moses sought election to the exalted post of governor of South Carolina.

CHAPTER FIVE

Governor Moses

IN 1872, THOUGH THE FUTURE might be problematic for South Carolina's Republicans, the present was bright. The federal government's proceedings against the Ku Klux Klan and other paramilitary forces associated with the Democrats made it virtually impossible for the Democratic party to mount a credible campaign in 1872. With the Klan temporarily quiet, the Democrats could not hope to intimidate black voters or to prevent the Republican party's black militias from maintaining physical control of the ballot boxes—and thus the capacity to determine the outcome of the voting—in most South Carolina counties. Hence, the Democrats did not bother to nominate a gubernatorial candidate and refrained from competing even for local offices in some counties.

At the same time, factional struggles within the Republican party gave rise to a party split and the presence of two Republican tickets on the statewide ballot. The Republican gubernatorial nomination had been seriously sought by three individuals, Frank Moses and two of the state's most prominent carpetbaggers, Attorney General Daniel Chamberlain and Reuben Tomlinson, the state auditor. Tomlinson was a Quaker from Pennsylvania. He had come to South Carolina in 1862 to educate freed slaves on the Sea Islands that had been seized by the Union army at the beginning of the war. After the Confederate surrender, Tomlinson was appointed head of the Freedmen's Bureau's educational efforts in the state and was later elected to the state legislature.

Tomlinson and his supporters were allied with the national Liberal Republican faction that broke from the Republican convention and nominated Horace Greeley for president. Hoping to win Democratic support, Greeley and the Liberal Republicans attacked the corruption associated with the first Grant administration and called for an end to the military occupation of the South. With such a platform, of course, Tomlinson had no hope of winning South Carolina's Republican gubernatorial nomination. Federal troops were critical to the party's continued existence in the state. Accordingly, Tomlinson and his small group of allies, led by former governor Orr, bolted the convention and organized their own conclave. This breakaway convention endorsed Tomlinson's candidacy. The defectors hoped to attract the support of Democrats and at least some Republicans. This was mere wishful thinking. South Carolina's Republican voters were mainly black and now voted under the direction of the militias. The state's Democrats, for their part, had decided to boycott the election. Tomlinson received barely a third of the popular vote.

As to Chamberlain, the attorney general could count on the support of many of the party's carpetbaggers such as Comptroller General John Naegle, and some of the scalawags. Though few in number, by virtue of education and contacts in the North these individuals continued to play an important role in the Republican party's leadership stratum. Like Chamberlain himself, many of the party's white officials and activists viewed Republican dependence on federal troops and black voters as a situation that would be untenable in the long run. And like Chamberlain himself, many white Republicans had little love for blacks and craved acceptance in polite (white) society. Unlike Tomlinson's bolters, though, Chamberlain's followers understood that in the short run they could not hope for more than a small number of white votes and would need substantial support among blacks if they were to have any hope of success. Chamberlain also understood that he could not afford to offend the national Republican administration that controlled federal patronage and the Union army.

Accordingly, Chamberlain and his followers spoke in a political code that would be understood by the state's white citizens but would not be overtly offensive to blacks. Chamberlain spoke out for political reform, economy in government, and an end to corruption. In fact, Chamberlain and his reformers were no less corrupt than those they attacked. Their goal was not to rid South Carolina of corrupt influences. Corruption was a code word for the policies, programs, and practices associated with black participation in the state's political affairs. In opposing corruption, the reform wing of the Republican party was signaling to white voters that it was prepared to delimit black political involvement and open the way for expansion of white political power, albeit under Republican auspices.

Finally, there was Moses. With a solid base of support among blacks—who comprised 115 of the convention's 148 delegates—there was never any doubt that Moses would secure the Republican nomination. Moses had spent several months actively campaigning. He attended the military balls organized by black militia companies and gave numerous parties for his black supporters. The white press made much of the fact that in February 1872 Moses was billed for six cases of champagne, six cases of whiskey, one case of brandy, and a cask of ale. Later he purchased six boxes of cigars, another case of champagne, twelve cases of carbonated water, and five thousand cheap cigars.[1]

Moses was strongly supported by the Union League, whose state president, Francis Cardozo, was nominated for secretary of state on the Moses ticket. Another Union League veteran and black Republican stalwart, Richard Gleaves, was nominated for lieutenant governor. Moses's name was placed in nomination by H. J. Maxwell, a black delegate from Orangeburg. Maxwell praised Moses as "a native Carolinian of high family, character, education and culture, who, upon reconstruction, had come forward to lead the poor colored men to self-government while [others] held aloof. His record, since, had been honest, consistent and brilliant," Maxwell averred.[2] Moses's nomination was seconded by his old political ally R. H. Cain. Cain told the convention that although Moses was a member of a prominent South Carolina family, he had become a champion of the poor and oppressed and was, thus, the candidate of the "bone and sinew" of the state.[3] As Moses accepted the nomination, he declared that so long as God gave him strength he would make his duty to the state the guiding star of his political and personal life.[4] According to white Democrats, who saw sexual implications in this relationship between a Jew and blacks, Moses secured the nomination by providing prostitutes for the black delegates to the Republican state convention. Moses had "cultivated the black women and the high brown of his state. When the Republican convention met . . . the ladies supporting Moses circulated among the boys to gratify passions for the asking."[5]

After Moses was nominated, about a third of the delegates carried out their threat to leave the convention and proceeded to nominate Tomlinson on a Reform Republican ticket. To some extent, the split in the Republican camp simply reflected clashes of personal ambition. At its heart, however, the split emerged from a fundamental division in the Republican camp—a division involving race. Race divided the Republicans in two ways. It split blacks and whites, and at the same time, divided white Republicans with divergent attitudes toward blacks. Much of the state Republican leadership was white, while virtually all of the party's voting strength was black. In the war's immediate aftermath, this division could not be avoided. There simply were not enough African Americans with the education and experience needed to operate a political party and state government. In the beginning, the help of carpetbaggers and scalawags was essential.

By 1872, however, blacks had learned a good deal about the practice of politics. Hundreds had served in state and county posts, and hundreds more had served as officials in the Union League and the state militia. It was not long before black politicians began to resent their junior partnership in the Republican party and demanded a greater share of the state's top leadership positions. Black politicians said that the Republican party had been too much "a black man's party with a white man's offices."[6] Struggles between black and white factions over nominations, appointments, and the allocation of state funds broke out in South Carolina as they did in a number of southern states during this period. Blacks were no longer content to be the Republican party's "hewers of wood and drawers of water," while white Republicans complained they were now being subjected to a new "color line."

As early as 1869, a coalition of black legislators including Rainey, Whipper, Elliott, Nash, and DeLarge had forced Governor Scott to appoint an African American to head the state land office. By 1872, blacks were demanding and receiving a larger share of both the top statewide elective offices and state legislative seats. In the first Republican campaign after the 1868 constitution, the party nominated only one black candidate for a statewide elective office—Francis Cardozo for secretary of state. Four years later, on the Moses ticket, the Republican party nominated blacks for four of the seven statewide positions. African Americans were nominated for and subsequently elected to the office of lieutenant governor, secretary of state, state treasurer, and adjutant and inspector general. Four of the state's five members of the U.S. House of Representatives were black. Republicans were also slating blacks for an ever larger share of the state's legislative seats. In 1868, though they cast nearly 100 percent of the Republican party's votes, blacks accounted for only 88 of 135, or 65 percent, of the South Carolina House and Senate seats held by the Republicans. By 1872 blacks held 106 of 130, or 81 percent of the Republican seats. These changes in the distribution of political power were accompanied not only by conflicts between black and white Republicans but also by divisions within the white Republican leadership. White carpetbaggers and scalawags could see that their role in the Republican party would soon be sharply curtailed. There were virtually no white Republican voters in the state, and as the black leadership stratum grew and gained political confidence, their need for white allies would inevitably diminish. For some white Republicans, this was an inevitable process, to be neither feared nor resisted.

Moses, for example, was firmly allied with the leading black politicians of the day, including Cardozo, Cain, and Elliott, and he counted on their support in campaigns and in the state legislature. The 1872 Moses ticket reflected these alliances. Moses led the state's first black-majority ticket. For other Republicans, however, the solution to the problem of growing black power was a realignment of political forces that might bring at least some white voters into the Republican party. Such Republicans generally called for reform and an end to "corruption" in government. By this they meant the adoption of policies that would placate whites and reduce the role of blacks in the political process. One practitioner of this tactic was Attorney General Daniel Chamberlain who courted white support by calling for reduced state taxation and spending as well as an end to corruption.

It was this division among white Republicans on issues of race that, more than anything else, led to the split at the 1872 Republican state convention. Tomlinson's dissenters had no chance of winning the general election in 1872, and in the absence of a Democratic gubernatorial candidate, the Moses ticket won handily. Most white voters stayed home, professing to see no difference between the two candidates. The *Edgefield Advertiser* advised the "good people" of South Carolina to "simply look upon the entire contest as a struggle between thieves and plunderers, and have no preference between the combatants. . . . Let us pray!"[7] South Carolina's Democrats were biding their time while divisions among the state's Republicans continued to fester.

Once nominated, Moses campaigned vigorously to make certain that his black supporters went to the polls in adequate numbers. Moses relied heavily on the state militias, many of whose officers he had appointed in his capacity as adjutant general. Moses had allowed these officers considerable latitude in their handling of the state funds allocated to their units. This gave Moses a loyal following in what had become the most important element of the Republican electoral machine. For good measure, in his capacity as Speaker, Moses had exercised considerable influence over the appointment of each county's election commissioners. The majority of them were Moses supporters and likely to make certain that votes were counted in a manner favorable to their candidate.

Despite effectively controlling the state's electoral machinery, Moses campaigned vigorously among black voters statewide. As was typical of campaigns during that era—North and South—Moses and his agents handed out gifts to the voters who came to see him. Poor blacks received shirts and small bags of hominy meal. Some were given small-denomination state pay certificates. These were state notes that could be cashed by the bearer and were often used as political favors. Everywhere, boisterous crowds of blacks yelled, "Hoo-ray for General F. J. Moses Jr."[8]

Even after his election, Moses continued to cultivate close ties to his impoverished black constituents. His former hometown newspaper, the *Sumter News,* castigated Governor Moses for

> devoting himself day and night, and with tireless alacrity, to corporal works of mercy, feeding the hungry, with a little flour here, a modicum of meal and grist there, and a small amount of sugar and coffee yonder; clothing the naked with breeches, jackets, waistcoats and cravats; shoeing the bare-footed; covering the hatless and bonnetless; and sending tea, chicken broth, painkiller, Dalby's Carminative, and other good and medicinal things to the sick and afflicted among his colored brethren and sisters. His charity was overflowing, and his good deeds are loudly applauded, by every colored tongue in the community. [The *News* was furious that] funds extorted from the honest, industrious taxpayers of the county should be thus wasted upon the . . . good-for-nothing vagabonds of Sumter County . . . because they happen to be friends and supporters of "our native young governor."[9]

Governor Moses

Moses was sworn in by his father, the chief justice, in December 1872. His inaugural address consisted of the usual promises and platitudes. He averred that he would faithfully discharge his duties to all the people of the state. He sought to prove "by the enactment of just laws and their impartial administration" that in South Carolina "the highest private liberty" was "consonant with the greatest public good."[10] For the most part, the state's white press professed to be satisfied with the new governor's remarks and hopeful that he would pursue a wise course of action in office. The *Marion Star* said Moses should be given a fair chance to be a good governor. "The plan of giving a man a bad name and then gibbeting him has not worked well in South Carolina."[11] Similarly, the *Darlington Southerner* hoped that Moses might "disappoint the evil prognostics of his enemies."[12] Moses's hometown newspaper, however, claimed to know Moses too well to be taken in by his rhetoric. "We hope for the best from the new regime," opined the *Sumter News,* "but we have, however, such implicit and abiding confidence, in this gentleman and his associates, that we do not hesitate to assert that they will renew the work of plunder, if they dare attempt it."[13] This was the opening shot in what soon became an unrelenting attack on the Moses administration by the state's white press.

Moses's first task on assuming office was to address the state's financial crisis. The tax base was being eroded by the ongoing decline in land values coupled with increased tax resistance on the part of white land owners. In 1871 nearly one-third of the state's taxes, more than $1 million, were uncollected. A measure of mismanagement, coupled with four years of attacks by the Democrats—and some Republicans—had ruined South Carolina's credit. The state could not meet its current obligations in such critical areas as education and security. Immediately after taking office, Moses told the legislature that there was not enough money in the state treasury to meet the state's obligations.

For four years, the Scott administration had borrowed heavily to finance the state's ambitious plans for education, land redistribution, and economic development, as well as to establish a large black military force. There was, to be sure, a certain amount of fraud associated with South Carolina's financial affairs. State funds were deposited in a bank established by a group of state officials; appropriations were diverted from their intended use; more bonds were issued than authorized; and so on. These minor frauds, however, could not account for the state's financial difficulties. The real problem was that for four years the state's credit had been subjected to a relentless attack. South Carolina could borrow only at extremely high rates of interest and was compelled to sell its bonds at a steep discount, usually less than 50 cents on the dollar. Beginning in 1868, the white press had warned that the state would never be able to pay its "bayonet bond" debts issued by a "bogus legislature." This media campaign was bolstered by various taxpayers unions and taxpayers conventions that trumpeted the same message and soon convinced the northern media and northern investors that South Carolina was an extremely poor credit risk.

At the beginning of the Moses administration, there was much discussion about the idea of debt repudiation. In the late nineteenth century, it was not uncommon for states to renege on all or part of their debt. After the Civil War, at least twelve states, including Minnesota and Michigan, were forced to repudiate debts, and others came close to so doing.[14] South Carolina had already stopped paying interest on its bonds and bondholders were afraid the state might default on all its debt. Moses proposed that the state issue about $8 million in new bonds, which would be offered to bondholders in place of their existing bonds. By reducing its debt to $8 million, the state could afford to resume paying interest and bondholders, for their part, would receive some value for their currently worthless paper.

Most of the state's bondholders indicated that they would not accept Moses's offer and demanded that the state resume interest payments on the existing bonds. In April 1873 Morton, Bliss, and Company, New York bankers who had purchased several million dollars worth of South Carolina bonds at a deep discount, demanded that the state's comptroller levy a new tax to pay the interest due on the bonds. The comptroller refused and the bank hired none other than former attorney general Daniel Chamberlain, now an attorney in private practice in Charleston, to take its case to court. The bank asked the court to issue a writ of mandamus ordering the state comptroller to levy the tax. A variety of taxpayer organizations intervened in the case asserting that the bonds in question had been fraudulently issued. The state, for its part, argued that the power to levy taxes had not been delegated to the comptroller but belonged, instead, to the state legislature. The court held that under South Carolina law, the comptroller had the power to levy a tax and issued an order of mandamus requiring him to raise taxes sufficiently to pay the next two installments on a portion of the state's bonds.[15]

Whether this new tax could be collected any more successfully than the existing taxes was an open question. Rather than risk answering this question in the negative, Moses sought to begin the process of restoring the state's credit. In October 1873 Moses called a special session of the state legislature to consider the debt problem. Moses informed the legislature that the state's financial situation was much worse than his predecessor had said. The state owed its creditors some $15 million in long-term debt; $5.3 million in short-term "floating" debt; and an interest arrears of $2.3 million for a total of more than $22.6 million.[16] This was a staggering sum, the equivalent of approximately 500 million in today's dollars, and far more than a small and impoverished state could hope to repay.

Moses proposed a three-part solution to the debt crisis. First, he reminded the legislature of the ratification of a constitutional amendment during his last term as Speaker. This amendment provided that no further debt or obligation, "either by the loan of the credit of the state, by guarantee, endorsement or otherwise," could be created by the legislature unless submitted to the state's voters and approved by a two-thirds majority.[17] Moses interpreted this to mean that the demands by some creditors that the state's entire floating debt be funded at par value was out of the question. Because of the state's poor credit rating, this debt had generally been sold below its nominal value and Moses asserted that to now fund it at par value would violate the state's constitution by increasing the public debt of the state without the now-required popular referendum. Creditors would have to settle for less or nothing at all. Second, Moses asked the legislature to respond to the writ of mandamus requiring the comptroller to impose a new tax levy to support interest payments on the state's bonds by depriving the state's comptroller of the power to levy taxes. The legislature enacted the necessary legislation and the writ of mandamus was defeated.

Most important, Moses proposed a consolidation of the state's outstanding debt. This entailed issuing new bonds in amounts equal to 50 percent of the face value of some $11.5 million of the state's long-term debt. These new bonds would pay interest of 6 percent and would mature in twenty years.[18] Moses reasoned that the state's creditors would be willing to accept this nominal loss. The state's bonds were selling at about fifteen cents on the dollar and no interest was being paid at all. "Now it is evident," said Moses, "that it is to the interest of every bondholder that the debt be reduced in volume to a reasonable limit so that the payment of interest may be resumed." Bondholders would benefit immediately because "while this new bond would represent upon its face a sum [less than] the face value of the old bond, the market value of the new bond would undoubtedly be . . . greater than the present value of the old."[19]

At its special session, the legislature took no further action. At its regular session, though, later the same month, the legislature enacted Moses's proposal in the form of a "consolidation act." This act authorized the exchange of outstanding state bonds for new bonds, which would bear on their face the words "consolidation bonds," equal to 50 percent of the face value of the bonds surrendered.[20] The legislature also invalidated some $6 million in bonds deemed to have been fraudulently issued. These two actions promised to reduce South Carolina's bonded indebtedness by $10 million or more to a level that the state might be able to sustain.[21] As Moses anticipated, the state's creditors preferred a fraction of something to 100 percent of nothing and accepted the scaling down of the debt. To make certain that the state's creditors would not balk, Moses had the legislature add a proviso to its funding bill declaring that the state would never levy a tax to support interest payments on any bonds covered by the act that were not exchanged for consolidation bonds.[22]

Moses's actions relieved, but did not fully resolve, the state's fiscal problems. Over the next several years, the state encountered a number of stumbling blocks, including the failure of South Carolina Bank and Trust, in which hundreds of thousands of dollars in state funds had been deposited, recurrent charges of bond frauds, and several instances in which the state was briefly unable to collect sufficient taxes to meet its current interest payments.[23] Nevertheless, the actions of the Moses administration began the process through which South Carolina gradually recovered from the debt crisis of the early 1870s. By the end of Moses's term as governor, South Carolina securities were considered a "good buy" in the financial marketplace.[24] And by the time the Democrats returned to power in 1876, the state's debt had been reduced to a manageable $7.1 million.[25] The Robber Governor had begun the process of restoring South Carolina's financial viability.

Integrating Public Institutions

Though South Carolina's immediate fiscal crisis had been alleviated and the state's long-term financial outlook had improved, in the short term the Moses administration lacked the financial resources to even consider new programs or initiatives. Moses hoped that restoring the state's credit would allow the government to fund its schools and maintain the large militia forces on which it depended. One area, however, in which the Moses administration was able to take significant action was the integration of the university and other state educational institutions.

Under an act of 1869, the state university was prohibited from making "any distinction in the admission of students, or the management of the university on account of race, color or creed."[26] However, between 1869 and 1873 no black students applied to the university and no black faculty sought appointments. The university was, in principle, open to blacks. In practice, it was understood that the university was open only to whites. Blacks who sought an education beyond the elementary level could attend one of the institutes established by various missionary societies or Claflin University in Orangeburg, which was supported by a wealthy Boston family and offered theological and teachers' training. Some prominent white politicians suggested that the state university should remain an all-white institution and the Citadel Academy in Charleston might become an all-black college.[27]

Although no blacks attended the state university, two members of the board of regents were black, and whites thought it was only a matter of time before blacks sought to take advantage of their formal right to enroll. White enrollments gradually declined in anticipation of this looming calamity. The father of two white students said, "I suppose that the S.C. University will go up the spout, under the new regime of the Carpet bagger and Scalawags and negroes."[28]

White fears of integrated educational facilities were realized in 1873. A new board of regents had been elected in 1872 consisting of four blacks and three whites, with Moses serving as the chairman. At the same time, the state legislature provided that the newly created State Normal School (teachers college), which would presumably enroll a great many black students, would be located in a building on the state university campus. University faculty members would be required to lecture to the Normal students and these students would also have the right to use the university library. Several professors resigned rather than teach blacks and the board replaced them with faculty members more sympathetic to black education.[29] Subsequently, the board dismissed several other professors who were known to oppose the admission of blacks to the university and brought in new faculty members, including Richard T. Greener, who was Harvard's first black graduate.

In October 1873 the first black student arrived for classes at the state university. He was none other than Henry E. Hayne, a prominent Republican politician then serving as secretary of state. Hayne hoped to earn a medical degree at the university. The moment Hayne set foot on the campus, the three members of the university's medical faculty resigned. In accepting their resignations the board issued a statement, signed by Moses and the other members, indicating that the board wished to place on the record its conviction "that the resignations of these gentlemen were caused by the admission as a student of the medical department of the University of . . . a gentleman against whom said professors can suggest no objection except, in their opinion, his race."[30]

South Carolina's Democratic press denounced Hayne's admission to the university. The *Charleston News and Courier* acknowledged that blacks had the abstract right to attend the university but, until now, had possessed a "wise" sense of propriety that had prevented them from taking advantage of this right. Now, the university would be destroyed without doing the Negroes "a particle of good."[31] The *Chester Reporter* claimed that Hayne "did not want to study medicine. He only entered for the purpose of submitting the professors to the test." The professors, said the *Reporter,* had acted with "commendable dignity" in resigning.[32]

Following Hayne's matriculation, a number of other prominent black politicians, including Francis Cardozo, enrolled in the university. Like Hayne, these individuals hoped to demonstrate to the state's blacks that the university was now open to them. Virtually all the school's white students promptly left. Few blacks, however, could afford the costs associated with university attendance, and despite an effort by the state government to recruit South Carolinians then studying out of state, only a handful of students attended the school's classes. Moses asked the state legislature for help, and early in 1874, the legislature, in one of its few new undertakings, provided for 124 scholarships of two hundred dollars each, distributed among the state's counties, to help defray the living expenses of state university students. The *Columbia Daily Phoenix* denounced the scholarships as "a scheme to buy students . . . [that] was no doubt suggested by the practical difficulty that, notwithstanding the gates of the college are flung wide open . . . none have gone in."[33]

Many of the first scholarship students could not pass the university's entrance exams and were sent for remedial work to the university's preparatory department. Gradually, however, classrooms filled with students, including a number of poor up-country whites who had received scholarships. Overall, about 10 percent of the scholarships went to whites.[34] Moses informed the state legislature that the university was flourishing. He called it the "healthy child of the present administration" and expressed the hope that "the narrow spirit of bigotry and prejudice had been banished from its portals."[35] Moses's views were disputed by the *News and Courier,* which declared, "Governor Moses gives us ruin and calls it prosperity."[36] Many white South Carolinians left the state to attend college elsewhere. Improbably enough, more than forty found their way to Union College in Schenectady, New York, which was happy to receive a tuition windfall.[37] Other white Carolinians remained in the school. Indeed, twelve of the twenty-three men who graduated from the university's law school between 1873 and 1876 were white, and several went on to practice law in the state.[38]

Black students benefited greatly from the instruction they received at the state university and from the scholarships that allowed them to attend college.[39] At least three of the faculty members brought in by the new administration were quite distinguished. William Main held a master's degree in engineering from the University of Pennsylvania and was a well-known mining engineer. Fisk Brewer had taught ancient languages at Yale. Richard Greener later became a law professor at Howard University and a U.S. diplomat in Russia. Their students, who went on to become prominent members of the black community, included twelve ministers, eleven lawyers, ten college professors, five physicians, four diplomats, and many other professionals.[40] Whites did not consider these accomplishments to have any merit nor would they give the Moses administration credit for making higher education available to blacks for the first time in South Carolina's history. To whites, the scholarships were simply another form of corruption that could be blamed on the Robber Governor. Soon after Democrats took control of the state in 1876, they closed the university and rid themselves of the scholarships—and the scholars.

As governor, Moses chaired the board governing South Carolina's institute for the education of the deaf and blind located in Cedar Spring. In 1873 the board ordered the institute to accept black students and to teach them in the same classes and house them in the same facilities as white students. Rather than carry out this order, the officers and teachers of the institute resigned en masse and the facility was closed. Far from castigating the teachers and officials for abandoning their charges, the Democratic press claimed these events were evidence of the callousness and indifference of the Moses administration to the plight of the deaf and blind children of the state. In 1876 the Hampton administration reopened the institute with separate classrooms and dormitories for black and white children.

The Making of the Robber Governor

Bishop Gilbert Haven of the Methodist Episcopal Church of Massachusetts visited South Carolina in 1874 and returned impressed by the accomplishments of the Moses administration. He described new schools, the integrated state university, and a variety of state services available to poor black people.[41] Most histories of South Carolina during Reconstruction, however, are influenced by the portrait of Moses and his allies carefully painted by his Democratic foes. William A. Dunning was the turn-of-the-century historian whose critique of Reconstruction inspired the eponymous "Dunning school" of historians who accepted as fact the version of events promulgated by conservative southern whites. Dunning reserved particular venom for Frank Moses. Under Moses, he claimed, South Carolina was "thoroughly Africanized." The state had become a "shameless caricature of government" under the administration of this man of "notoriously bad character."[42] Another turn-of-the-century historian called Moses a "degenerate" who was "lost to every moral sense." How else could his conversion to Radicalism be explained?[43] Even contemporary historians tend to gloss over accomplishments that might be credited to the Moses administration and devote virtually all their attention to the various forms of corruption linked to Moses and his political allies. To this day, in South Carolina, Moses retains the label given him by his enemies— the Robber Governor.

Moses and other Republican leaders did engage in various forms of corrupt activity. But they were not simply lining their own pockets. They were compelled to distribute jobs, money, and favors to mobilize popular support and maintain a party machine capable of competing against foes who were more experienced in the political realm, better organized, supported by a potent set of media allies, and ultimately, more proficient in the political uses of violence than the Republicans. What the Democratic press called corruption was one of the few tools available to the Republicans.

Democratic politicians and the Democratic press routinely attacked all the Republicans. They ridiculed the black politicians as buffoons who aped the manners of their white masters. They castigated the various carpetbaggers and scalawags as petty thieves Their most vicious and venomous attacks, however, were usually directed at Frank Moses. Day after day, week after week, South Carolina newspapers attacked the governor. They accused him of a string of vile crimes and declared that his middle initial, "J.," stood for Judas. An entire paper, the *Colleton Gazette,* was founded by the Democrats for the express purpose of vilifying Frank Moses.[44] What made Moses a special target? He lived what Charles Sumner preached. Moses associated freely and openly with blacks. He had black friends. He invited blacks to his home. Whatever else they did, the other white Republicans did not violate the most fundamental tenet of South Carolina's moral code. South Carolina whites were determined to prove, as Julian Buxton put it, "that a man who had betrayed his race to associate with the Negroes on terms of absolute equality, even social equality, was necessarily a moral degenerate."[45]

To fully illustrate Moses's moral degeneracy, the white press engaged in what today would be called "opposition research." The press carefully investigated his financial dealings, examined the intimate details of his personal life, and interviewed his associates, colleagues, neighbors, and friends looking for information that could be used against him. A "vast right-wing conspiracy" was organized against Frank Moses. Somehow, Moses's personal financial records found their way into the pages of the *Augusta Constitutionalist*.[46] When Moses declared bankruptcy, the full details of every filing and disclosure were acquired by the *Charleston News and Courier*.[47] When Moses had a falling out with his friends, the Rollin sisters, the latter were persuaded to reveal every detail of their relationship with Moses to the eager readers of the *Colleton Gazette*.[48]

In contemporary American politics, newspaper revelations of wrongdoing on the part of public officials are typically followed by demands for legislative hearings. The hearings, in turn, fuel demands for court proceedings and, perhaps, the incarceration of the unfortunate target of the process. Generally speaking, these revelations, hearings, and so forth do not arise accidentally. They are usually a carefully coordinated political tactic. I have elsewhere called this tactic RIP—revelation, investigation, and prosecution—and often enough it is a political epitaph for its subjects.[49] Contemporary Democrats and Republicans have used RIP attacks against one another quite regularly, often with considerable success. Rumors and revelations in the press led to the Watergate hearings, the Iran-Contra hearings, the Whitewater hearings, and so on. These hearings, in turn, have provided ammunition for the prosecution of government officials, led to a presidential resignation, and prompted the impeachment of a president. Most of those subjected to RIP attacks have almost certainly been guilty of some form of wrongdoing. But every politician, if not every adult, has at one time or another done something that, if fully investigated and revealed by the media, would be embarrassing, if not illegal.

Frank Moses was an easy target for these sorts of attacks. The Democratic press had little difficulty finding much to reveal, but

the state legislature, firmly in Republican hands, would not cooperate by conducting hearings and investigations. Republican control
of the legislature was, however, not an insurmountable problem.[50]
The functional equivalents of legislative investigations were carried out by various taxpayers' conventions organized by Moses's
Democratic opponents following up on the accusations and revelations trumpeted by the media. Late in 1873, after Moses had
used a special legislative session to deprive the comptroller of the
power to levy taxes, the Democratic media blasted the governor for
his alleged financial improprieties and claimed that he planned to
raise taxes himself. The *Orangeburg Times* demanded that citizens
"make an effort to arrest this outrageous spoliation before you are
hopelessly and ignominiously enslaved. . . . Protest at Washington
against further taxation under such a filthy, disgusting loathsome
state government and ask to be made a territorial dependency, or
a conquered province, anything rather than the football of Moses
and his crew." The *Times* and other Democratic papers called for
a convention that would investigate Moses's crimes and identify
remedies.[51]

Within a few weeks, a convention of citizens was called, consisting of those who were opposed to the "frauds and corruptions which
prevail" and were in favor of "honest government with exact and
equal justice to all."[52] The convention listened to testimony from
various of Moses's foes and found that the tax law was "cumbrous,
obscure, and intricate." Tax assessments, said the convention, were
made improperly and frequently in secret. The administration had
utterly ruined the credit of the state and corruption prevailed in
nearly all the departments of the government. This same convention
promoted the idea of encouraging white emigration from Europe to
South Carolina to overcome white numerical inferiority in the state.
The Democratic press was pleased that this convention of eminent
and disinterested citizens had confirmed press accounts of events
and demanded that something be done. As had been suggested by
the press, the convention made provisions for the formation of "tax
unions" in every county that would continue harassing the Moses

administration. The Democratic press trumpeted the slogan "old men in the tax unions and young men in the rifle clubs." The Republican press, for its part, averred that the taxpayers' convention was the work of the former ruling class, which hoped to regain the power it had lost through secession. This response seemed closer to the truth.

Democrats could reveal and investigate, but they usually could not prosecute to complete the RIP process. Before 1876 most of the state's law enforcement and prosecutorial agencies were in Republican hands. In 1873, however, a factional struggle within the Republican party led to Moses's indictment on the serious charges of abetting fraud and grand larceny, charges that threatened to end his political career and, potentially, send him to prison.[53] Moses's legal troubles were related to his attempt to gain control of a newspaper.[54] The *Columbia Union-Herald* was the state's most important daily Republican newspaper.[55] Its publisher, Thaddeus Andrews, had decided to sell the paper, and Republican politicians were concerned about who the paper's purchaser might be. Moses apparently heard a rumor that his opponents within the Republican party might acquire the *Union-Herald*. He said that he "heard from reliable sources that an attempt was being made to obtain control of the paper by those whose views did not coincide with [his] as to the financial policy to be pursued, and the adoption of which views would, therefore, in [his] opinion, have been injurious and hurtful."[56] Moses determined that he would seek to acquire "political control" of the *Union Herald* and to use it as an instrument to counter attacks against his administration and publicize his own views.

Moses arranged a complex deal in which state funds would be used to acquire a half interest in the paper for the Republicans, which would, in effect, place the *Union-Herald* under his control. Before the transaction could be completed, however, Andrews lost control of the paper to his creditors, and Moses invalidated the state payment order that had been issued to Andrews. In the meantime, one of Andrews's political cronies, John L. Humbert, the state-appointed treasurer of Orangeburg County, paid Andrews two thousand dollars based on the original payment order, which both men now knew to have been revoked. Humbert was arrested and charged with "defalcation," or attempting to embezzle state funds. Unfortunately for Moses, the state solicitor whose jurisdiction encompassed Orangeburg was E. L. Butz, a white Republican who detested Moses and was allied with Daniel Chamberlain, who hoped to replace Moses as governor. The solicitor secured an indictment against Moses, charging him with having advised Humbert to pay the now invalid debt to Andrews. The county judge had little choice but to issue a warrant for Moses's arrest.

Moses denied the charge and refused to surrender to the Orangeburg County sheriff who had been sent to serve the warrant. Instead, Moses ordered four companies of the state militia to surround his official residence and office to prevent any action by the Orangeburg sheriff. Accompanied by black militiamen in red uniforms, Moses rode around the capital in an open carriage to express his contempt for his foes.[57] He also had one of his allies issue a warrant for the arrest of the hapless Orangeburg County sheriff.

While onlookers gaped at the show, Moses negotiated with Chamberlain. Moses threatened to appoint only Democratic election commissioners to supervise next October's elections if his indictment was not dropped. This would certainly give the election to the Democrats and end Chamberlain's hope of becoming the state's governor. If, on the other hand, Chamberlain was able to get the charges against him dropped, Moses agreed to step aside and not seek the 1874 Republican gubernatorial nomination.[58] Chamberlain agreed to these terms and, accompanied by Congressman Robert Elliott, a longtime Moses ally, Chamberlain hurried to the Orangeburg court. To the judge, Chamberlain argued that based on the traditional English theory that a king can do no wrong, the chief executive of the state could not be arrested and prosecuted while in office. He would first have to be impeached by the state legislature. Since the legislature was not in session, it would have to be called into session by Governor Moses, who seemed unlikely to call a special session for the purpose of his own impeachment. Whether for jurisprudential or political reasons, the Republican judge upheld Chamberlain's argument and quashed the case against the governor. Once the charges were dropped, Moses denied having made any deal and said he planned to run for reelection in 1874.

Moses's reputation for fraud extended far beyond South Carolina. Constant attacks on Moses in the southern press were soon echoed by the northern Democratic press and by Republican papers opposed to the Grant administration. The most important of these was Horace Greeley's *New York Tribune*. It was the *Tribune's* correspondent James S. Pike who dubbed Moses the Robber Governor and whose accounts of the corrupt administration of the "Israelite" with a "thrifty eye to the main chance" helped make Moses an infamous figure everywhere in the nation.[59] Pike disliked blacks, and his newspaper, though Republican, opposed the Grant administration.[60] For Pike, exposing corruption in South Carolina served a double purpose. He was able to expose the villainy of Sambo and, simultaneously, demonstrate that the Grant administration, itself corrupt, supported an even more corrupt satellite regime in the South. For the northern press more generally, though, Frank Moses was an especially tempting target. This was a period in America when Jews were beginning to be ostracized and excluded from polite society. The idea of the rude, money-grubbing Jew who lacked the refinement and moral standards of Christian Americans was becoming a common theme in the popular press.[61]

That Moses and his father were both married to Christians and linked to blacks was, to the press, a sign of their political and sexual perversity. In a widely reprinted story, the *New York Herald* exposed the vices of the entire Moses clan. "The governor of the state sits in the synagogues of Africans, messes with them and dines and coquettes," observed the scandalized reporter. How did a Jew ever become the governor of the state? The *Herald* knew the answer— predatory sexuality. "The Hebrews [in South Carolina] hardly got beyond the countenance of such females as they wooed and won until the era of scalawaggery [began]. Then . . . they arrived at their revenge, commonly with the rejected negroes. . . . Two of them are now on the bench and one is governor. . . . They are intermarried with Christians. Shylock and Bassanio meet in them and they have the plausibility of Portia."[62]

Against this backdrop, accounts of the financial and moral corruption of the Israelite Franklin Moses, Jewnier, fit the increasingly mean spirit of the times. Here was a Jew who stole, who socialized with blacks, inviting blacks into his home and even dancing with dusky maidens, as the papers liked to say. The story of Moses brought together so many popular themes, Jews, blacks, political corruption, even hints of illicit interracial sex. The political cartoonists, especially America's most influential editorial cartoonist Thomas Nast, made much of these themes. Nast was a Republican and friendly with President Grant. At the same time, he was an outspoken nativist who associated nonwhite, non-Protestant groups with debauchery and thievery. Nast's clever cartoons on the cover of *Harper's Weekly* emphasized Moses's Jewishness and linked him to political corruption and the crimes of blacks, always presented as apelike creatures. The words of Pike and drawings of Nast, more than the crimes of Moses himself—crimes that were decidedly petty in the context of the period—made the Robber Governor a national political figure.

Moses's Downfall

As the 1874 elections approached, Moses seemed determined to run for reelection. His main opponent within the Republican party would clearly be former attorney general Daniel Chamberlain. In the wake of Moses's failed attempt to acquire control of the *Union-Herald,* a consortium led by Chamberlain had succeeded. Now the state's most important Republican paper joined the Democratic press in condemning Moses. "He has thwarted the efforts of the Treasurer to bring to a strict accountability the treasurers. . . . He encouraged the extravagant and corrupt members of the legislature. He pardoned those convicted of fraud. He promised immunity to the dishonest but undetected."[63]

Despite these denunciations by the Republican press, Moses remained a powerful figure in South Carolina and could reasonably expect to be renominated by his party. He controlled the state militia and commanded a loyal following among the state's black voters. Events outside the state, however, would soon drive Moses from office. Given the publicity surrounding the Robber Governor and the media attention that had been focused on South Carolina's black government, the national Republican party had come to view its South Carolina wing as a political liability. On the national level, the Republicans were generally regarded as a corrupt bunch. The term "Grantism" had come to stand for a form of politics whose chief currencies were cash and favors.[64] Republicans had enough troubles without being saddled with what the press depicted as a bunch of thieving Sambos and their Israelite robber governor leader.

South Carolina's Republicans were informed by their allies in Washington that the state had become a political liability for the entire party and needed to quickly improve its reputation. Congressman Robert Elliott told Carolinians that he had learned in his travels outside the state that "to mention South Carolina is to merit the sneers of the Commonwealths of the North."[65] Elliott warned that northern Republican leaders threatened to abandon their South Carolina colleagues if something was not done to improve the state's reputation. This was by no means an idle threat. South Carolina's Republicans, who depended on the federal government's patronage and military support, could not afford to alienate their friends in Washington.

President Grant himself confided in a group of Democrats that South Carolina under Moses was "badly governed and overtaxed."[66] And Republican Thomas Mackey reported that the president had told him that he wanted the state's Republicans to reform themselves. "And while the president speaks calmly of all the great battles in which he participated," said Mackey, "yet when I talked to him of South Carolina, his apparently pulseless lips quiver, his veins and his eyes enlarge, and he says, 'You must stop the robbery!' " In particular, Grant was reported to have denounced Moses. The president was reported to have asked, "Why don't you convict Moses?"[67] Grant was rumored to be considering supporting a Democrat in the 1874 gubernatorial race if Moses won the state's Republican nomination. These reports from Washington were eagerly trumpeted by Chamberlain's *Union-Herald*. "The Republicans of this state must see to it that in the coming election every county shall elect none but honest and competent men, without stain or reproach on their private or public reputations," the paper warned, "or we shall be driven out of the house of our friends as a leprosy and a curse."[68]

Under pressure from the Grant administration, the state's black Republican leadership, including Congressman Robert Elliott, abandoned Moses and agreed to support the candidate favored by Washington, Daniel Chamberlain. Chamberlain was, in truth, no less corrupt than Moses or any other Republican. In some respects he was personally more corrupt, generally stealing to line his own pockets rather than to build a party machine. Chamberlain had been a leader of the major bond frauds, including the Greenville and Columbia Railroad fraud that had plagued the state. But he had a patrician demeanor, was popular in Washington, and had spent his time in South Carolina courting the white elite rather than kissing black babies. The national Republican leadership was very worried about appearances, and Chamberlain would diminish the appearance of impropriety.

Though the state Republican leadership would not support him, Moses might have considered bolting from the party and campaigning on his own. He still controlled the state militia, the key cog in the Republican electoral machinery. The militia's commander, Beverly Nash, remained loyal to Moses and might have been able to mobilize black voters for the governor. Such a strategy, however, would have been quite risky. By 1874 South Carolina's white paramilitary forces had been rearmed and reorganized. Indeed, throughout Moses's two years in office, white rifle clubs were formed throughout the state.[69] These generally replaced the Ku Klux Klan network and pretended to be social clubs, holding parades, picnics, festivals, and balls.

The oldest of these rifle clubs, the Carolina Rifle Club of Charleston, had been organized in 1869 for the purpose of "the promotion of social intercourse and the enjoyment of its members by means of target shooting and such other amusements as they may determine."[70] The club was organized in military ranks, but without military titles. The club's captain was called the president, the lieutenants were vice presidents, sergeants were called wardens, and corporals were named directors.[71]

Behind the pretense, the clubs engaged in military training, held regular drills, and stockpiled rifles and ammunition. Their purpose was to intimidate blacks, drive away the black state militia, and destroy the Republican party. In August 1874 white rifle companies instigated several confrontations with black militiamen. In the town of Ridge Spring, a white rifle club ordered a group of black militiamen to stop drilling. When the blacks refused, they were attacked by a force of three hundred armed whites. In Edgefield, which was patrolled by Ned Tenant, a prominent black militia officer, hundreds of heavily armed whites attacked the militia company of seventy or eighty blacks and forced it to disarm. Only the prompt arrival of federal troops prevented a massacre. Moses's request to the president for more federal troops to protect the black citizens of Edgefield was ignored by an administration anxious to limit its involvement in the affairs of South Carolina.

The growing power of white paramilitary forces meant that black militiamen would not be able to control the voting process unless they themselves were protected by federal troops. The Grant administration would certainly not allow its troops to intervene to help the Robber Governor win reelection. Frank Moses had no choice but to step aside and watch Daniel Chamberlain secure the 1874 Republican gubernatorial nomination.

Moses's downfall was celebrated by the state's white press. The *Sumter News*, now renamed the *True Southron*, said, "Tatterdemalion I, of South Carolina is dead. He is dead as a herring, dead as a nit, aye, is dead beyond all hope of resuscitation, reanimation, or resurrection, and will never trouble friend or foe, any more."[72] Why was Chamberlain preferable to Moses? While Chamberlain was a thief and plunderer, said the *Southron,* unlike Moses, he was not a "miscegenator."[73]

Though Moses's political career had apparently come to an end, there would be one last stand. At the first session of the state legislator after the 1874 elections, Moses was nominated for judge of the third judicial circuit, which included Sumter. Chamberlain was able to block Moses and a black nominee, Frank Whipper, on the grounds that they lacked ability, character, and learning. "Legal learning, a judicial spirit, and a high and unblemished personal character should mark every man who shall be elected [to the South Carolina bench]. If all these qualities are not attainable," said Chamberlain, "let the one quality of personal integrity never be lost sight of."[74]

This setback for Moses's nomination was only temporary. When the legislature convened for its second session, his name was placed in nomination again by W. E. Johnston, a black senator from Sumter. This time, Chamberlain was absent from the capital and not able to block the election. Chamberlain's absence was no accident. Chamberlain had been scheduled to deliver an address in Greenville. House Speaker Robert Elliott had assured the governor that no action would be taken on judicial nominations during his absence. Elliott, however, had no intention of keeping his promise. In response to pressure from the national Republican administration, Elliott had supported Chamberlain for governor against his longtime ally, Moses. As part of the deal, Elliott became Speaker of the South Carolina House, a position he preferred to continuing service in the U.S. Congress.

Before long Elliott came to loathe the new governor. In a few short months, Chamberlain had made it clear that his goal was to tie himself securely to the state's white establishment and give short shrift to his black supporters. Chamberlain was widely quoted as having said that he was opposed to too many black Republicans in office because he wanted to keep the Republican party from going over to "negroism."[75] Elliott was sure Chamberlain intended to betray black rights and he became obsessed with the matter of Chamberlain's duplicity.[76] Elliott was determined to undo his mistake in any way he could, including resurrecting the Robber Governor. As soon as Chamberlain was out of the city, Elliott brought the question of judicial appointments to the floor of the House. Elliott spoke on behalf of the eight Republican nominees, including Moses and Whipper. He declared that Whipper, in particular, had been opposed by some only because of his skin color. The vote was taken and Moses and Whipper, along with the other six Republican nominees, were elected.

News of Moses's election was greeted with elation by his black supporters. According to the *True Southron,* "There was whooping and yelling and hats thrown up to the ceiling, etc., and the ex-governor, who was sitting outside to hear the result, was borne in by his supporters and he was almost pulled to pieces in their vain endeavors to get a shake of his hand."[77] For the most part, black South Carolinians continued to support Moses. To the black citizens of the state, he was not the Robber Governor but was, rather, the only white politician who seemed genuinely blind to racial differences. When Moses was later indicted by the Hampton regime, some blacks went to jail rather than testify against him.[78]

Whites had a different view of Moses. For years December 16, the date of his election, was remembered as Black Thursday in South Carolina. Governor Chamberlain feared that the political resurrection of Frank Moses in the Republican party would undermine his own efforts to court conservative support. Chamberlain quickly returned to Columbia where he told the *News and Courier,* "I look upon [the election of Moses and Whipper] as a horrible disaster— a disaster equally great to the state, to the Republican party and, greatest of all, to those communities which shall be doomed to feel the full effects of Moses and Whipper on the bench. . . . Of Moses, no honest man can have different opinions. . . . The reputation of Moses is covered deep with charges, which are believed by all who are familiar with the facts, of corruption, bribery, and the utter prostitution of all his official powers, to the worst possible purposes. This calamity is infinitely greater in my judgement, than any which has yet fallen on this state, or, I might add, upon any part of the South. Moses as governor is endurable compared with Moses as judge."[79]

In Sumter, where Moses would serve as judge, huge crowds of blacks and whites assembled in the city streets. Several thousand whites gathered to protest Moses's appointment and to vow armed resistance to any effort he might make to take office. The leader of the throng said, "We meet to tell Franklin J. Moses, Jr., that he shall never preside as a judge in Sumter court house unless he is seated there by federal bayonets."[80] A prominent Jewish Sumterite, Charles Moise, declared, "I say the time has come for resistance! Should F. J. Moses, Jr., by any legal trickery, attempt to ascend the steps of the courthouse to take his seat as judge, I, Charles H. Moise, forty-six years of age, with a wife and ten children to support, am ready [to] unite with a band of determined men, and with muskets on our shoulders, defend that temple of justice from desecration."[81] Voicing the sentiments of the local Jewish community and its fear of being associated with the Moses clan, Moise sought to portray the problem as one of excessive parental indulgence. The elder Moses, "instead of compelling his son to earn an honest living by honest labor, encourages and assists him to aspire to positions for which he is utterly unfit."[82] Several thousand blacks gathered in support of Moses and to declare that they would protect him if need be. Both crowds included armed men and bloodshed seemed likely. A riot was narrowly averted.[83]

On December 25, 1875, Governor Chamberlain issued a statement asserting that he would refuse to present commissions to Whipper and Moses. The governor asserted their elections had been unconstitutional because their predecessors had been entitled to full four-year terms even though they had been elected only to fill the last two years of unexpired terms. Hence, said Chamberlain, the seats to which Moses and Whipper had been appointed were not vacant. Whipper mounted an unsuccessful court challenge to the governor's actions. Moses never attempted to take his seat. Chamberlain's action made the governor extremely popular among South Carolina's white citizens. Many Democrats declared that the party should endorse Daniel Chamberlain for reelection in 1876.[84] Chamberlain believed that his plan to build a firm base of support among the state's conservative whites was succeeding, and he hoped that he would run for reelection without a Democratic opponent.

As for Frank Moses, he was finished in South Carolina politics. Like the Wicked Witch of the West, Moses was not only merely dead; politically, at least, he was really most sincerely dead.

CHAPTER SIX

Exiled from the Promised Land

FRANK MOSES WAS thirty-seven when his term as governor ended. He had little money and few prospects. The Robber Governor's assets consisted of approximately a hundred dollars in cash and some personal effects.[1] If he was a thief, apparently he was not a very good one. Over the next two years, he worked unsuccessfully as a lobbyist and wrote Republican campaign materials in preparation for the 1876 elections. He considered running for the state legislature but had no money for a campaign.

In the meantime, things seemed to be going well for Governor Chamberlain and the Republican party. Chamberlain vigorously courted South Carolina's whites and had some success in winning their favor. After his election Chamberlain presented the legislature with a program that reduced taxes and cut expenditures. He vetoed nineteen bills that might have increased expenditures in one way or another.[2] Chamberlain also supported efforts to oust a number of Republican officials on charges of fraud and official corruption. The Republican state treasurer Niles Parker was tried and found guilty of official malfeasance. State senator Robert Smalls was found guilty of breach of public trust. Frank Moses's uncle Montgomery Moses, a judge, was impeached and removed from office.[3]

The conservative press, including the *Darlington Southerner,* the *Edgefield Advertiser,* and the *Charleston News and Courier* found much to praise in Chamberlain's management of the state's affairs. The *Advertiser* called Governor Chamberlain South Carolina's "only hope."[4] The *Southerner* said Chamberlain stood against corruption "like a rock, firm and immovable."[5] The July 18, 1876, issue of the *Courier* summarized Chamberlain's accomplishments. According to the newspaper, Chamberlain had corrected Moses's abuse of the pardoning power; he had reduced the state's indebtedness; he had amended the tax laws so as to ensure greater uniformity in property assessments; and he had reduced legislative expenses and state salaries. The *Courier* saw many reasons for white Carolinians to support Governor Chamberlain.[6] Indeed, the *Courier* advised white Democrats not to nominate a gubernatorial candidate in 1876 if Chamberlain was the Republican nominee. Large segments of the state's white business class agreed with the *Courier*, praising Chamberlain for his orderly and legalistic reforms and promising to support him against the "Radical Ring."[7]

But while Chamberlain was building support among Democrats, his policies were producing deep divisions within the Republican party. Most white Republicans supported the governor; most black Republicans, led by Robert Elliott, opposed him. One observer said, "The darkies here are deadly enemies to him now, and will get him out of the way if they can."[8] The lines were not entirely racial. Some black Republicans, seeing no viable alternative, supported Chamberlain, while U.S. senator John Patterson and former state treasurer Niles Parker sought to organize opposition to the governor. When Chamberlain moved to prosecute Parker on charges of malfeasance, Parker threatened to expose Chamberlain's own past misdeeds. Chamberlain's somewhat self-righteous response was published by the *Courier*: "My evils have heretofore come from the friendship of bad men. Perhaps I shall fare better if I now have their hatred."[9] Chamberlain believed that his enemies hated him "for being more decent than they."[10] Divisions between pro- and anti-Chamberlain forces within South Carolina's Republican party became so bitter that during a floor fight at the 1876 state party convention, pistols were drawn and spectators fled from the galleries.[11]

Ultimately, Chamberlain's efforts to win the support of native whites had little chance of success. White conservatives liked Chamberlain. He seemed to share many of their views, particularly their disdain for blacks. From the white Democratic perspective, Chamberlain was certainly the best of all the Republicans. By 1875, however, white Carolinians were no longer convinced that their only choices lay within the Republican party. Democrats had taken control of several state governments and the U.S. House of Representatives in what was widely viewed as the northern public's repudiation of Radical Reconstruction.[12] Once in control of the House, Democrats were able to sharply increase political pressure on the Grant administration to further reduce the federal military presence in the South. Democrats calculated that the removal of federal forces would be followed by a rapid collapse of Republican governments in the old Confederacy. This, in turn, would give the Democratic party additional strength in Congress and enhance the party's chances in future presidential contests. The Republicans could also count votes, and they feared that a continuation of Radical policies would further alienate northern voters. As a result, federal support for the South's Republican governments was waning. Several southern states had been "redeemed" by their native whites, and even Mississippi, a state with a majority black population similar to South Carolina's, had recently been returned to white control. Advocates of "straight-out Democracy" pointed to the "Mississippi plan" of coordinated violence, economic pressure, and political action as a blueprint for redeeming South Carolina from Republican rule.

The various rifle clubs and saber clubs for whites were already active in the 1874 election. No Democratic gubernatorial nominee had opposed Chamberlain that year, but a group of independent Republicans had bolted from the convention and nominated John Green, a native white Republican who appealed for conservative support by promising good government and fiscal reform. Though Green had no chance of carrying the state, Democratic paramilitary forces mounted what became a practice drill on his behalf, instigating a number of armed confrontations with black militias and murdering several black militiamen and politicians. "Pitchfork" Ben

Tillman, later a U.S. senator, was a leader of Democratic paramilitary forces in 1874. Tillman's forces helped Democrats carry Shaw's Mill, a precinct with five times as many black voters as whites, by driving off the black militia and terrorizing black voters to prevent them from coming to the polls.[13]

Violence continued after the election. White rifle clubs in Edgefield mobilized after a rumor spread that black militia captain Ned Tenant was responsible for fires at local plantations. Over the next several days, white paramilitaries killed or wounded a number of blacks and disarmed Tenant's forces. The violence did not abate until the federal government sent an infantry company to patrol the county.

Nonetheless, violence waned in the early months of Chamberlain's administration as the governor's overtures to the white community convinced some that the new chief executive might merit their support. The Republican legislature's election of Moses and Whipper to the bench was a turning point for whites. Although Chamberlain might be acceptable, he was isolated within his own party. Whites congratulated the governor for turning back the appointments but saw in the legislature's effort a dark conspiracy that had to be resisted by force of arms. The *Courier* declared that the election of Moses and Whipper was an effort by the Republicans to "Africanize" the state.[14] This was the last straw, "the last feather to break the camel's back," as another paper put it.[15] Even out-of-state observers understood that the Moses and Whipper nominations would galvanize the Democrats against the Republican government. "A rumpus has begun in South Carolina," said the correspondent for the *Cincinnati Commercial,* "which will end in the white people getting control of the state. . . . The whites are aroused; the color line is drawn. . . . [Whites see] no escape from Moses and Whipper on the bench but the complete overthrow of the so-called party which elected them."[16]

In the wake of the abortive Republican effort to appoint Moses and Whipper to the bench, whites dismissed Chamberlain as a "mere adventurer from Massachusetts" and mobilized an all-out struggle to seize control of the state.[17] Many whites were encouraged by events in Mississippi. The federal government had stood by as white paramilitary forces drove the Republicans from power in that state.[18] Now, South Carolinians thought it was time for "actions as shall result in the overthrow and banishment of the faction which has so long ruled, robbed and degraded us."[19] Between the fall of 1875 and the summer of 1876, white opinion in South Carolina seemed to settle on the idea that the Republicans—Chamberlain included—must be driven out by any means necessary.

The most effective of these means was violence. Democratic gun clubs, saber clubs, and the like stepped up their campaign of terror and intimidation aimed at destroying the black militias and compelling blacks and whites to abandon the Republican party. The Republican leader Joseph Crews was assassinated by Democratic gunmen. Other Republicans were threatened or beaten. The most horrific incident was the July 1876 Hamburg Massacre. Hamburg was a mainly black hamlet in Aiken County near Edgefield, not far from the Georgia border. On the Fourth of July the county's state militia company was parading through the town in honor of the national holiday. A confrontation broke out between the militia and two armed white men but no shots were exchanged. Seizing the opportunity, white paramilitary forces attacked the black militiamen. Ben Tillman later explained, "The leading white men of Edgefield had determined to seize the first opportunity that the negroes might offer them to provoke a riot and teach the negroes a lesson . . . by killing as many of them as was justifiable."[20]

The black militia exchanged fire with the white rifle companies and killed a white man. With more armed whites arriving, the black militiamen barricaded themselves in a house. The white paramilitary groups had an artillery piece and fired shrapnel at the militia company. The militiamen ran and at least one was killed and many more captured. After several hours the white paramilitaries began to execute their captives, shooting them through the head, one by one. After several were murdered the remainder were set free. Ben

Tillman recalled, "We were all tired but more than satisfied with the result."[21] In the aftermath of the massacre, a number of men were charged with murder and other offenses, but not one was brought to trial. President Grant deplored the massacre, declaring it "cruel, bloodthirsty, wanton and unprovoked." He promised whatever assistance he could provide for which he could find law or constitutional power.[22] In the end, the president found neither as he waited for his term and Republican rule in the South to come to an end.

Against this backdrop of white violence, Democrats fielded a candidate for the first time since the beginning of Reconstruction. Not surprisingly, he was Gen. Wade Hampton, the state's greatest war hero and most prominent citizen. Hampton took the high road, marching across the state with an entourage of three thousand mounted guards. He was met everywhere by cheering and festive white crowds. At the end of October he arrived in Charleston where he was greeted by thousands of admirers welcoming the general as he symbolically liberated the city from its occupiers.

While Hampton kept his own hands clean, as had been his practice throughout Reconstruction, his supporters, led by Martin Gary, launched a new campaign of terror against the Republicans and their black supporters.[23] Leading Republican politicians were physically attacked and Chamberlain, seeking reelection to a second term, found that everywhere he spoke he was surrounded by hostile cordons of armed men wearing the red shirts that marked them as Hampton supporters.[24] Preparations for the election as well as election day itself were marred by shootings, riots, and other forms of violence instigated mainly by white Democrats against black and white Republicans. When the votes were tallied, Hampton seemed to have defeated Chamberlain by a vote of 92,261 to 91,127. Thousands of blacks had risked their lives to vote, but apparently it had not been enough to carry the day. Voting fraud, however, had been widespread, and Republicans asserted that Democrats had stolen the election. Indeed, in two counties, the number of Democratic votes cast exceeded the total number of possible voters in the counties.[25]

The state constitution provided that in the case of a disputed election the legislature would choose the new governor. However, because of a complicated series of events, two legislative bodies—one controlled by the Democrats and one by the Republicans—claimed to be the legitimately elected South Carolina legislature. The Democratic group declared Hampton to be the new governor while the Republicans asserted that Chamberlain had been reelected. To the delight of the Democrats, the state's supreme court refused to invalidate the election returns. Republicans declared that the decision represented Chief Justice Moses's revenge against Chamberlain for refusing to allow his son to sit on the South Carolina bench. Chief Justice Moses was disparaged by northern Republican papers as a Jew who was "homely as a stump fence."[26] Justice Moses died unexpectedly, before he could issue any further opinions on the matter. The Democratic papers declared that old Moses was well known to have favored the election of Hampton.

For a time, it seemed that the outcome of the election would be decided by force. In any armed clash, the Democratic party's paramilitary forces would almost certainly have routed the state militiamen mustered by Chamberlain and his supporters. Republicans, though, appealed to the federal government for help, hoping that the federal troops stationed in Columbia would disperse the various Democratic rifle clubs and support the Chamberlain administration's claim to power. For a time, the federal army commander in Columbia deployed his troops to protect the Republican governor and legislature. In March 1877 the newly elected president Rutherford B. Hayes summoned both Chamberlain and Hampton to Washington. The substance of the discussions was confidential, but shortly after meeting with both men Hayes ordered federal forces to withdraw from Columbia. Without the support of the federal military, the Republican governor and many legislators bowed to the inevitable and turned their posts over to the Democrats.

Some historians have argued that Hayes's decision to abandon his fellow Republicans in South Carolina and the other southern states was prompted by the circumstances of his own election. The

1876 presidential contest had ended with no majority in the electoral college and a dispute over the nineteen electoral votes of South Carolina, Louisiana, and Florida. Hayes needed all nineteen votes to defeat the Democratic candidate, Samuel Tilden, who had actually polled more popular votes than his Republican rival. Faced with a growing national crisis, Congress created a bipartisan electoral commission to settle the matter. As the commission deliberated, Hayes's aides negotiated with Wade Hampton's emissaries as well as those representing Louisiana Democrats. Hayes agreed that if elected he would recognize Hampton as governor of South Carolina, Democrat Francis Nicholls as governor of Louisiana, and would order remaining federal forces in the South not to interfere with what was called "home rule."[27] In the wake of this agreement, Hayes was awarded all nineteen of the disputed electoral votes and the presidency. Reconstruction was over.

In the wake of their victory, Democrats began cleansing the state of all vestiges of Republican rule. To this end, the Hampton government began, where possible, removing Republican officeholders from their positions. The government established a Commission on Public Frauds to investigate the involvement of Republicans in a variety of improper bond and railroad transactions, among other misdeeds. Finally, the Hampton government brought indictments against twenty-five former Republican officeholders, of whom four were actually brought to trial and three convicted.

The South Carolina fraud investigation produced hundreds of pages of documents and testimony affirming that the Republicans had been a corrupt bunch.[28] Conveniently, the involvement of prominent Democrats in the various shady schemes was overlooked. The commission sought to show that state debt certificates had been illegally issued, railroad shares had been manipulated, state legislators had accepted bribes, and legislators had accepted kickbacks from contractors. Virtually every prominent Republican—but not a single Democrat—was named in the report. To the state's press, the fraud report was conclusive proof that the Radical government had been little more than a criminal enterprise that had been properly overthrown by the heroic Hampton and his red-shirted followers. And that was the report's purpose—to provide "moral evidence" to incriminate the Republicans in the court of public opinion.[29] The name of Franklin Moses did not figure very prominently in the report. Moses testified briefly, admitting some minor financial sleight of hand.[30] Others testified that Moses had, at one time or another, defrauded the state of a few dollars, often to reward some worthy Republican. All in all, the infamous Robber Governor turned out to have played a fairly minor role in the various crimes identified by the commission.

Of the twenty-five Republicans indicted for criminal activities and official misconduct, only three were convicted—Francis Cardozo, Robert Smalls, and Cass Carpenter, a former tax agent and newspaper editor who had incurred the wrath of Governor Hampton.[31] Moses was briefly arrested but never charged. Those arrested were questioned individually and secretly, and they were sworn to reveal neither the questions they were asked nor the answers they gave.[32] Detainees who later violated their oath told the northern press that the state's authorities had mainly been interested in eliciting testimony against former governor Chamberlain, the only Republican that Hampton still considered even a remote threat. Presumably, Moses would have been only too happy to tell what he knew about Chamberlain and his allies. At any rate, Moses was not indicted, despite having once been hailed as the notorious Robber Governor.

The three men convicted of involvement with various public frauds soon won official pardons in what amounted to an exchange of prisoners between state and federal authorities. The federal government had indicted a number of white South Carolinians involved in the political violence of 1876. Some of these men were well-known Democrats who had been engaged in violent action to help bring the new state administration into power. Their trial and possible conviction would be embarrassing to Hampton and the other Democrats. Accordingly, Governor Hampton proposed to President Hayes that the state government would stop prosecuting Republicans if the federal government would drop its cases against the Democrats.[33] After some maneuvering by both sides, a deal was struck. South Carolina pardoned the convicted Republicans and the U.S. government refrained from prosecuting the several Democrats it had indicted.

As Democratic rule took hold in South Carolina, the memory of Reconstruction began to fade. Most of the state's scalawags "crossed Jordan" by returning to the Democratic fold and making peace with their neighbors. Some even held minor political office in later years. Those scalawags who refused to renounce their Republicanism found themselves subject to reprisals and even violence at the hands of their fellow South Carolinians.[34] Old governor Perry declared that Moses should take his thirty pieces of silver and his scalawag friends and depart for New York, New England, or Australia.[35] Most scalawags, however, tried to remain in their home state.

Most of the carpetbaggers, including South Carolina's two carpetbagger governors, left the state. Former governor Robert Scott returned to Napoleon, Ohio, where he became involved in real estate. Daniel Chamberlain opened a law practice in New York City, eventually became a professor of constitutional law at Cornell University, and often returned to South Carolina to visit (white) friends. In a Massachusetts speech in 1890, Chamberlain declared that since 1876, South Carolina's blacks had been treated extremely well. "The Negro has never known such an era of advancement and prosperity in all that benefits a citizen and free man as the period since 1876."[36] A few years later, Chamberlain wrote that the idea that blacks could be politically or socially equal to whites should be abandoned. He observed that many whites found blacks physically repulsive. "I freely acknowledge that repulsion," he declared.[37] In 1904 Chamberlain wrote that the major cause of the race problem in the South was the propensity of black men to rape white women. When blacks stopped raping white women, Chamberlain opined, racial problems would diminish.[38]

Some of the blacks who became prominent in South Carolina

during Reconstruction remained in the state, even participating in politics for a time. After receiving a pardon from Hampton, Robert Smalls represented South Carolina in the U.S. House of Representatives until 1887. At the expiration of his term, Smalls received a federal appointment as collector of the port of Beaufort.[39] William Whipper was active in South Carolina politics in the 1880s and 1890s. Others were able to pursue successful careers outside South Carolina. After his pardon, Francis Cardozo moved to Washington, D.C., where he eventually became the principal of a black high school. A historically black high school in the District of Columbia is named for him. Robert B. Elliott practiced law for many years in New Orleans, and Richard Cain was elected a bishop of the AME church, serving in Texas, Louisiana, New York, New Jersey, and Pennsylvania. Other prominent blacks were not so fortunate. Former congressman Joseph Rainey failed in business in Washington, D.C. One-time congressman and lieutenant governor Alonzo Ransier found employment as a day laborer in Charleston. Former lieutenant governor Richard Gleaves spent his last years as a waiter and steward at the Jefferson Club in Washington, D.C.[40] According to legend, Gleaves was once called upon to serve Wade Hampton, who had been elected to the Senate by his fellow citizens.

Within a few years, historians Francis Simkins and Robert Woody observe, "the principals of the Reconstruction regime vanished from the public life of the state as completely as if they had been made to do long terms in the state penitentiary."[41] One might add that the principles of the Reconstruction regime vanished along with its principals. After 1876 the Republican party of South Carolina gradually disintegrated, unable to contest elections or protect its voters from reprisals and intimidation.[42] Robert Elliott became the party chairman and blacks remained loyal to the party as long as they could. But after the debacle of 1876, Republicans were unable to campaign on a statewide basis.[43] Within two decades, blacks had been almost completely extruded from the political life of South Carolina. They were effectively barred by the state's 1895 constitution from voting or holding office until the civil rights revolution, nearly a century later, shook up the politics of the state. Most South Carolinians believed that during Reconstruction, the Republicans had been led by "the most unprincipled, brutal leaders ever known" and that Reconstruction and Republicanism had been synonymous with the horror of "Negro domination."[44]

Coda

A ND WHAT OF FRANKLIN MOSES? After winning his release from state custody, Moses left South Carolina. He deserted his wife and stole from his mother.[1] He spent time in New York, Chicago, Boston, and other northern cities, eking out a living as a petty grifter. He was arrested in Cambridge, Massachusetts, and convicted of having obtained thirty-four dollars under false pretenses. He was arrested in Chicago for writing forty-two dollars worth of bad checks. Moses told anyone who would listen that he had been treated unfairly. "I want to say right now," he told one reporter, "that the bulk of the stealing . . . was before I came into the Governorship. I had nothing to do with Scott and Parker and Patterson and their New York man, Kimpton."[2] Moses spent three years in the Massachusetts state prison before being pardoned by the governor, and three months in a Detroit jail. He told a judge that his life had been ruined by his addiction to cocaine.[3] Moses was reduced to begging. A New York editor received a note from Moses, in pencil on soiled paper, evidently written from a jail cell. It read: "Respected Sir—In the bitterness of despair I ask you to come and see me and listen to my story. Out of the thousands who I have helped, not one will remember now a ruined man. The good that I have done my fellow man will far outweigh the evil. I am alone in this great city with none to help or assist. I only ask you to listen and to judge. Will your humanity lead you to come?"[4]

Moses understood full well why he had been hated and ostracized in South Carolina. It was not his occasional failure to observe the eighth commandment. Rather, it was his continual violation of the first commandment of southern life—the one regarding race relations. Moses told a New York reporter, "I wanted to be governor. . . . I saw there was but one way—make myself popular with the niggers. . . . My life was ruined. I was made an outcast. I did not dare even to go back to Sumter. I had to meet my own father even in secret. I am now an outcast."[5] Years later, Moses might categorize his relationship with blacks in purely instrumental terms. But none of the other white politicians who used blacks to win power had found it necessary to accept them as friends and equals. Moses was the only one who actually lived the life others preached.

As a result, Moses was, indeed, an outcast. Back in South Carolina, his wife had divorced him and most of his relatives in Sumter who bore the family surname changed their names to DeLeon or Harby to avoid any link to Frank Moses.[6] Some histories of South Carolina's Jewish community fail to even mention Frank Moses. One history of the Jewish community of Charleston lists ten individuals named Moses, but no Franklin Moses.[7] Barnett Elzas's authoritative 1905 volume *The Jews of South Carolina: From the Earliest Times to the Present Day* mentions Frank Moses as the "notorious governor of South Carolina from 1872 to 1874" but declares that he was neither brought up in nor in any way affiliated with the state's Jewish community.[8] To other South Carolinians, Moses became a figure of legend. He was no longer simply a man. He had become, along with other infamous carpetbaggers and scalawags, a "vampire" or "phantasmagorical ghost" associated with ghostly doings and horrors.[9] One Moses who resolutely kept the family name was Frank's son, Col. Franklin J. Moses, USMC. This colonel Moses fought in the Spanish-American War, in Nicaragua, and in China; he died while commanding a marine brigade in the occupation of Vera Cruz in 1914. Obituaries said that he was from Sumter, South Carolina, and was the grandson of the late South Carolina chief justice Franklin Moses. They made no mention of his father.[10]

On December 11, 1906, Franklin Moses was found dead, apparently of asphyxiation and under suspicious circumstances, in a rooming house in Winthrop, Massachusetts. He was sixty-eight years old. There was some talk of an investigation, but the death of a drifter without ties to the community apparently did not warrant the expenditure of police resources. Moses's death was barely noticed by the press even in his home state. In South Carolina and the nation as a whole, the principals and principles of Reconstruction had nearly disappeared so there was no one to care that the Israelite Franklin Moses, Jewnier, the only white man in South Carolina who had given a damn about blacks, had died.

NOTES

Chapter One: A Southern Moses

1. Julian Thomas Buxton Jr., "Franklin J. Moses, Jr.: The Scalawag Governor of South Carolina" (undergraduate thesis, Princeton University, 1950), 13.

2. R. H. Woody, "Franklin J. Moses, Jr., Scalawag Governor of South Carolina, 1872–74," *North Carolina Historical Review* 10, no. 2 (April 1933): 112.

3. Woody, 111.

4. Hyman Rubin III, *South Carolina Scalawags* (Columbia: University of South Carolina Press, 2006), xv.

5. Christopher Dell, "Franklin J. Moses: Proto–New Dealer and Reconstruction Governor," paper presented to the Conference on the South, the Citadel, April 1981.

6. Richard Zuczek, *State of Rebellion: Reconstruction in South Carolina* (Columbia: University of South Carolina Press, 1996), 162–64. See also Stephen Kantrowitz, *Ben Tillman and the Reconstruction of White Supremacy* (Chapel Hill: University of North Carolina Press, 2000).

7. *Harper's Weekly,* September 19, 1874.

8. For a general history of Reconstruction see Eric Foner, *Reconstruction: America's Unfinished Revolution* (New York: Harper, 1988).

9. Hannah Arendt, *The Origins of Totalitarianism*, rev. ed. (New York: Harcourt, 1967).

10. Quoted in Robert McKenzie and Allan Silver, *Angels in Marble: Working-Class Conservatives in Urban England* (Chicago: University of Chicago Press, 1968).

11. John Mearsheimer and Stephen Walt, *The Israel Lobby and U.S. Foreign Policy* (New York: Farrar, Straus, and Giroux, 2007).

12. Marc Dollinger, *Quest for Inclusion: Jews and Liberalism in Modern America* (Princeton: Princeton University Press, 2000).

13. Eric L. Goldstein, *The Price of Whiteness: Jews, Race, and American Identity* (Princeton: Princeton University Press, 2006). See also Karen Brodkin, *How Jews Became White Folks* (New Brunswick, N.J.: Rutgers University Press, 2006).

14. Benjamin Ginsberg, *The Fatal Embrace: Jews and the State* (Chicago: University of Chicago Press, 1993), 146.

15. Buxton, 190.

16. Stella Suberman, *The Jew Store* (Chapel Hill, N.C.: Algonquin Books, 2001).

17. Historical Research Department of the Nation of Islam, *The Secret Relationship between Blacks and Jews* (Chicago: Latimer, 1991).

18. Robert N. Rosen, *The Jewish Confederates* (Columbia: University of South Carolina Press, 2000), 17.

19. Charles Reznikoff, *The Jews of Charleston* (Philadelphia: Jewish Publication Society, 1950), 85.

20. Harry Scheiber, *Jacob N. Cardozo: Economic Thought in the Antebellum South* (New York: Columbia University Press, 1966). All quotes by Cardozo in this chapter are from this work.

21. Rosen. Also Bertram W. Korn, *American Jewry and the Civil War* (Philadelphia: Jewish Publication Society, 1951).

22. Barnett A. Elzas, *The Jews of South Carolina: From the Earliest Times to the Present Day* (Philadelphia: Lippincott, 1905).

23. Elzas, 107.

24. Elzas, 71.

25. Gary Phillip Zola, *Isaac Harby of Charleston, 1788–1828: Jewish Reformer and Intellectual* (Tuscaloosa: University of Alabama Press, 1994), 3.

26. Zola, 4.

27. Elzas, chap. 12.

28. Elzas, 248–49.

29. Rosen, 117.

30. Elzas, 226.

31. Elzas, 233. The family members included Israel Nunez and Albert Luria, sons of Raphael Moses, who changed their names to honor old family connections.

32. Harry Simonhoff, "1868: Franklin J. Moses: Chief Justice of South Carolina," *Journal of the Southern Jewish Historical Society* 1, no. 1, 23.

33. Elzas, 197.

34. U. R. Brooks, *The Politics of Bench and Bar,* vol. 1 (Columbia, S.C.: State Co., 1908).

35. Brooks, 34.

36. Walter Edgar, *South Carolina: A History* (Columbia: University of South Carolina Press, 1998), 334.

37. *Sumter Watchman*, Dec. 20, 1859, quoted in Buxton, 22.

38. Elzas, 198.

39. Brooks, 33.

40. Buxton, 8.

41. Buxton, 5.

42. Mary Boykin Chesnut, *A Diary from Dixie*, ed. by Ben Ames Williams (Cambridge: Harvard University Press, 1980).

43. John S. Reynolds, *Reconstruction in South Carolina* (Columbia, S.C.: State Co., 1905), 99–100.

44. Emory S, Thomas, *The Confederacy as a Revolutionary Experience* (Englewood Cliffs, N.J.: Prentice-Hall, 1971), 19.

45. Buxton, 12.

46. Woody, 113.

47. Woody, 113.

48. Joseph J. Ellis, *His Excellency, George Washington* (New York: Knopf, 2004), 38.

49. Buxton, 18.

50. Chesnut, 38.

51. James M. Morgan, *Recollections of a Rebel Reefer* (Boston: Houghton Mifflin, 1917), 318.

52. Edgar, 363.

53. Emory Thomas, *The Confederate Nation* (New York: Harper and Row, 1979), chap. 11.

54. Charles Cauthen, *South Carolina Goes to War, 1860–1865* (Chapel Hill: University of North Carolina Press, 1950), 135.

55. Edgar, 375.

56. Cauthen, 137.

57. Edgar, 363.

58. Cauthen, 217.

59. Thomas, *Confederate Nation*, 284.

60. Thomas, *Confederate Nation*, 108.

61. "Franklin Moses, Jr., Formerly of South Carolina," *New York Times*, Dec. 26, 1878.

62. Buxton, 32.

63. Leonard Rogoff, "Is the Jew White? The Racial Place of the Southern Jew," *American Jewish History* 85, no. 3 (1997): 195–230.

64. Edgar, 373.

65. Cauthen, 183–84.

66. Edgar, 372.

67. Korn, 210.

68. Korn, 133.

69. Korn, 212.

70. John B. Jones, *A Rebel War Clerk's Diary* (Philadelphia: Lippincott, 1866), 1:213.

71. Korn, 214.

72. Korn, 213.

73. Korn, 210.

74. Rosen, 334.

Chapter Two: The Making of a Scalawag

1. Francis B. Simkins and Robert H. Woody, *South Carolina during Reconstruction* (Chapel Hill: University of North Carolina Press, 1932), 18.

2. Simkins and Woody, 21.

3. John Porter Hollis, *The Early Period of Reconstruction in South Carolina* (Baltimore: Johns Hopkins University Press, 1905), 27

4. Laura Webster, *The Operation of the Freedmen's Bureau in South Carolina* (Northampton, Mass.: Smith College, 1916).

5. Webster, 4.

6. Simkins and Woody, 30.

7. Simkins and Woody, 30.

8. Lillian A. Kibler, *Benjamin Perry: South Carolina Unionist* (Durham, N.C.: Duke University Press, 1946), 375.

9. Kibler, 313.

10. Quoted in Kibler, 396.

11. Walter Fleming, ed., *Documentary History of Reconstruction* (Cleveland: Arthur Clark Co., 1906), 47.

12. Kibler, 403.

13. Fleming, 47.

14. Simkins and Woody, 37.

15. "Franklin Moses, Jr., Formerly of South Carolina," *New York Times,* Dec. 26, 1878.

16. Julian Thomas Buxton Jr., "Franklin J. Moses, Jr.: The Scalawag Governor of South Carolina" (undergraduate thesis, Princeton University, 1950), 41.

17. Simkins and Woody, 41.

18. Simkins and Woody, 42.

19. Robert K. Ackerman, *Wade Hampton III* (Columbia: University of South Carolina Press, 2007).

20. Simkins and Woody, 43.

21. Simkins and Woody, 53.

22. Simkins and Woody, 55.

23. South Carolina House Journal, Reg. Sess., 1866, 32–35.

24. Simkins and Woody, 63.

25. John S. Reynolds, *Reconstruction in South Carolina* (Columbia, S.C.: State Co., 1905), 49.

26. Buxton, 46.

27. Buxton, 47.

28. *Sumter News*, Oct. 18, 1866.

29. *Sumter News*, July 19, 1866.

30. *Sumter News*, Oct. 18, 1866.

31. *Sumter News*, Oct. 11, 1866.

32. *Sumter News*, Dec. 13, 1866.

33. *Sumter News*, Aug. 16, 1866.

34. *Sumter News*, Oct. 18, 1866.

35. *Sumter News*, Nov. 1, 1866.

36. *Sumter News*, Oct. 4, 1866.

37. *Sumter News*, Oct. 4, 1866.

38. *Sumter News*, Dec. 13, 1866.

39. Simkins and Woody, 68.

40. Hollis, 69.

41. Simkins and Woody, 71.

42. Simkins and Woody, 71.

43. Simkins and Woody, 87.

44. Michael Fitzgerald, *The Union League Movement in the Deep South* (Baton Rouge: Louisiana State University Press, 1989).

45. Thomas Holt, *Black over White: Negro Political Leadership in South Carolina during Reconstruction* (Urbana: University of Illinois Press, 1979), 31.

46. Fitzgerald, 212.

47. Eric Foner, *Reconstruction: America's Unfinished Revolution* (New York: Harper and Row, 1988), 283.

48. Foner, 287.

49. Simkins and Woody, 81.

50. Reynolds, 79.

51. Simkins and Woody, 85.

52. Simkins and Woody, 84.

53. Foner, 292.

54. *Sumter News*, April 11, 1867.

55. *Sumter News*, March 21, 1867.

56. *Sumter News*, May 23, 1867.

57. *Sumter News*, April 11, 1867.

58. *Sumter News*, May 2, 1867.

59. "Franklin Moses, Jr., Formerly of South Carolina," *New York Times*, Dec. 26, 1878.

60. R. H. Woody, "Franklin Moses, Jr., Scalawag Governor of South Carolina, 1872–74," *North Carolina Historical Review* 10, no. 2 (April 1933): 115.

61. William L. King, *The Newspaper Press of Charleston, South Carolina* (Charleston: Edward Perry, 1872).

62. Foner, 282.

63. Ronald Lewis, "Cultural Pluralism and Black Reconstruction: The Public Career of Richard H. Cain," *Crisis* 85 (July 1978): 57–60.

64. *Sumter News*, Aug. 30, 1866.

65. *Sumter News*, June 22, 1867.

66. *Sumter News*, June 8, 1867.

67. *Sumter News*, May 2, 1867.

68. *Sumter News*, April 11, 1867.

69. *Sumter News*, Aug. 31, 1867.

70. Simkins and Woody, 89.

71. *Sumter News*, June 29, 1867.

72. *Sumter News*, Aug. 31, 1867.

73. *Sumter News*, July 27, 1867.

74. *Sumter News*, Aug. 31, 1867.

75. *Sumter News*, Sept. 14, 1867.

76. *Sumter News*, Sept. 21, 1867.

Chapter Three: Reinventing South Carolina's Government

1. Hyman Rubin III, *South Carolina Scalawags* (Columbia: University of South Carolina Press, 2006), xx.

2. John Porter Hollis, *The Early Period of Reconstruction in South Carolina* (Baltimore: Johns Hopkins University Press, 1905), 83.

3. Thomas Holt, *Black over White: Negro Political Leadership in South Carolina during Reconstruction* (Urbana: University of Illinois Press, 1979), 36.

4. William C. Hine, "Black Politicians in Reconstruction Charleston, South Carolina," *Journal of Southern History* 49, no. 4 (Nov. 1983): 559.

5. Eric Foner, *Freedom's Lawmakers: A Directory of Black Officeholders during Reconstruction* (Baton Rouge: Louisiana State University Press, 1996), 39.

6. Peggy Lamson, *The Glorious Failure: Black Congressman Robert Brown Elliott and the Reconstruction in South Carolina* (New York: Norton, 1973).

7. Quoted in Francis B. Simkins and Robert H. Woody, *South Carolina during Reconstruction* (Chapel Hill: University of North Carolina Press, 1932), 92.

8. *Charleston Mercury,* Feb. 5, 1868.

9. *Charleston Mercury,* Jan. 29, 1868.

10. *Charleston Mercury,* Jan. 28, 1868.

11. *Charleston Mercury,* Jan. 28, 1868.

12. Cal M. Logue, "Racist Reporting during Reconstruction," *Journal of Black Studies* 9, no. 3 (March 1979): 339.

13. *Charleston Mercury,* Jan. 15, 1868.

14. Logue, 349.

15. Rubin, 27.

16. Rubin, 27.

17. *Charleston Mercury,* Jan. 16, 1868.

18. *Sumter News,* Jan. 25, 1868.

19. Hollis, 90.

20. James S. Pike, *The Prostrate State: South Carolina under Negro Government* (New York: Appleton, 1874).

21. Mark Wahlgren Summers, *The Press Gang: Newspapers and Politics, 1865–1878* (Chapel Hill: University of North Carolina Press, 1994), 191–96.

22. Pike, 15.

23. Pike, 12.

24. Pike, 29.

25. Summers, chap. 12.

26. Foner, *Freedom's Lawmakers*, 577.

27. Foner, *Freedom's Lawmakers*, 290.

28. James S. Allen, *Reconstruction: The Battle for Democracy* (New York: International Publishers, 1937), 66–67.

29. Eric Foner, *Reconstruction: America's Unfinished Revolution* (New York: Harper, 1988), 305; Simkins and Woody, 82.

30. Foner, *Reconstruction*, 294–96.

31. Hine, 564.

32. *Proceedings of the Constitutional Convention of South Carolina* (New York: Arno Press, 1968), 136.

33. V. I. Lenin, *What Is to Be Done?* (New York: International Publishers, 1929), 15.

34. Simkins and Woody, 94.

35. W. E. B. Du Bois, *Black Reconstruction in America* (New York: Free Press, 1998), 200.

36. *Proceedings*, 828.

37. *Proceedings*, 829.

38. *Proceedings*, 729.

39. *Proceedings*, 735.

40. Simkins and Woody, 417.

41. *Proceedings*, 695.

42. *Proceedings*, 705.

43. *Proceedings*, 706.

44. Simkins and Woody, 100.

45. *Proceedings*, 227.

46. *Proceedings*, 437.

47. *Proceedings*, 427.

48. *Proceedings*, 427.

49. Julian Thomas Buxton Jr., "Franklin Moses, Jr.: The Scalawag Governor of South Carolina" (undergraduate thesis, Princeton University, 1950), 72.

50. Du Bois, 197.

51. Foner, *Reconstruction*, 309.

52. Du Bois, 198.

53. Foner, *Reconstruction,* 309.

54. Foner, *Reconstruction,* 309.

55. Michael Les Benedict, *A Compromise of Principle: Congressional Republicans and Reconstruction, 1863–1869* (New York: Norton, 1974), 258.

56. Foner, *Reconstruction,* 309.

57. Benedict, 273.

58. Foner, *Reconstruction,* 316.

59. Foner, *Reconstruction,* 310.

60. Foner, *Reconstruction,* 310.

61. Foner, *Reconstruction,* 71.

62. Carol Bleser, *The Promised Land: The History of the South Carolina Land Commission, 1869–1890* (Columbia: University of South Carolina Press, 1969), chap. 1.

63. Foner, *Reconstruction,* 329.

64. *Proceedings,* 118.

65. *Proceedings,* 107.

66. *Proceedings,* 115.

67. *Proceedings,* 113.

68. *Proceedings,* 114.

69. *Proceedings,* 115.

70. Joel Williamson, *After Slavery: The Negro in South Carolina during Reconstruction* (Chapel Hill: University of North Carolina Press, 1965), 156.

71. *Proceedings,* 147.

72. *Proceedings,* 146.

73. *Proceedings,* 196.

74. Bleser, 20.

75. *Proceedings,* 379.

76. *Proceedings,* 434.

77. *Proceedings,* 508.

78. Bleser, 97.

79. Bleser, 146–59.

80. Simkins and Woody, 107.

81. Simkins and Woody, 109

82. Walter L. Fleming, ed., *Documentary History of Reconstruction* (Cleveland: Arthur Clark, 1906), 1:456.

83. Simkins and Woody, 109.

84. Herbert Shapiro, "The Ku Klux Klan during Reconstruction," *Journal of Negro History* 49, no. 1 (Jan. 1964): 35–36.

85. Richard Zuczek, *State of Rebellion: Reconstruction in South Carolina* (Columbia: University of South Carolina Press, 1996), chap. 3.

86. Merrill Singer, "Symbolic Identity Formation in an African American Religious Sect: The Black Hebrew Israelites," in *Black Zion: African American Religious Encounters with Judaism,* ed. Yvonne Chireau and Nathaniel Deutsch (New York: Oxford University Press, 2000, 57.

Chapter Four: Speaker Moses

1. Francis B. Simkins and Robert H. Woody, *South Carolina during Reconstruction* (Chapel Hill: University of North Carolina Press, 1932), 122.

2. Eric Foner, *Reconstruction: America's Unfinished Revolution* (New York: Harper, 1988), 538.

3. Peggy Lamson, *The Glorious Failure: Black Congressman Robert Brown Elliott and the Reconstruction in South Carolina* (New York: Norton, 1973), 68.

4. Lamson, 69.

5. Hyman Rubin III, *South Carolina Scalawags* (Columbia: University of South Carolina Press, 2006), 102.

6. Herbert Shapiro, "The Ku Klux Klan during Reconstruction: The South Carolina Episode," *Journal of Negro History* 49, no. 1 (Jan. 1964): 35.

7. Foner, 303.

8. Charles Cummings, "The Scott Papers: An Inside View of Reconstruction," *Ohio History* 79, no. 2 (Spring 1970): 116.

9. Joel Williamson, *After Slavery: The Negro in South Carolina during Reconstruction* (Chapel Hill: University of North Carolina Press, 1965), 294.

10. *Atlantic Monthly,* 1901.

11. Quoted in Julian Thomas Buxton Jr., "Franklin Moses, Jr.: The Scalawag Governor of South Carolina" (undergraduate thesis, Princeton University, 1950), 93.

12. Buxton, 94.

13. Rubin, 114.

14. Williamson, 294.

15. Buxton, 104.

16. James S. Pike, *The Prostrate State: South Carolina under Negro Government* (New York: Appleton, 1874), 19.

17. Williamson, 202.

18. Buxton, 107.

19. Williamson, 338.

20. "Moses," *New Hampshire Sentinel*, June 25, 1874, 2.

21. Claude Bowers, *The Tragic Era: The Revolution after Lincoln* (Cambridge, Mass.: Houghton Mifflin, 1929), 350.

22. South Carolina House Journal, July 6, 1868, 9.

23. Simkins and Woody, 142.

24. Harry Simonhoff, "Franklin J. Moses: Chief Justice of South Carolina," *Journal of the Southern Jewish Historical Society* 1, no. 1 (Nov. 1958): 23–27.

25. Williamson, 292.

26. Williamson, 210.

27. Simkins and Woody, 432.

28. Williamson, 213.

29. Williamson, 229.

30. Williamson, 291.

31. Williamson, 149.

32. Carol Bleser, *The Promised Land: The History of the South Carolina Land Commission, 1869–1890* (Columbia: University of South Carolina Press, 1969), 64.

33. Bleser, 97.

34. Williamson, 158.

35. Williamson, 149.

36. Williamson, 149.

37. Williamson, 157.

38. John S. Reynolds, *Reconstruction in South Carolina* (Columbia, S.C.: State Co., 1905), 162.

39. Quoted in Williamson, 156.

40. Williamson, 158.

41. Simkins and Woody, 209.

42. Simkins and Woody, 202.

43. Simkins and Woody, 203.

44. Buxton, 100.

45. Reynolds, 266.

46. Simkins and Woody, 132.

47. Simkins and Woody, 162.

48. Robert N. Rosen, *The Jewish Confederates* (Columbia: University of South Carolina Press, 2000), 346.

49. Matthew Josephson, *The Politicos, 1865–1896* (New York: Harcourt Brace, 1938).

50. Mark Wahlgren Summers, *The Era of Good Stealings* (New York: Oxford University Press, 1993), 158.

51. Richard H. Abbott, *For Free Press and Equal Rights: Republican Newspapers in the Reconstruction South* (Athens: University of Georgia Press, 2004).

52. Robert H. Woody, *Republican Newspapers of South Carolina,* Southern Sketches Series no. 10 (Charlottesville, Va.: Historical Publishing, 1936).

53. Mark Wahlgren Summers, *The Press Gang: Newspapers and Politics, 1865–1878* (Chapel Hill: University of North Carolina Press, 1994), 197.

54. "Franklin Moses, Jr., Formerly of South Carolina," *New York Times,* Dec. 26, 1878.

55. Summers, *The Press Gang,* 195–96.

56. Rubin, 30.

57. Rubin, 30.

58. Richard Zuczek, *State of Rebellion: Reconstruction in South Carolina* (Columbia: University of South Carolina Press, 1996), 149.

59. Walter Edgar, *South Carolina: A History* (Columbia: University of South Carolina Press, 1998), 401.

60. Martin Shefter, *Political Parties and the State: The American Historical Experience* (Princeton: Princeton University Press, 1994), chaps. 2 and 3.

61. Shefter, 35–36.

62. "South Carolina and Her Robber Governor," *Troy Weekly Times,* June 18, 1874, 1.

63. "The Crimes of Moses, the Robber Governor," *New York Times,* June 11, 1874, 1.

64. South Carolina House Journal, Nov. 23, 1869, 3–4.

65. Edward F. Sweat, "The Union Leagues and the South Carolina Election of 1870," *Journal of Negro History* 41, no. 1 (Jan. 1976): 200–214.

66. Allen W. Trelease, *White Terror: The Ku Klux Klan Experience and*

Southern Reconstruction (Baton Rouge: Louisiana State University Press, 1971).

67. Nicholas Lemann, *Redemption: The Last Battle of the Civil War* (New York: Farrar, Straus, and Giroux, 2006).

68. Otis A. Singletary, *Negro Militia and Reconstruction* (Austin: University of Texas Press, 1957).

69. Simkins and Woody, 452.

70. Lamson, 88.

71. Zuczek, 75.

72. Singletary, chap. 3.

73. South Carolina House Journal, Nov. 23, 1869, 7–8.

74. Simkins and Woody, 178.

75. Reginald McGrane, *Foreign Bondholders and American State Debts* (New York: Macmillan, 1935), 348.

76. Simkins and Woody, 156.

77. "Message of His Excellency, Franklin J. Moses, Jr., Governor of South Carolina, to the Extra Session of the General Assembly," October 1873.

78. South Carolina House Journal, Nov. 23, 1869, 6.

79. Zuczek, *State of Rebellion.*

80. Shapiro, 41.

81. John A. Leland, *A Voice from South Carolina* (Charleston: Walker, Evans, and Cogswell, 1879), 49.

82. Lou Falkner Williams, *The Great South Carolina Ku Klux Klan Trials, 1871–1872* (Athens: University of Georgia Press, 1996), 23.

83. Shapiro, 43.

84. Trelease.

85. Shapiro, 43.

86. *Proceedings in the Ku Klux Klan Trials at Columbia, South Carolina, in the United States Circuit Court, November term, 1871* (Columbia, S.C.: Republican Printing Co., State Printers, 1872), 279–80.

87. Zuczek, 100.

88. Summers, *The Press Gang,* chap. 12.

89. Zuczek, 101.

90. Zuczek, 138–40.

91. Rubin, xviii.

92. Zuczek, 146.

93. Zuczek, 149.

94. Zuczek, 149.

Chapter Five: Governor Moses

1. Julian Thomas Buxton Jr., "Franklin J. Moses, Jr.: The Scalawag Governor of South Carolina" (undergraduate thesis, Princeton University, 1950), 123.

2. R. H. Woody, "Franklin Moses, Jr.: Scalawag Governor of South Carolina, 1872–74," *North Carolina Historical Review* 10, no. 1 (Jan. 1933): 120.

3. Peggy Lamson, *The Glorious Failure* (New York: Norton, 1973), 157.

4. Woody, "Franklin Moses," 120.

5. William A. Sheppard, *Red Shirts Remembered: Southern Brigadiers of the Reconstruction Period* (Atlanta: Ruralist Press, 1940), 5.

6. Frederick C. Bancroft, *The Negro in Politics* (New York: Pearson, 1885), 29.

7. Francis Butler Simkins and Robert H. Woody, *South Carolina during Reconstruction* (Chapel Hill: University of North Carolina Press, 1932), 467.

8. Buxton, 133.

9. *Sumter News,* March 27, 1873.

10. *South Carolina Senate Journal,* 1872–73, 39–43.

11. Quoted in *Sumter News,* Dec. 25, 1872.

12. Quoted in *Sumter News,* Dec. 25, 1872.

13. *Sumter News,* Dec. 12, 1872.

14. William A. Scott, *The Repudiation of State Debts* (Boston: Crowell, 1893).

15. Simkins and Woody, 182.

16. "Message of His Excellency Franklin J. Moses, Jr., Governor of South Carolina, to the Extra Session of the General Assembly," October 1873, 17.

17. Simkins and Woody, 167.

18. "Message of His Excellency," 28–30.

19. "Message of His Excellency," 20.

20. Scott, 87.

21. B. U. Ratchford, *American State Debts* (Durham: Duke University Press, 1941), 186.

22. Scott, 88.

23. Scott, 88.

24. Simkins and Woody, 168.

25. Alrutheus Ambush Taylor, *The Negro in South Carolina during the Reconstruction* (New York: Russell and Russell, 1924), 214.

26. Simkins and Woody, 440.

27. John S. Reynolds, *Reconstruction in South Carolina* (Columbia, S.C.: State Co., 1905), 231.

28. Joel Williamson, *After Slavery: The Negro in South Carolina during Reconstruction* (Chapel Hill: University of North Carolina Press, 1965), 232.

29. Daniel W. Hollis, *University of South Carolina,* vol. 2 (Columbia: University of South Carolina Press, 1956), 64–65.

30. Reynolds, 234.

31. Hollis, 67.

32. Hollis, 67.

33. Hollis, 71.

34. Reynolds, 263.

35. Henry Thompson, *Ousting the Carpetbagger from South Carolina* (Columbia, S.C.: Bryan Co., 1926), 68.

36. Hollis, 70.

37. Thompson, 68.

38. W. Lewis Burke Jr., "The USC School of Law," in *At Freedom's Door,* ed. James L. Underwood and W. Lewis Burke (Columbia: University of South Carolina Press, 2000), 115.

39. John Herbert Roper, "A Reconsideration: The University of South Carolina during Reconstruction," *Proceedings of the South Carolina Historical Association* (1974): 46–57.

40. Roper, 54.

41. James M. McPherson, *The Abolitionist Legacy: From Reconstruction to the NAACP* (Princeton: Princeton University Press, 1975), 41–42.

42. William A. Dunning, *Reconstruction: Political and Economic* (New York: Harper, 1907), 216.

43. Thompson, 63.

44. Buxton, 140.

45. Buxton, 140.

46. Woody, "Franklin Moses," 123.

47. Woody, "Franklin Moses," 123.

48. Buxton, 140.

49. Benjamin Ginsberg and Martin Shefter, *Politics by Other Means* (New York: Basic Books, 1990).

50. Benjamin Ginsberg and Martin Shefter "The Presidential Impeachment Process," in *Debating the Presidency,* ed. Richard J. Ellis and Michael Nelson (Washington, D.C.: CQ Press, 2006), 56–59.

51. Simkins and Woody, 182.

52. Simkins and Woody 182.

53. "The Crimes of Moses, the Robber Governor," *New York Times,* June 11, 1874, 1.

54. Woody, "Franklin Moses," 124–26.

55. Robert H. Woody, *Republican Newspapers of South Carolina,* Southern Sketches Series no. 10 (Charlottesville, Va.: Historical Publishing, 1936).

56. Woody, *Republican Newspapers,* 38.

57. Lamson, 197.

58. Lamson, 198.

59. James S. Pike, *The Prostrate State: South Carolina under Negro Government* (New York: D. Appleton, 1874), 107.

60. Robert F. Durden, "The Prostrate State Revisited: James Pike and South Carolina Reconstruction," *Journal of Negro History* 39, no. 2 (April 1954): 87–110.

61. Benjamin Ginsberg, *The Fatal Embrace: Jews and the State* (Chicago: University of Chicago Press, 1993), chap. 2.

62. "Southern Society: South Carolina Miscegenation," *Indianapolis Sentinel,* Nov. 1, 1874, 7.

63. Hyman Rubin III, *South Carolina Scalawags* (Columbia: University of South Carolina Press, 2006), 87.

64. Williamson, 400.

65. Rubin, 87.

66. Reynolds, 263.

67. "The President on South Carolina," *Jamestown Journal* 49, no. 11, (July 17, 1874): 2.

68. Williamson, 399.

69. Richard Zuczek, *State of Rebellion: Reconstruction in South Carolina* (Columbia: University of South Carolina Press, 1996), 139.

70. Thompson, 69.

71. Thompson, 69.

72. *True Southron,* Sept. 17, 1874.

73. *True Southron,* Oct. 1, 1874.

74. *Charleston News and Courier,* Dec. 20, 1875.

75. Rubin, 93.

76. Lamson, 227.

77. *True Southron,* Dec. 23, 1875.

78. Williamson, 397.

79. *Charleston News and Courier,* Dec. 20, 1875.

80. Buxton, 160

81. Woody, "Franklin Moses," 129.

82. *True Southron,* Jan. 6, 1876.

83. Buxton, 160.

84. Thompson, 88.

Chapter Six: Exiled from the Promised Land

1. "Franklin Moses, Jr., Formerly of South Carolina," *New York Times,* Dec. 26, 1878.

2. Walter Allen, *Governor Chamberlain's Administration in South Carolina* (New York: Putnam's, 1888), 88–104.

3. Francis B. Simkins and Robert H. Woody, *South Carolina during Reconstruction* (Chapel Hill: University of North Carolina Press, 1932), 476.

4. Allen, 110.

5. Allen, 110.

6. Simkins and Woody, 477.

7. Joel Williamson, *After Slavery: The Negro in South Carolina during Reconstruction* (Chapel Hill: University of North Carolina Press, 1965), 401.

8. Williamson, 403.

9. Williamson, 404.

10. Williamson, 404.

11. Williamson, 405.

12. William Gillette, *Retreat from Reconstruction* (Baton Rouge: Louisiana State University Press, 1979).

13. Richard Zuczek, *State of Rebellion: Reconstruction in South Carolina* (Columbia: University of South Carolina Press, 1996), 146.

14. Zuczek, 153.

15. Zuczek, 153.

16. Walter L. Fleming, ed., *Documentary History of Reconstruction,* vol. 2 (Cleveland: Arthur H. Clark, 1907), 405–6.

17. John A. Leland, *A Voice from South Carolina* (Charleston: Walker, Evans, and Cogswell, 1879), 137.

18. Nicholas Lemann, *Redemption: The Last Battle of the Civil War* (New York: Farrar, Straus, and Giroux, 2006).

19. Zuczek, 153.

20. Stephen Kantrowitz, *Ben Tillman and the Reconstruction of White Supremacy* (Chapel Hill: University of North Carolina Press, 2000), 67.

21. Hyman Rubin III, *South Carolina Scalawags* (Columbia: University of South Carolina Press, 2006), 105.

22. Fleming, 407.

23. William A. Sheppard, *Red Shirts Remembered: Southern Brigadiers of the Reconstruction Period* (Atlanta: Ruralist Press, 1940).

24. Allen, 349.

25. Simkins and Woody, 514.

26. "A Scalawagger, a Carpet-Bagger, and a Nigger," *New Hampshire Sentinel,* Jan. 4, 1877, 1.

27. Foner, 580–81.

28. *Report of the Joint Investigating Committee on Public Frauds and the Election of the Hon. J. J. Patterson to the United States Senate, Made to the General Assembly of South Carolina at the Regular Session, 1877–78* (Columbia, S.C.: Calvo and Patton, 1878).

29. William J. Cooper Jr., *The Conservative Regime: South Carolina, 1877–1890* (Columbia: University of South Carolina Press, 2005), 30.

30. *Report of the Joint Investigating Committee,* 552.

31. W. Lewis Burke, "Post-Reconstruction Justice: The Prosecution and Trial of Francis Lewis Cardozo," *53 S.C.L. Rev. 361* (Winter 2002).

32. "Wade Hampton's Domain," *New York Times,* Aug. 20, 1877, 1.

33. Cooper, 30.

34. Rubin, 114.

35. Lillian Kibler, *Benjamin F. Perry, South Carolina Unionist* (Durham, N.C.: University of North Carolina Press, 1946), 497.

36. Simkins and Woody, 544–45.

37. *Atlantic Monthly,* April 1901.

38. Wilton B. Fowler, "A Carpetbagger's Conversion to White Supremacy," *North Carolina Historical Review* 43, no. 3 (Summer 1966): 301.

39. Simkins and Woody, 547.

40. Eric Foner, *Freedom's Lawmakers* (Baton Rouge: Louisiana State University Press, 1993), 87.

41. Simkins and Woody, 544.

42. James Patton, "The Republican Party in South Carolina, 1876–1895," *University of North Carolina James Sprunt Studies in History and Political Science* 31 (1949): 93–111.

43. George Brown Tindall, *South Carolina Negroes, 1877–1900* (Columbia: University of South Carolina Press, 1952), chap. 3.

44. Patton, 110.

Coda

1. Edward P. Mitchell, *Memoirs of an Editor* (New York: Scribner's, 1924), 327.

2. R. H. Woody, "Franklin J. Moses, Jr., Scalawag Governor of South Carolina, 1872–74," *North Carolina Historical Review* 10 no. 2 (April 1933): 131.

3. Julian Thomas Buxton Jr., "Franklin Moses, Jr.: The Scalawag Governor of South Carolina" (undergraduate thesis, Princeton University, 1950), 178.

4. Mitchell, 327.

5. Woody, 131.

6. Robert N. Rosen, *The Jewish Confederates* (Columbia: University of South Carolina Press, 2000), 347.

7. Solomon Breibart, *Explorations in Charleston's Jewish History* (Charleston: History Press, 2005).

8. Barnett A. Elzas, *The Jews of South Carolina: From the Earliest Times to the Present Day* (Philadelphia: Lippincott, 1905), 199.

9. Stephen Kantrowitz, *Ben Tillman and the Reconstruction of White Supremacy* (Chapel Hill: University of North Carolina Press, 2000), 116.

10. "Col. F. J. Moses Dead," *New York Times,* Sept. 27, 1914.

INDEX

Chamberlain, Daniel: bonds and, 139, 141–43, 156–57; as candidate, 149–50, 173; as carpetbagger, 102, 187; *Charleston Mercury* and, 88; *Columbia Union-Herald* and, 170, 172; Constitutional Convention and, 71, 76–77; corruption and, 172, 178; Elliott and, 172, 174–75; as governor, 178–80; Hampton and, 183, 184–85, 186; land commission and, 86, 117; Moses and, 168, 170, 175–77; railroads and, 122, 123; Republican party and, 153; social strata of, 106; white views of, 181–82

chambers of commerce, 141

Charleston: Carolina Rifle Club of, 173; Civil War and, 27, 28, 35; riots in, 131. *See also* Fort Sumter

Charleston and Savannah railroad, 121

Charleston Mercury (newspaper), 72–73, 74, 88, 96–97

Chilton, William, 31–32

civil rights, 110–11

Civil Rights Act, 47, 111

Civil War: Jews in, 15, 17–18; Moses during, 25, 26–27, 28–29

code, political, 150

Colleton Gazette (newspaper), 164, 165

Colored People's Convention, 46, 112

Columbia Union-Herald (newspaper), 167–69, 170, 172

compromisers, 59, 65

constabulary, 131–32, 137

constitution, adoption of, 98

Constitutional Convention: education and, 82–84, 113–14; equality before law and, 84–85; exclusion of blacks from, 40–41; land and, 87–96; members of, 70–73; motivations of members of, 76–77; outcome of, 96–97; political rights and, 79–82; press attacks on, 72–75; public finance and, 85–87; second, 55–56; views of blacks by,

42–43; white reaction to, 75–76

corruption: armed services fund and, 133; Chamberlain and, 172, 178; as code word, 150; evaluation of, 2; Pike and, 169; politics of, 124–27, 132, 164; railroad construction and, 122–24; scholarships as, 162

court Jews, 22, 34

credit of state: attacks on, 140–42, 143, 156; repair of, 155–59

Crews, Joseph: assassination of, 146, 182; Constitutional Convention and, 71; as scalawag, 102–3; state militia and, 133, 135–37

Curtis, George W., 3

Davis, Jefferson, 23, 27

debt crisis, 155–59

debt repudiation, 156

DeLarge, Robert: Constitutional Convention and, 77, 87; family of, 9; foreclosure sales and, 93–94; land commission and, 86, 117; loan program and, 95, 96; on poll taxes, 80; press attacks on, 72; state land office and, 152

DeLeon, Thomas Cooper, 14

Democratic party: after 1876 victory, 185–86; bond sales and, 140–41; Chamberlain and, 179–80; convention of, 97–98; in election of 1872, 148; Hampton and, 103–5; paramilitary forces of, 130, 180–81; power of, 105; Reconstruction and, 187; school system and, 115; state officials from, 103; violence and, 99, 105–6, 182–83

Disraeli, Benjamin, 5–6

economic development, and railroad lines, 120–24

Edgar, Walter, 126

Edgefield, 28, 131, 173, 181

education: Constitutional Convention and, 82–84; integration of public schools, 114–15, 159–63;

public, creation of system of, 112–15; in South, 11, 112
election commissioners, 153–54
elections: of 1867, 57–58, 66; of 1868, 98–99; of 1870, 136–37; of 1872, 148–51, 153–54; of 1874, 170, 171, 173, 180–81; of 1876, 183–85
Elliott, Robert B.: as attorney, 188; Chamberlain and, 172, 174–75, 179; Constitutional Convention and, 72, 77; judicial nominations and, 174–75; as leader, 101; Moses and, 102, 153, 168; on reputation of South Carolina, 171; on slave trade, 85; state land office and, 152
Elzas, Barnett, 20, 191
Enforcement Act, 144–46
equality before law, and Constitutional Convention, 84–85
Euphradian Society, 107

Fatal Embrace, The: Jews and the State (Ginsberg), ix
federal troops: black, 39–41, 144; home rule and, 185; in Laurens County, 136; removal of, 180; in South Carolina, 130–31
Field Order 15, 37, 91–92
Fifteenth Amendment, 75
financial crisis, 155–59
First South Carolina artillery regiment, 26
Foner, Eric, ix
Foote, Henry, 31
foreclosure sales, 92–94, 138
Fort Sumter, 1–2, 24–25, 26
Fourteenth Amendment, 47–48, 49, 53, 99
fraud: armed services fund and, 133; bonds and, 158; Chamberlain and, 178; in election of 1876, 183–84; investigations of, 185–86; land commission and, 117–18; Moses and, 122–23, 169; in state financial affairs, 155–56

freedmen: courting of, 62, 63–65, 66–67; evolution of Moses's thinking about, 59–62; land redistribution and, 75–76, 89, 90–92, 94–95, 115–20
Freedmen's Bureau: homestead loans and, 95; officials from, 101–2; Republican party and, 104; role of, 36, 37–38; schools established by, 113; Tomlinson and, 148

Garrison, William Lloyd, 79
Gillmore, Quincy, 40
Gleaves, Richard, 150, 188
graft, and Moses, 134
Grant, Ulysses S.: anti-Semitism of, 33; Enforcement Act and, 145; Fifteenth Amendment and, 75; on Hamburg Massacre, 183; South Carolina and, 171–72
Grantism, 171
Greeley, Horace, 91, 149, 169
Greener, Richard T., 160, 162
Greenville and Columbia railroad, 121–23, 172

Hamburg Massacre, 182–83
Hampton, Wade, III: on black troops, 39–40; boycott strategy of, 55–56, 58, 60, 66; as candidate, 183, 184–85; compromisers and, 59; as Democrat, 103–5; insurgency and, 3; Ku Klux Klan and, 145–46; Moise and, 17; planter aristocracy and, 116; status of, 43–44
Harby, Isaac, 14
Hayes, Rutherford B., 184–85
Hayne, Henry, 77–78, 117, 160–61
Hellhole Swamp, 117–18
historians, attacks on Moses by, 163–64
Howard, Oliver O., 37

Inglis, John, 41
integration of public schools, 114–15, 159–63

Jacobs, Myer, 16–17
Jews: agrarian radicalism and, 31–32; alliance with blacks, 7–9, 32–33; ostracism of, 169–70; social marginality of, 5–7; in South Carolina, 5, 15–18; in southern society, 10–15, 33–34
Johnson, Andrew: Moses on, 53; Perry and, 38; Reconstruction and, 46, 47, 48–49
Jones, John Beauchamps, 32

Kansas-Nebraska Act, 13
Ku Klux Klan, 99, 130, 144–46, 172–73

land commission, 86, 96, 116–18
land issues: confiscation, 89–90, 95, 116; foreclosure sales, 92–94, 138; loans to purchase homesteads, 95–96; Moses and, 94–96; overview of, 88–89; redistribution, 75–76, 89, 90–92, 94–95, 115–20; taxation, 116–17, 118–20. *See also* land commission
Laurens County, 131, 135–37
Lee, Samuel, 63, 101
legislative apportionment, 42, 79, 81
legislature, expenses of, 139
legislature, programs and policies of: civil rights, 110–11; consolidation act, 158–59; economic development, 120–24; education, 112–15; land redistribution, 115–20; overview of, 109–10
Levy, Chapman, 16
Liberal Republican faction, 149
Lincoln, Abraham, 22, 23, 25, 33
low-country whites, 104, 106–7
loyalty oaths, 39, 41

Mackey, Albert G., 70–71, 73
Mackey, E. W. M., 74
Mackey, Thomas J., 107–8, 127, 171–72
marginality: of Jews, 5–7; as precarious position, 9

martial law, 36–37, 45
McGrath, Andrew, 27, 36
McKinlay, William, 77–78, 80
Meade, George, 40
missionaries, views of, 51
Mississippi plan, 180, 182
Moise, E. W., 17, 25, 64
Mordecai, M. C., 17
Morris Island, 26, 27
Moses, Emma Buford Richardson (wife), 21, 190, 191
Moses, Franklin I. (father): addresses to freedmen by, 64; as chief justice, 110–11, 154, 184; as circuit judge, 45; as constitutional convention delegate, 41, 42; life and career of, 18–20; Pickens and, 23; secession and, 23; as state senator, 44–45
Moses, Franklin J. (son), 191
Moses, Franklin J., Jr.: as adjutant and inspector general, 98–99, 133, 134; ambition of, 66–69; arrest of, 186; birth and education of, 20; on black legislator deaths, 144; on black voters, 128; as candidate, 150–51, 153–54; career of, 1–3, 23, 54; as chair of board of regents, 160; during Civil War, 25, 26–27, 28–29; *Columbia Union-Herald* and, 167–69; as constitutional convention delegate, 58, 69, 87–88; death of, 192; downfall of, 170–77, 190–91; as editor, 49–54, 59–62, 64–66, 68–69; Elliott and, 102; as ex-governor, 178; failure of, 10; Fort Sumter and, 24–25; as governor, 154–59; in historical record, ix–xi; as horseman, 20–21; inaugural address of, 154–55; indictment of, 167; as judicial nominee, 174–77; land commission and, 86; as living what Sumner preached, 109, 164, 191; marriage of, 21–22; as provost judge, 41–42, 62; as Robber Governor, 2, 3, 163–70; as Speaker, 109–10; on

state revenue, 137, 143; taxes on land and, 118–20

Moses, Jane McLelland (mother), 19

Moses, Meyer (great-grandfather), 18

Moses, Montgomery (uncle), 178

Moses, Myer (grandfather), 18

mulatto delegates to Constitutional Convention, 77

Nash, Beverly, 101, 152, 172

Nast, Thomas, cartoons by, 125, 170. *See also illustrations*

national guard. *See* state militia companies

North Carolina Historical Review (journal), x

nullification crisis, 3, 19

Orr, James L.: compromisers and, 59; Constitutional Convention and, 43; election of, 43, 44; on Fourteenth Amendment, 47–48; as scalawag, 103; Sickles, Canby, and, 54; Tomlinson and, 149

paramilitary forces: Democratic party and, 130, 146; Hamburg Massacre and, 182–83; rifle clubs, 172–73, 180–81

pardons: by Johnson, 39; of men convicted of public fraud, 186; by Moses, 127; of Moses, 190. *See also illustrations*

Parker, Niles: bond commission and, 139; as carpetbagger, 102; Chamberlain and, 179; fraud and, 178; land commission and, 117; railroads and, 122. *See also illustrations*

Patterson, John J. "Honest John," 102, 122, 123, 179

Perry, Benjamin F., 38–41, 43, 58–59, 187

Phillips, Philip, 13

Pickens, Francis W., 22–23, 24, 25–26, 41

Pike, James S.: attacks on South Car-

olina by, 74–75; horse race and, 108; interactions of, 125; purpose of, in exposing corruption, 169; review of book by, 126

planter aristocracy: disenfranchisement of, 128; land and, 89–90, 116; political rights of, 79; up-country whites and, 104

political rights, 79–82

poll taxes, 80–81, 114, 115

press: Chamberlain and, 178–79; defense of freedom of, 88. *See also* cartoons, editorial; press, attacks by; press, Northern; *specific newspapers*

press, attacks by: bond sales and, 140–41; charges of corruption in, 125–26; on constitution, 96–97; on Constitutional Convention, 72–75; on Moses, 73–74, 154, 155, 164–67, 170, 173–74; on Republican government, 100

press, Northern: manipulation of, 125–26; Moses and, 169; trials of Klansmen and, 146

property: seizure of, 37; taxes on, 85–86, 138

public finance, and Constitutional Convention, 85–87

race, and Republican party, 151–53

racism: of federal troops, 131; in Northern press, 126

Radical legislature. *See illustrations*

Radical Republicans, 46, 51–52, 67, 90

railroad lines, 120–24, 172

Rainey, Joseph, 93–94, 152, 188

rallies, political, 63–64

Ransier, Alonzo: as constitutional convention delegate, 77; Democratic party rule and, 188; land issues and, 93–94, 95; leadership of, 87; on right to vote, 80

Reconstruction: and Democratic party, 187; land redistribution and, 89; overview of, 3–5; story told of, ix; violence and, 147

suffrage, black: constitutional convention and, 42–43; in election of 1867, 55, 57; views of, after Civil War, 46, 79
Summers, Mark Wahlgren, 125
Sumner, Charles: on black congressman, 101; land confiscation and, 89; as Radical Republican, 46, 47, 52
Sumter, South Carolina, 28, 176
Sumter, Thomas, 18
Sumter News (press): on Constitutional Convention, 73–74; editorials in, x, 59–62, 64–66, 68–69; on Governor Moses, 154; on Moses, 107; Moses as editor of, 50–54

taxes: constitution and, 85–87; on defeated southern states, 37; for education, 82–83, 114, 115; on land, 116–17, 118–20; poll, 80–81, 114, 115; on property, 85–86, 138
taxpayer conventions, 166–67
tax resisters, 138, 155
Tenant, Ned, 173, 181
Thirteenth Amendment, 44
Tillman, Benjamin Ryan "Pitchfork Ben," 3, 147, 180–81, 182–83
Tomlinson, Reuben, 148–49, 151, 153

Union League of America: and election of 1867, 57–58, 66; Moses and, 51, 150; organization of, 56–57; Republican party and, 56–57, 104, 129–30; role of, 101
university, integration of, 159–63
up-country whites, 104, 106, 135

vices attributed to Moses family, 169–70
violence: Democratic party and, 99, 105–6, 182–83; effect of, 146–47; and election of 1874, 180–81; in politics, 128; against Union League, 129–30; by whites, 143–47, 186–87

Whipper, Frank, 174, 175, 176–77
Whipper, William, 81–82, 108, 152, 188
whites: low-country, 104, 106–7; poor, during Civil War, 29–31; reaction of, to Constitutional Convention, 75–76; Republican party, views of by, 181–82; up-country, 104, 106, 135; violence by, 143–47, 186–87. See also Ku Klux Klan; paramilitary forces; planter aristocracy
Whittemore, B. F., 87, 102
Williamson, Joel, 108
Woodward, Thomas, 58
Woody, Robert Hilliard, x, 124, 188

Yulee, David, 13